Aruna Kranthi Godishala

Computer organization & operating systems

Rajkumar Banoth
Aruna Kranthi Godishala

Computer organization & operating systems

Scholars' Press

Imprint

Cover image: www.ingimage.com

Publisher:
Scholars' Press
is a trademark of
International Book Market Service Ltd., member of OmniScriptum Publishing Group
17 Meldrum Street, Beau Bassin 71504, Mauritius

ISBN: 978-613-8-94946-6

Acknowledgements

Writing a book is harder than I thought and more rewarding than I could have ever imagined. None of this would have been possible without my best friend and wife, **Mrs.Gidishala Aruna Kranthi**. She stood by me during every struggle and all my successes. That is true relationship.

I'm eternally grateful to my Mother, who took in an extra mouth to feed when she didn't have to. She taught me discipline, tough love, manners, respect, and so much more that has helped me succeed in life. I truly have no idea where I'd be if she hadn't given me a roof over my head or became the father figure whom I desperately needed at that age.

Although this period of my life was filled with many ups and downs, my time in the Copenhagen University Denmark and Haramaya University Ethiopia was worth it. My time in the industry wouldn't have been made possible without Tue beri who taught me the honest mortgage game.

To my family. To my in-laws **Dr.G.Hanumatha Rao** and **Mrs.Subhasini** (Teacher): for always being the persons I could turn to during those dark and desperate years. they sustained me in ways that I never knew that I needed. To my little Daughter **Aadhya Kruthi:** thank you for letting me know that you had nothing but great memories of me. So thankful to have you in my life.

Finally, to all those who have been a part of my getting there: Brother B.Sammaiah, Son B.Bhanu Prakash , Daughter B.Manasa . To the true friends Azmera Megya, Dr.Narsimha, Dr.Prapreddy.

Dr.B. Rajkumar, He has received his **B. Tech** degree from National Institute of Technology **(NIT)**, Hamirpur, Himachal Pradesh, INDIA, in the Department of Computer Science & Engineering. He has received his M**. Tech and PhD** from Jawaharlal Nehru Technological University **(JNTUH)**, Hyderabad, Telangana,INDIA, in the Department of Computer Science & Engineering. He has Published 16 Hi-indexed SCI and Scopus International Journals, He has Presented 6 International Conference papers and invitee speaker for 3 international conference.

He is a Session Speaker for 7 AICTE Sponsored FDP's in India. Membership in Professional bodies: **IEEECS senior** member, The Institution of Engineers (INDIA) Member, **LMISTE, MCSI**, Member of Research Gate, He has published 4 text books in international publishing houses. He filed 2 patents out of which one in India and one in Europe. He has awarded the best instructor excellence from CISCO Global Academy for the Years 2011,12,17,18 and 2019. He also awarded as best Teacher for the year 2010 at SREC. He has awarded **a CCNA** and **Cyber Security Operations** Certified Trainer, and He is running the CISCO Networking Local Academy and trained around 4000+ graduates and MNC Employees around the world. He has 16+ years of teaching Experience in the Department of Computer Science & Engineering in various countries like Denmark (Europe) Ethiopia (Africa) and in INDIA, currently he is working as an Assistant Professor in Copenhagen University, Denmark which is the world 70th ranked university. He was awarded as best Instructor in Haramaya universities Ethiopia. He has Participated in **IUCEE FLT-2009** at INFOSYS MYSORE on "29th June to 3rd July, 2009, participated in and conducted many faculty developments Programs, participated in and conducted many workshops on like "TESTING TOOLS, MICROSOFT&IEG/JKC, IBM Tivoli and DB2, MICROSOFT.NET, CANVAS LMS, Moodle LMS, AWS Cloud etc.". More than 42 M. Tech students have done their project under his guidance in India.

Preface

This book is designed with the goal of providing a comprehensive understanding of the structure of a computer and its operations, the RTL and Micro-level operations and control in a computer, the concepts of I/O and memory organization and operating systems. Able to visualize the organization of different blocks in a computer, able to use micro-level operations to control different units in a computer, able to use Operating systems in a computer in a single textbook. In addition, the book contains an entire chapter on computer organization and operating systems.

This book covers both the fundamentals of computer organization and operating systems. Separate chapters are allocated to cover design methodologies of simple and complex combinational and sequential circuits. The book covers Basic Structure of Computers , Register Transfer Language and Micro Operations, Micro Programmed Control, The Memory System, Input-Output Organization, Operating Systems Overview, memory organization, Principles of Deadlock, File System Interface and File System Implementation.

We wrote this book as a text for an introductory course in operating systems at the junior or senior undergraduate level or at the first-year graduate level. We hope that practitioners will also find it useful. It provides a clear description of the concepts that underlie operating systems.

The book also covers computer architecture concepts from instruction set architecture, including the architecture for secure execution, pipelining and parallelism, and memory hierarchy. An attempt is made to provide numerous examples that illustrate the applications of pipelining and parallelism to increase concurrency and reduce or hide latency (two factors that affect performance). Program code examples are also used to illustrate the link between CPU architecture and a compiler and between programming methodologies and performance.

Overview of Chapters

There are 5 chapters in this book.

Chapter-1

Basic Structure of Computers: Computer Types, Functional Unit, Basic OPERATIONAL Concepts, Bus Structures, Software, Performance, Multiprocessors and Multi Computers, Data Representation, Fixed Point Representation, Floating – Point Representation.

Register Transfer Language and Micro Operations: Register Transfer Language, Register Transfer Bus and Memory Transfers, Arithmetic Micro Operations, Logic Micro Operations, Shift Micro Operations, Arithmetic Logic Shift Unit, Instruction Codes, Computer Registers Computer Instructions– Instruction Cycle, Memory – Reference Instructions, Input – Output and Interrupt, STACK Organization, Instruction Formats, Addressing Modes, DATA Transfer and Manipulation, Program Control, Reduced Instruction Set Computer.

Chapter-2

Micro Programmed Control: Control Memory, Address Sequencing, Microprogram Examples, Design of Control Unit, Hard Wired Control, Microprogrammed Control

The Memory System: Basic Concepts of Semiconductor RAM Memories, Read-Only Memories, Cache Memories Performance Considerations, Virtual Memories Secondary Storage, Introduction to RAID.

Chapter-3

Input-Output Organization: Peripheral Devices, Input-Output Interface, Asynchronous Data Transfer Modes, Priority Interrupt, Direct Memory Access, Input –Output Processor (IOP), Serial Communication; Introduction to Peripheral Components, Interconnect (PCI) Bus, Introduction to Standard Serial Communication Protocols like RS232, USB, IEEE 1394

Chapter-4

Operating Systems Overview: Overview of Computer Operating Systems Functions, Protection and Security, Distributed Systems, Special Purpose Systems, Operating Systems Structures-Operating System Services and Systems Calls, System Programs, Operating Systems Generation

Memory Management: Swapping, Contiguous Memory Allocation, Paging, Structure of The Page Table, Segmentation, Virtual Memory, Demand Paging, Page-Replacement Algorithms, Allocation of Frames, Thrashing Case Studies - UNIX, Linux, Windows

Principles of Deadlock: System Model, Deadlock Characterization, Deadlock Prevention, Detection and Avoidance, Recovery from Deadlock.

Chapter-5

File System Interface: The Concept of a File, Access Methods, Directory Structure, File System Mounting, File Sharing, Protection.

File System Implementation: File System Structure, File System Implementation, Directory Implementation, Allocation Methods, Free-Space Management.

REFERENCES:

1. *Computer Organization – Carl Hamacher, Zvonks Vranesic, Safea Zaky, Vth Edition, McGraw Hill.*
2. *Computer Systems Architecture – M. Moris Mano, IIIrd Edition, Pearson*
3. *Operating System Concepts- Abraham Silberchatz, Peter B. Galvin, Greg Gagne, 8th Edition, John Wiley.*
4. *Computer Organization and Architecture – William Stallings Sixth Edition, Pearson*
5. *Structured Computer Organization – Andrew S. Tanenbaum, 4th Edition PHI*
6. *Fundamentals of Computer Organization and Design - Sivaraama Dandamudi Springer Int. Edition.*
7. *Operating Systems – Internals and Design Principles, Stallings, sixth Edition–2009, Pearson Education.*
8. *Modern Operating Systems, Andrew S Tanenbaum 2nd Edition, PHI.*
9. *Principles of Operating Systems, B.L. Stuart, Cengage Learning, India Edition.*
10. *https://www.javatpoint.com/os-tutorial*
11. *https://www.cs.uic.edu/~jbell/CourseNotes/OperatingSystems/*
12. *https://www.tutorialspoint.com/operating_system/index.htm*
13. *https://www.tutorialspoint.com/*

Table of Content

Chapter-1	Page No
Basic Structure of Computers:	2
Computer Types	2
Functional Unit	4
Basic OPERATIONAL Concepts	5
Bus Structures	7
Software	8
Performance	9
Multiprocessors and Multi Computers	11
Data Representation	12
Fixed Point Representation	28
Floating – Point Representation	35
Register Transfer Language and Micro Operations:	41
Register Transfer Language	41
Register Transfer Bus and Memory Transfer	45
Arithmetic Micro Operations	49
Logic Micro Operations	61
Shift Micro Operations	68
Arithmetic Logic Shift Unit	71
Instruction Codes	73
Instruction Cycle	80
Memory – Reference Instructions	82
Input – Output and Interrupt	89
STACK Organization	
Instruction Formats	97
Addressing Modes	102
Data Transfer and Manipulation	108
Program Control	115
Reduced Instruction Set Computer	123

Chapter-2	Page No
Micro Programmed Control:	129
Control Memory	131
Address Sequencing	134
Microprogram Examples	139
Micro Instruction Format	141
Symbolic Micro Instruction	144
The Memory System:	147
MAIN Memory	150
Basic Concepts of Semiconductor RAM Memories	151
Read-Only Memories	152
Memory Connection to CPU	164
Cache Memory	166
Virtual Memory	174
Introduction to RAID	181
Chapter-3	186
Input-Output Organization:	186
Peripheral Devices	187
Input-Output Interface	188
Direct Memory Access	189
COA-Asynchronous Data Transfer Modes	195
COA-Priority Interrupt	201
Input –Output Processor (IOP)	204
Serial Communication	207
RS232	211
IEEE 1394	212
Peripheral Component Interconnect(PCI)	214
Interconnect (PCI) Bus	214
USB	215

Chapter-4	Page No
Operating Systems Overview:	218
Overview of Computer Operating Systems Functions	218
overview	219
Types of Operating System	222
Operating System Services	225
User Operating-system Interface	226
Operating Systems Structures	231
Systems Calls	234
Types of System Calls	237
Operating Systems Generation	241
Protection and Security	242
Memory Management:	247
Swapping	250
Contiguous Memory Allocation	252
Fragmentation	253
Segmentation	255
Paging	257
Hardware Support	261
Protection	262
Shared pages	264
Structure of The Page Table	265
Virtual Memory	267
Demand Paging	268
Page-Replacement Algorithms	270
Allocation of Frames	274
Thrashing	276
Principles of Deadlock:	278
System Model	278
Deadlock Characterization(Necessary Conditions)	280
Deadlock Prevention	281

Deadlock Avoidance	285
Recovery from Deadlock	286
Chapter-5	
File System Interface:	290
The Concept of a File	290
Access Methods	293
Directory Structure	295
File System Mounting	299
File Sharing	301
Consistency Semantics	303
Protection	304
File System Implementation:	308
File System Structure	308
File System Implementation	310
Directory Implementation	313
Allocation Methods	314
Free-Space Management	319

Computer Organization and Operating System

Dr.Rajkumar Banoth

Godishala Aruna Kranthi

Chapter-1

Introduction

Computer Architecture in general covers three aspects of computer design namely: Computer Hardware, Instruction set Architecture and Computer Organization. Computer hardware consists of electronic circuits, displays, magnetic and optical storage media and communication facilities. Instruction set Architecture is programmer visible machine interface such as instruction set, registers, memory organization and exception handling. Two main approaches are mainly CISC (Complex Instruction Set Computer) and RISC (Reduced Instruction Set Computer) Computer Organization includes the high level aspects of a design, such as memory system, the bus structure and the design of the internal CPU.

Computer Types

Computer is a fast electronic calculating machine which accepts digital input, processes it according to the internally stored instructions (Programs) and produces the result on the output device. The internal operation of the computer can be as depicted in the figure below:

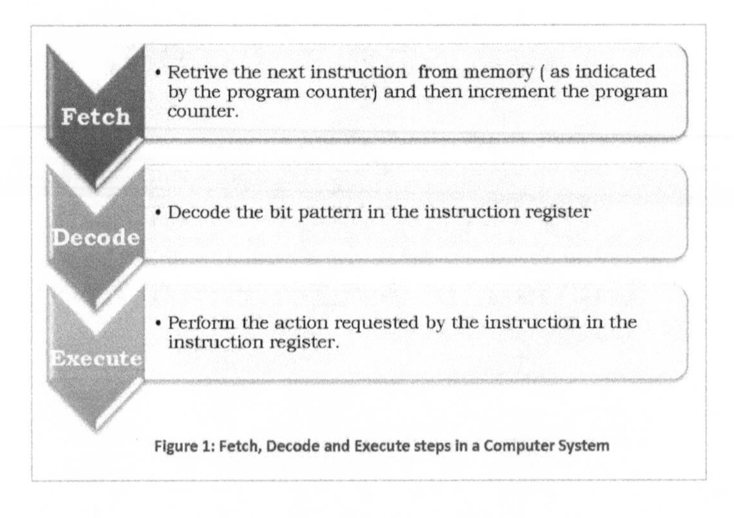

Figure 1: Fetch, Decode and Execute steps in a Computer System

The computers can be classified into various categories as given below:

Micro Computer

Laptop Computer

Work Station

Super Computer

Main Frame

Hand Held

Multi core

Micro Computer:

A personal computer; designed to meet the computer needs of an individual. Provides access to a wide variety of computing applications, such as word processing, photo editing, e-mail, and internet.

Laptop Computer:

A portable, compact computer that can run on power supply or a battery unit. All components are integrated as one compact unit. It is generally more expensive than a comparable desktop. It is also called a Notebook.

Work Station:

Powerful desktop computer designed for specialized tasks. Generally used for tasks that requires a lot of processing speed. Can also be an ordinary personal computer attached to a LAN (local area network).

Super Computer:

A computer that is considered to be fastest in the world. Used to execute tasks that would take lot of time for other computers. For Ex: Modeling weather systems, genome sequence, etc (Refer site: http://www.top500.org

Main Frame:

Large expensive computer capable of simultaneously processing data for hundreds or thousands of users. Used to store, manage, and process large amounts of data that need to be reliable, secure, and centralized.

Hand Held:

It is also called a PDA (Personal Digital Assistant). A computer that fits into a pocket, runs on batteries, and is used while holding the unit in your hand. Typically used as an appointment book, address book, calculator and notepad.

Multi Core:

Have Multiple Cores – parallel computing platforms. Many Cores or computing elements in a single chip. Typical Examples: Sony Play station, Core 2 Duo, i3, i7 etc.

Functional Units

A computer in its simplest form comprises five functional units namely input unit, output unit memory unit, arithmetic & logic unit and control unit. Figure 2 depicts the functional units of a computer system.

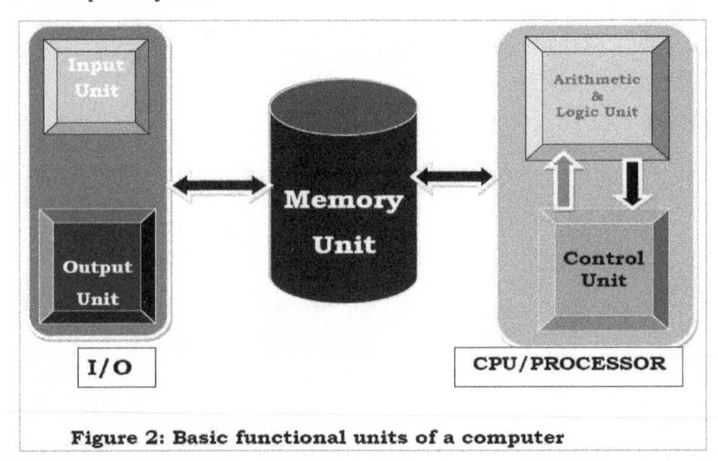

Figure 2: Basic functional units of a computer

Let us discuss about each of them in brief:

1. Input Unit: Computer accepts encoded information through input unit. The standard input device is a keyboard. Whenever a key is pressed, keyboard controller sends the code to CPU/Memory.

Examples include Mouse, Joystick, Tracker ball, Light pen, Digitizer, Scanner etc.

2. Memory Unit: Memory unit stores the program instructions (Code), data and results of computations etc. Memory unit is classified as:

1.Primary /Main Memory and 2. Secondary Memory

Primary memory is a semiconductor memory that provides access at high speed. Run time program instructions and operands are stored in the main memory. Main memory is classified again as ROM and RAM. ROM holds system programs and firmware routines such as BIOS, POST, I/O Drivers that are essential to manage the hardware of a computer. RAM is termed as Read/Write memory or user memory that holds run time program instruction and data. While primary storage is essential, it is volatile in nature and expensive. Additional requirement of memory could be supplied as auxiliary memory at cheaper cost.

Secondary memories are non volatile in nature.

Arithmetic and logic unit: ALU consist of necessary logic circuits like adder, comparator etc., to perform operations of addition, multiplication, comparison of two numbers etc.

Output Unit: Computer after computation returns the computed results, error messages, etc. via output unit. The standard output device is a video monitor, LCD/TFT monitor. Other output devices are printers, plotters etc.

Control Unit: Control unit co-ordinates activities of all units by issuing control signals. Control signals issued by control unit govern the data transfers and then appropriate operations take place. Control unit interprets or decides the operation/action to be performed. The operations of a computer can be summarized as follows: A set of instructions called a program reside in the main memory of computer.

The CPU fetches those instructions sequentially one-by-one from the main memory, decodes them and performs the specified operation on associated data operands in ALU. Processed data and results will be displayed on an output unit. All activities pertaining to processing and data movement inside the computer machine are governed by control unit.

Basic Operational Concepts

An Instruction consists of two parts, an Operation code and operand/s as shown below:

OPCODE OPERAND/s

Let us see a typical instruction

ADD LOCA, R0

This instruction is an addition operation.

The following are the steps to execute the instruction:

Step 1: Fetch the instruction from main memory into the processor

Step 2: Fetch the operand at location LOCA from main memory into the processor

Step 3: Add the memory operand (i.e. fetched contents of LOCA) to the contents of register RO

Step 4: Store the result (sum) in RO.

The same instruction can be realized using two instructions as Load LOCA, R1 Add R1, RO

The steps to execute the instructions can be enumerated as below:

Step 1: Fetch the instruction from main memory into the processor

Step 2: Fetch the operand at location LOCA from main memory into the processor Register R1

Step 3: Add the content of Register R1 and the contents of register RO

Step 4: Store the result (sum) in RO.

Figure 3 below shows how the memory and the processor are connected. As shown in the diagram, in addition to the ALU and the control circuitry, the processor contains a number of registers used for several different purposes. The instruction register holds the instruction that is currently being executed.

The program counter keeps track of the execution of the program. It contains the memory address of the next instruction to be fetched and executed. There are n general purpose registers RO to Rn-1 which can be used by the programmers during writing programs.

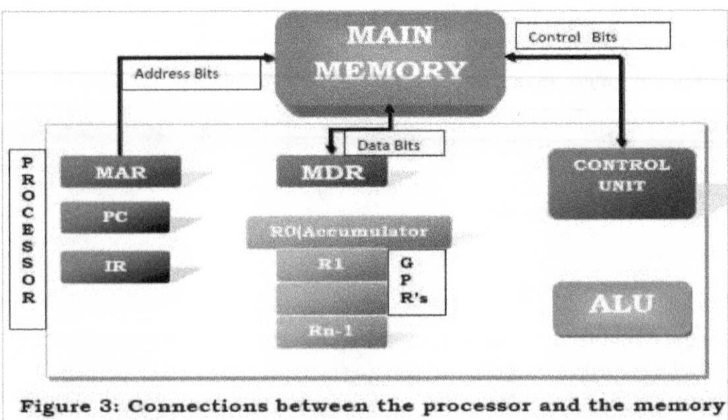

Figure 3: Connections between the processor and the memory

The interaction between the processor and the memory and the direction of flow of information is as shown in the diagram below:

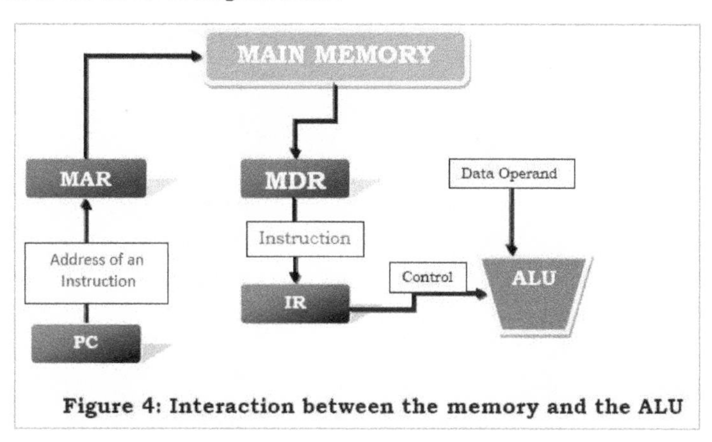

Figure 4: Interaction between the memory and the ALU

BUS STRUCTURES

Group of lines that serve as connecting path for several devices is called a bus (one bit per line). Individual parts must communicate over a communication line or path for exchanging data, address and control information as shown in the diagram below.

Printer example – processor to printer. A common approach is to use the concept of buffer registers to hold the content during the transfer.

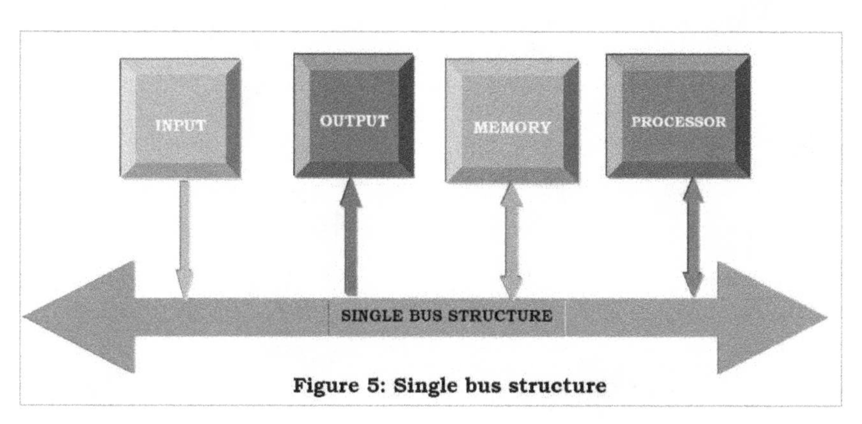

Figure 5: Single bus structure

SOFTWARE

If a user wants to enter and run an application program, he/she needs a System Software. System Software is a collection of programs that are executed as needed to perform functions such as:

- Receiving and interpreting user commands
- Entering and editing application programs and storing them as files in secondary storage devices
- Running standard application programs such as word processors, spread sheets, games etc.
- Operating system - is key system software component which helps the user to exploit the below underlying hardware with the programs.

USER PROGRAM and OS ROUTINE INTERACTION

Let's assume computer with 1 processor, 1 disk and 1 printer and application program is in machine code on disk. The various tasks are performed in a coordinated fashion, which is called multitasking. **t0, t1 ...t5** are the instances of time and the interaction during various instances as given below:

t0: the OS loads the program from the disk to memory

t1: program executes

t2: program accesses disk

t3: program executes some more

t4: program accesses printer t5: program terminates

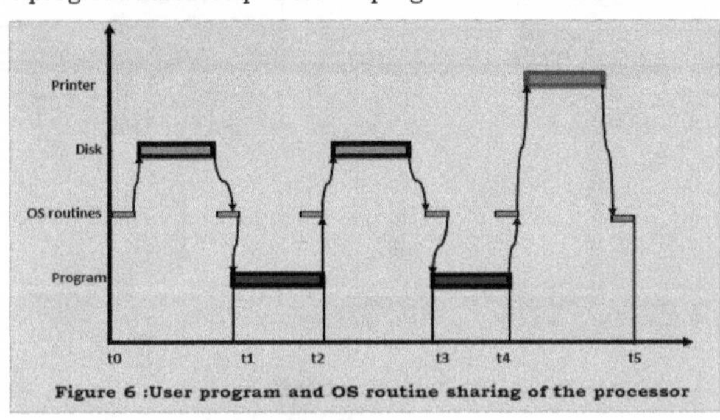

Figure 6 :User program and OS routine sharing of the processor

PERFORMANCE

The total time required to execute a program is the most important measure of performance for a computer. (t0-t5 of earlier example). Compiler, instruction set and hardware architecture, program all have impact on performance.

Basic Performance Equation:

The basic performance equation is given by **T = (N * S) / R**

where

T = execution time,

N = number of instructions,

S = average cycles per instruction,

R = clock rate in cycles per second

CACHING

Commonly used data are copied to on-processor memory (cache) to reduce access time. Small memories can be made with higher speed than large ones. In a computer, we need both.

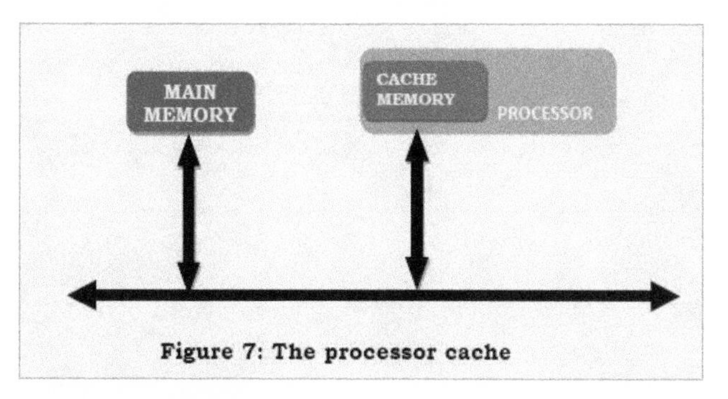

Figure 7: The processor cache

PIPELINING and SUPERSCALR OPERATION

Pipelining: Like a production line, instruction execution overlapped so greater parallelism is achieved. Superscalar operation: Execute several instructions simultaneously using multiple ALU's.

CISC vs RISC

Reduced instruction set computer

–Large N, small S

Complex instruction set computer

–Small N, large S

COMPILER

Translates high level language such as C, C++ and Java to machine instructions. Aims to reduce N×S

PERFORMANCE MEASUREMENT

Benchmark refers to standard task used to measure how well a processor operates. To evaluate the performance of Computers, a non-profit organization known as SPEC-System Performance Evaluation Corporation employs agreed-upon application programs of real world for benchmarks. Accordingly, it gives performance measure for a computer as the time required to execute a given benchmark program. The SPEC rating is computed as follows .

$$SPEC\ Rating = \frac{Running\ Time\ on\ a\ Reference\ Computer}{Running\ Time\ on\ a\ Test\ Computer}$$

MULTIPROCESSORS AND MULTICOMPUTERS

Multicomputer

A computer made up of several computers. The term generally refers to an architecture in which each processor has its own memory rather than multiple processors with a shared memory. Distributed computing deals with hardware and software systems containing more than one processing. Element or storage element, concurrent processes, or multiple programs, running under a loosely or tightly controlled regime. A multicomputer may be considered to be either a loosely coupled NUMA computer or a tightly coupled cluster. Multi computers are commonly used when strong computer power is required in an environment with restricted physical space or electrical power. Common suppliers include Mercury Computer Systems, CSPI, and SKY Computers. Common uses include 3D medical imaging devices and mobile radar. In distributed computing a program is split up into parts that run simultaneously on multiple computers communicating over a network. Distributed computing is a form of parallel computing, but parallel computing is most commonly used to describe program parts running simultaneously on multiple processors in the same computer. Both types of processing require dividing a program into parts that can run simultaneously, but distributed programs often must deal with heterogeneous environments, network links of varying latencies, and unpredictable failures in the network or the computers.

Multiprocessor

A multiprocessor system is simply a computer that has more than one CPU on its motherboard. If the operating system is built to take advantage of this, it can run different processes (or different threads belonging to the same process) on different CPUs. Multiprocessing is the use of two or more central processing units (CPUs) within a single computer system. The term also refers to the ability of a system to support more than one processor and/or the ability to allocate tasks between them.[1] There are many variations on this basic theme, and the definition of multiprocessing can vary with context, mostly as a function of how CPUs are defined (multiple cores on one die, multiple chips in one package, multiple packages in one system unit, etc.).

Data Representation

Introduction

The digital computer is a digital system that performs various computational tasks. The word ***digital*** implies that the information in the computer is represented by variables that take a limited number of discrete values. These values are processed internally by components that can maintain a limited number of discrete states. The decimal digits 0, 1, 2, 9, for example, provide 10 discrete values. The first electronic digital computers, developed in the late 1940s, were used primarily for numerical computations. In this case the discrete elements are the digits. From this application the term ***digital computer*** has emerged. In practice, digital computers function more reliably only if two states are used. Because of the physical restriction of components, and because human logic tends to be binary (i.e. true-or-false, yes-or-no statements), digital components that are constrained to take discrete values are further constrained to take only two values and are said to be ***binary***.

Objectives:

After studying this unit, the learner will be able to

- Explain various units of a digital computer
- Understand different data types
- Explain fixed and floating point number representation
- Discuss various binary and error detection codes

Digital Computers

Digital computers use the binary number system, which has two digits: 0 and 1. A binary digit is called a ***bit***. Information is represented in digital computers in groups of bits. By using various coding techniques, groups of bits can be made to represent not only binary numbers but also other discrete symbols, such as decimal digits or letters of the alphabet.

By the judicious use of binary arrangements and by using various coding techniques, the groups of bits are used to develop complete sets of instructions for performing various types of computations. In contrast to the common decimal numbers that employ the base 10 system, binary numbers use a base 2 system with two digits: 0 and 1.

The decimal equivalent of a binary number can be found by expanding it into a power series with a base of 2.

For example, the binary number 1001011 represents a quantity that can be converted to a decimal number by multiplying each bit by the base 2 raised to an integer power as follows: 1 x 26 + 0 x 25 + 0 x 24 + 1 x 23 + 0 x 22 + 1 x 21 + 1 x 20 = 75

The seven bits 1001011 represent a binary number whose decimal equivalent is 75. However, this same group of seven bits represents the letter K when used in conjunction with a binary code for the letters of the alphabet. It may also represent a control code for specifying some decision logic in a particular digital computer.

In other words, groups of bits in a digital computer are used to represent many different things. This is similar to the concept that the same letters of an alphabet are used to construct different languages, such as English and French. A computer system is sometimes subdivided into two functional entities: hardware and software.

The ***hardware*** of the computer consists of all the electronic components and electromechanical devices that comprise the physical entity of the device.

Computer ***software*** consists of the instructions and the data that the computer manipulates to perform various data-processing tasks.

A sequence of instructions for the computer is called a ***program***. The data that are manipulated by the program constitute the ***data base***. A computer system is composed of its hardware and the system software available for its use.

The ***system software*** of a computer consists of a collection of programs whose purpose is to make more effective use of the computer.

The programs included in a systems software package are referred to as the ***operating system***. They are distinguished from application programs written by the user for the purpose of solving particular problems.

For example, a high-level language program written by a user to solve particular data-processing needs is an ***application program***, but the compiler that translates the high-level language program to machine language is a ***system program***.

The customer who buys a computer system would need, in addition to the hardware, any available software needed for effective operation of the computer. The system software is an indispensable part of a total computer system. Its function is to compensate for the differences that exist between user needs and the capability of the hardware.

The hardware of the computer is usually divided into three major parts as shown in Fig. 8.

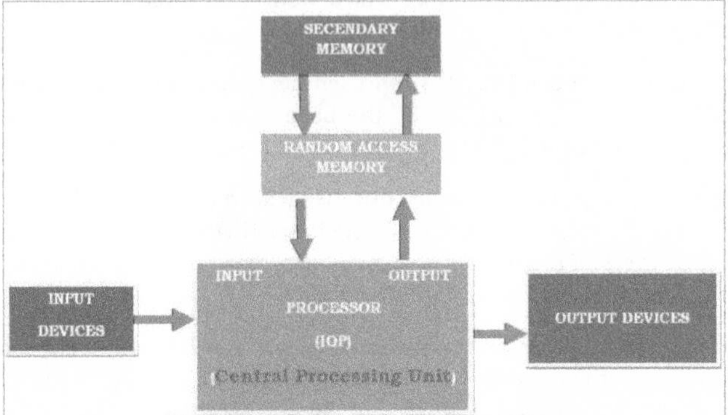

Fig. 8: Block diagram of a digital computer

The ***Central Processing Unit (CPU)*** contains an ***Arithmetic and Logic Unit (ALU)*** for manipulating data, a number of registers for storing data, and control circuits for fetching and executing instructions. The memory of a computer contains storage for instructions and data. It is called a ***Random Access Memory (RAM)*** because the CPU can access any location in memory at random and retrieve the binary information within a fixed interval of time.

The ***Input-Output Processor (IOP)*** contains electronic circuits for communicating and controlling the transfer of information between the computer and the outside world. The input and output devices connected to the computer include keyboards, printers, terminals, magnetic disk drives, and other communication devices. This book provides the basic knowledge necessary to understand the hardware operations of a computer system.

The subject is sometimes considered from three different points of view, depending on the interest of the investigator. When dealing with computer hardware it is customary to distinguish between what is referred to as computer organization, computer design, and computer architecture.

Computer organization is concerned with the way the hardware components operate and the way they are connected together to form the computer system. The various components are assumed to be in place and the task is to investigate the organizational structure to verify that the computer parts operate as intended.

Computer design is concerned with the hardware design of the computer. Once the computer specifications are formulated, it is the task of the designer to develop hardware for the system. Computer design is concerned with the determination of what hardware should be used and how the parts should be connected. This aspect of computer hardware is sometimes referred to as ***computer implementation***.

Computer architecture is concerned with the structure and behavior of the computers as seen by the user. It includes the information formats, the instruction set, and techniques for addressing memory. The architectural design of a computer system is concerned with the specifications of the various functional modules, such as processors and memories, and structuring them together into a computer system.

Data Types

Binary information in digital computers is stored in memory or processor registers. Registers contain either data or control information. Control information is a bit or a group of bits used to specify the sequence of command signals needed for manipulation of the data in other registers. Data are numbers and other binary-coded information that are operated on, to achieve required computational results.

The data types found in the registers of digital computers may be classified as being one of the following categories:

(1) numbers used in arithmetic computations,

(2) letters of the alphabet used in data processing, and

(3) other discrete symbols used for specific purposes.

All types of data, except binary numbers, are represented in computer registers in binary-coded form. This is because registers are made up of flip-flops and flip-flops are two-state devices that can store only 1's and 0's. The binary number system is the most natural system to be used in a digital computer. But sometimes it is convenient to employ different number systems, especially the decimal number system, since it is used by people to perform arithmetic computations.

Number Systems

As we know, the number system is a form of expressing the numbers. In **number system conversion**, we will study to convert a number of one base, to a number of another base. There are a variety of number systems such as binary numbers, decimal numbers, hexadecimal numbers, octal numbers, which can be exercised.

In this article, you will learn the conversion of one base number to another base number considering all the base numbers such as decimal, binary, octal and hexadecimal with the help of examples. Here, the following number system conversion methods are explained.

- Binary to Decimal Number System
- Decimal to Binary Number System
- Octal to Binary Number System
- Binary to Octal Number System
- Binary to Hexadecimal Number System
- Hexadecimal to Binary Number System

The general representation of number systems are;

- Decimal Number – Base 10 – N_{10}
- Binary Number – Base 2 – N_2
- Octal Number – Base 8 – N_8
- Hexadecimal Number – Base 16 – N_{16}

Number System Conversion Methods

Number system conversions deal with the operations to change the base of the numbers. For example, to change a decimal number with base 10 to binary number with base 2. We can also perform the arithmetic operations like addition, subtraction, multiplication on the number system. Here, we will learn the methods to convert the number of one base to the number of another base starting with the decimal number system. The representation of number system base conversion in general form for any base number is;

Number System Conversion Table

Binary Numbers	Octal Numbers	Decimal Numbers	Hexadecimal Numbers
0000	0	0	0
0001	1	1	1
0010	2	2	2
0011	3	3	3
0100	4	4	4
0101	5	5	5
0110	6	6	6
0111	7	7	7
1000	10	8	8
1001	11	9	9
1010	12	10	A
1011	13	11	B
1100	14	12	C
1101	15	13	D
1110	16	14	E
1111	17	15	F

Table 1. Number System Conversion

$(Number)_b = d_{n-1}\ d_{n-2}$——$.d_1\ d_0\ .\ d_{-1}\ d_{-2}$ —- d_{-m}

In the above expression, $d_{n-1}\ d_{n-2}$——$.d_1\ d_0$ represents the value of integer part and $d_{-1}\ d_{-2}$ — - d_{-m} represents the fractional part.

Also, d_{n-1} is the Most significant bit (MSB) and d_{-m} is the Least significant bit (LSB).

Decimal to Other Bases

Converting a decimal number to other base numbers is easy. We have to divide the decimal number by the converted value of the new base.

Decimal to Binary Number:

Suppose if we have to convert **decimal to binary,** then divide the decimal number by 2.

Example 1. Convert $(25)_{10}$ to binary number.

Solution: Let us create a table based on this question.

Operation	Output	Remainder
25 ÷ 2	12	1(MSB)
12 ÷ 2`	6	0
6 ÷ 2	3	0
3 ÷ 2	1	1
1 ÷ 2	0	1(LSB)

Table .2

Therefore, from the above table, we can write,

$(25) = (11001)_2$

Decimal to Octal Number:

To convert decimal to octal number we have to divide the given original number by 8 such that base 10 changes to base 8.

Let us understand with the help of an example.

Example 2: Convert 128_{10} to octal number.

Solution: Let us represent the conversion in tabular form.

Operation	Output	Remainder
128÷8	16	0(MSB)
16÷8	2	0
2÷8	0	2(LSB)

Therefore, the equivalent octal number = 200_8

Table .3

Decimal to Hexadecimal:

Again in decimal to hex conversion, we have to divide the given decimal number by 16.

Example 3: Convert 128_{10} to hex.

Solution: As per the method, we can create a table;

Therefore, the equivalent hexadecimal number is **80_{16}**

Operation	Output	Remainder
128÷16	8	0(MSB)
8÷16	0	8(LSB)

Here MSB stands for a Most significant bit and LSB stands for a least significant bit.

Table .4

Other Base System to Decimal Conversion

Binary to Decimal:

In this conversion, binary number to a decimal number, we use multiplication method, in such a way that, if a number with base n has to be converted into a number with base 10, then each digit of the given number is multiplied from MSB to LSB with reducing the power of the base. Let us understand this conversion with the help of an example.

Example 1. Convert $(1101)_2$ into a decimal number.

Solution: Given a binary number $(1101)_2$.

Multiplying each digit from MSB to LSB with reducing the power of the base number 2.

$1 \times 2^3 + 1 \times 2^2 + 0 \times 2^1 + 1 \times 2^0$

$= 8 + 4 + 0 + 1$

$= 13$

Therefore, $(1101)_2 = (13)_{10}$

Octal to Decimal:

To convert octal to decimal, we multiply the digits of octal number with decreasing power of the base number 8, starting from MSB to LSB and then add them all together.

Example 2: Convert 22_8 to decimal number.

Solution: Given, 22_8

$2 \times 8^1 + 2 \times 8^0$

$= 16 + 2$

$= 18$

Therefore, $22_8 = 18_{10}$

Hexadecimal to Decimal:

Example 3: Convert 121_{16} to decimal number.

Solution:

$1 \times 16^2 + 2 \times 16^1 + 1 \times 16^0$

$= 16 \times 16 + 2 \times 16 + 1 \times 1$

$= 289$

Therefore, $121_{16} = 289_{10}$

Hexadecimal to Binary Shortcut Method

To convert hexadecimal numbers to binary and vice versa is easy, you just have to memorize the table given below.

Hexadecimal Number	Binary
0	0000
1	0001
2	0010
3	0011
4	0100
5	0101

6	0110
7	0111
8	1000
9	1001
A	1010
B	1011
C	1100
D	1101
E	1110
F	1111

Table 5.Hexadecimal to Binary

You can easily solve the problems based on hexadecimal and binary conversions with the help of this table.

Example: Convert $(89)_{16}$ into a binary number.

Solution: From the table, we can get the binary value of 8 and 9, hexadecimal base numbers. 8 = 1000 and 9 = 1001

Therefore, $(89)_{16} = (10001001)_2$

Octal to Binary Shortcut Method

To convert octal to binary number, we can simply use the table. Just like having a table for hexadecimal and its equivalent binary, in the same way, we have a table for octal and its equivalent binary number.

Octal Number	Binary
0	000
1	001
2	010
3	011
4	100
5	101
6	110
7	111

Table 6.Octal to Binary

Example: Convert $(214)_8$ into a binary number.

Solution: From the table, we know,

$2 \rightarrow 010$

$1 \rightarrow 001$

$4 \rightarrow 100$

Therefore, $(214)_8 = (010001100)_2$

Decimal Representation

The binary number system is the most natural system for a computer, but people are accustomed to the decimal system. One way to solve this conflict is to convert all input decimal numbers into binary numbers, let the computer perform all arithmetic operations in binary and then convert the binary results back to decimal for the human user to understand. However, it is also possible for the computer to perform arithmetic operations directly with decimal numbers provided they are placed in registers in a coded form.

Decimal numbers enter the computer usually as binary-coded alphanumeric characters. These codes, introduced later, may contain from six to eight bits for each decimal digit. When decimal numbers are used for internal arithmetic computations, they are converted to a binary code with four bits per digit.

Binary Code:

A binary code is a group of n bits that assume up to 2^n distinct combinations of 1's and 0's with each combination representing one element of the set that is being coded.
For example, a set of four elements can be coded by a 2-bit code with each element assigned one of the following bit combinations; 00, 01, 10, or 11. A set of eight elements requires a 3-bit code, a set of 16 elements requires a 4-bit code, and so on.

A binary code will have some unassigned bit combinations if the number of elements in the set is not a multiple power of 2.The 10 decimal digits form such a set. A binary code that distinguishes among 10 elements must contain at least four bits, but six combinations will remain unassigned.

Binary-Coded Decimal

Numerous different codes can be obtained by arranging four bits in 10 distinct combinations. The bit assignment most commonly used for the decimal digits is the straight binary assignment listed in the first 10 entries of given Table .

This particular code is called binary-coded decimal and is commonly referred to by its abbreviation BCD.

Decimal number	Binary-coded decimal (BCD) number	
0	0000	↑
1	0001	
2	0010	
3	0011	Code
4	0100	for one
5	0101	decimal
6	0110	digit
7	0111	
8	1000	
9	1001	↓
10	0001 0000	
20	0010 0000	
50	0101 0000	
99	1001 1001	
248	0010 0100 1000	

Table 7: Binary Coded Decimal (BCD) Numbers

It is very important to understand the difference between the conversion of decimal numbers into binary and the binary coding of decimal numbers. For example, when converted to a binary number, the decimal number 99 is represented by the string of bits 110001 1, but when represented in BCD, it becomes 1001 1001 .

The only difference between a decimal number represented by the familiar digit symbols 0, 1, 2, ... , 9 and the BCD symbols 0001, 0010, ... , 1001 is in the symbols used to represent the digits-the number itself is exactly the same. A few decimal numbers and their representation in BCD are listed in Table .

N	100 1110	.	010 1110
O	100 1111	(	010 1000
P	101 0000	+	010 1011
Q	101 0001	$	010 0100
R	101 0010	*	010 0100
S	101 0011	)	010 1001
T	101 0100	-	010 1101
U	101 0101	/	010 1111
V	101 0110	,	010 1100
W	101 0111	=	011 1101
X	101 1000		
Y	101 1001		
Z	101 1010		

Table 8: American Standard Code for Information Interchange (ASCII)

Complements

Complements are used in digital computers for simplifying the subtraction operation and for logical manipulation. There are two types of complements for each base ***r*** system: the ***r's*** complement and the ***(r-1)'s*** complement. When the value of the base ***r*** is substituted in the name, the two types are referred to as the 2's and 1's complement for binary numbers and the 10's and 9's complement for decimal numbers.

(r-1)'s Complement

Given a number N in base r having n digits, the *(r-1)'s* complement of N is defined as $(r^n - 1) - N$.

For decimal numbers $r = 10$ and $r - 1 = 9$, so the *9's* complement of N is $(10^n - 1) - N$.

Now, 10^n represents a number that consists of a single *1* followed by *n 0s*.

$10^n - 1$ is a number represented by *n 9s*. For example, with $n = 4$ we have $10^4 = 10000$ and $10^4 - 1 = 9999$.

It follows that the *9's* complement of a decimal number is obtained by subtracting each digit from *9*. For example, the *9's* complement of *546700* is *999999 – 546700 = 453299* and the *9's* complement of *12389* is *99999 –12389 = 87610*.

For binary numbers, $r = 2$ and $r - 1 = 1$, so the 1's complement of N is $(2^n - 1) - N$. Again, 2^n is represented by a binary number that consists of a *1* followed by *n 0s*.

$2^n - 1$ is a binary number represented by *n 1s*. For example, with $n = 4$, we have $2^4 = (10000)_2$ and $2^4 - 1 = (1111)_2$. Thus the *1's* complement of a binary number is obtained by subtracting each digit from *1*. However, the subtraction of a binary digit from *1* causes the bit to change from *0 to 1* or from *1 to 0*. Therefore, the *1's* complement of a binary number is formed by changing *1s into 0s* and *0s into 1s*.

For example, the *1's* complement of *1011001* is *0100110* and the *1's* complement of *0001111* is *1110000*. The *(r – 1)'s* complement of octal or hexadecimal numbers are obtained by subtracting each digit from *7 or F* (decimal 15) respectively.

(r 's) Complement

The *r 's* complement of an *n* digit number N in base r is defined as $r^n - N$ for $N \neq 0$ and 0 for $N = 0$. Comparing with the *(r – 1)'s* complement, we note that the *r 's* complement is obtained by adding *1* to the *(r – 1)'s* complement since $r^n - N = [(r^n - 1) - N] + 1$. Thus the *10's* complement of the decimal *2389* is *7610 + 1 = 7611* and is obtained by adding *1* to the *9's* complement value. The *2's* complement of binary *101100* is *010011 + 1 = 010100* and is obtained by adding *1* to the *1's* complement value. Since *10n* is a number represented by a *1* followed by *n 0s*, then $10^n - N$, which is the *10's* complement of *N*, can be formed also by leaving all least significant *0s* unchanged, subtracting the first non-zero least significant digit from *10*, and then subtracting all higher significant digits from *9*.

The *10's* complement of *246700* is *753300* and is obtained by *leaving the two zeros unchanged*, subtracting *7 from 10*, and subtracting the *other three digits from 9*. Similarly, the *2's* complement can be formed by leaving all least significant *0's* and the first *1* unchanged, and then replacing *1s by 0s* and *0s by 1s* in all other higher significant bits.

The *2's* complement of *1101100* is *0010100* and is obtained by *leaving the two low-order 0s and the first 1 unchanged,* and then replacing *1s by 0s* and *0s by 1s* in the other four most significant bits. In the definitions above it was assumed that the numbers do not have a radix point. If the original number *N* contains a radix point, it should be removed temporarily to form the *r's* or *(r-1)'s* complement. The radix point is then restored to the complemented number in the same relative position. It is also worth mentioning that the complement of the complement restores the number to its original value. The *r's* complement of *N* is $r^n - N$. The complement of the complement is $r^n - (r^n - N) = N$ giving back the original number.

Subtraction of Unsigned Numbers

The direct method of subtraction taught in elementary schools uses the borrow concept. In this method we borrow a 1 from a higher significant position when the minuend digit is smaller than the corresponding subtrahend digit. This seems to be easiest when people perform subtraction with paper and pencil. When subtraction is implemented with digital hardware, this method is found to be less efficient than the method that uses complements.

The subtraction of two ***n*** digit unsigned numbers $M - N\ (N \neq 0)$ in base ***r*** can be done as follows:

1. ***Add the minuend M to the r's complement of the subtrahend N.***
   This performs $M + (r^n - N) = M - N + r^n$.
2. ***If*** $M \geq N$***, the sum will produce an end carry*** r^n ***which is discarded, and what is left is the result*** $M - N$.
3. ***If*** $M < N$***, the sum does not produce an end carry and is equal to*** $r^n - (N - M)$***, which is the r's complement of*** $(N - M)$***. To obtain the answer in a familiar form, take the r's complement of the sum and place a negative sign in front.***

Consider, for example, the subtraction 72532 – 13250 = 59282.

The 10's complement of 13250 is 86750.

Therefore: M = 72532

10's complement of N = +86750

Sum = 159282

Discard end carry 105 = -100000

Answer =59282

Since we are dealing with unsigned numbers, there is really no way to get an unsigned result for the second example. When working with paper and pencil, we recognize that the answer must be changed to a signed negative number. When subtracting with complements, the negative answer is recognized by the absence of the end carry and the complemented result. Subtraction with complements is done with binary numbers in a similar manner using the same procedure outlined above. Using the two binary numbers X = 1010100 and Y = 1000011, we perform the subtraction X – Y and Y – X using 2's complements:

X =	1010100
2's complement of Y =	+0111101
Sum =	10010001
Discard end carry 2^7 =	−10000000
Answer: X − Y =	0010001
Y =	1000011
2's complement of X =	+0101100
Sum =	1101111

There is no end carry. Answer is negative 0010001 = 2's complement of 1101111

Fixed-Point Representation

Positive integers, including zero, can be represented as unsigned numbers. However, to represent negative integers, we need a notation for negative values. In ordinary arithmetic, a negative number is indicated by a minus sign and a positive number by a plus sign. Because of hardware limitations, computers must represent everything with 1s and 0s, including the sign of a number. As a consequence, it is customary to represent the sign with a bit placed in the leftmost position of the number. The convention is to make the sign bit equal to 0 for positive and to 1 for negative.

In addition to the sign, a number may have a ***binary (or decimal) point***. The position of the binary point is needed to represent fractions, integers, or mixed integer-fraction numbers. The representation of the binary point in a register is complicated by the fact that it is characterized by a position in the register.

There are two ways of specifying the position of the binary point in a register: by giving it a fixed position or by employing a floating-point representation. The fixed-point method as-

The two positions most widely used are (1) a binary point in the extreme left of the register to make the stored number a fraction, and (2) a binary point in the extreme right of the register to make the stored number an integer. In either case, the binary point is not actually present, but its presence is assumed from the fact that the number stored in the register is treated as a fraction or as an integer. The floating-point representation uses a second register to store a number that designates the position of the decimal point in the first register. Floating-point representation is discussed further in the next section.

Integer Representation

When an integer binary number is positive, the sign is represented by 0 and the magnitude by a positive binary number. When the number is negative, the sign is represented by 1 but the rest of the number may be represented in one of three possible ways:

1. ***Signed-magnitude representation***
2. ***Signed-1's complement representation***
3. ***Signed-2's complement representation***

The signed-magnitude representation of a negative number consists of the magnitude and a negative sign. In the other two representations, the negative number is represented in either the 1's or 2's complement of its positive value.

As an example, consider the signed number 14 stored in an 8-bit register. +14 is represented by a sign bit of 0 in the leftmost position followed by the binary equivalent of 14: 00001110. Note that each of the eight bits of the register must have a value and therefore 0's must be inserted in the most significant positions following the sign bit.

Although there is only one way to represent +14, there are three different ways to represent -14 with eight bits.

In signed-magnitude representation	*1*	*000111 0*
In signed-1's complement representation	*1*	*111000 1*
In signed-2's complement representation	*1*	*111001 0*

The signed-magnitude representation of -14 is obtained from +14 by complementing only the sign bit. The signed-1's complement representation of -14 is obtained by complementing all the bits of +14, including the sign bit. The signed-2's complement representation is obtained by taking the 2's complement of the positive number, including its sign bit. The signed-magnitude system is used in ordinary arithmetic but is awkward when employed in computer arithmetic.

Therefore, the signed-complement is normally used. The 1's complement imposes difficulties because it has two representations of 0 (+0 and -0). It is seldom used for arithmetic operations except in some older computers. The 1's complement is useful as a logical operation since the change of 1 to 0 or 0 to 1 is equivalent to a logical complement operation.The following discussion of signed binary arithmetic deals exclusively with the signed-2's complement representation of negative numbers.

Arithmetic Addition

The addition of two numbers in the signed-magnitude system follows the rules of ordinary arithmetic. If the signs are the same, we add the two magnitudes and give the sum the common sign. If the signs are different, we subtract the smaller magnitude from the larger and give the result the sign of the larger magnitude. For example, (+25) + (-37) = -(37 – 25) = -12 and is done by subtracting the smaller magnitude 25 from the larger magnitude 37 and using the sign of 37 for the sign of the result. This is a process that requires the comparison of the signs and the magnitudes and then performing either addition or subtraction.

+ 6	00000110	-6	1111101 0
+ 13	00001101	+13	0000110 1
--- --	-------------	-----	---------- ---
+ 19	00010011	+7	0000011 1
+ 6	00000110	-6	1111101 0
- 13	11110011	-13	1111001 1
--- -	-------------	-----	---------- ---
-7	11111001	-19	1110110 1

By contrast, the rule for adding numbers in the signed-2's complement system does not require a comparison or subtraction, only addition and complementation. The procedure is very simple and can be stated as follows: ***Add the two numbers, including their sign bits, and discard any carry out of the sign (leftmost) bit position.*** Numerical examples for addition are shown below.

Note that negative numbers must initially be in 2's complement and that if the sum obtained after the addition is negative, it is in 2's complement form.

In each of the four cases, the operation performed is always addition, including the sign bits. Any carry out of the sign bit position is discarded, and negative results are automatically in 2's complement form. The complement form of representing negative numbers is unfamiliar to people used to the signed-magnitude system. To determine the value of a negative number when in signed-2's complement, it is necessary to convert it to a positive number to place it in a more familiar form. For example, the signed binary number 11111001 is negative because the leftmost bit is 1.Its 2's complement is 00000111, which is the binary equivalent of +7. We therefore recognize the original negative number to be equal to -7.

Arithmetic Subtraction

Subtraction of two signed binary numbers when negative numbers are in 2's complement form is very simple and can be stated as follows: ***Take the 2's complement of the subtrahend (including the sign bit) and add it to the minuend (including the sign bit). A carry out of the sign bit position is discarded.*** This procedure stems from the fact that a subtraction operation can be changed to an addition operation if the sign of the subtrahend is changed.

This is demonstrated by the following relationship:

$$(\pm A) - (+B) = (\pm A) + (-B)$$

$$(\pm A) - (-B) = (\pm A) + (+B)$$

But changing a positive number to a negative number is easily done by taking its 2's complement. The reverse is also true because the complement of a negative number in complement form produces the equivalent positive number.

Consider the subtraction of (-6) – (-13) = +7. In binary with eight bits this is written as 11111010– 11110011. The subtraction is changed to addition by taking the 2's complement of the subtrahend (-13) to give (+13). In binary this is 11111010 + 00001101 = 100000111. Removing the end carry, we obtain the correct answer 00000111 (+7). It is worth noting that binary numbers in the signed-2's complement system are added and subtracted by the same basic addition and subtraction rules as unsigned numbers.

Therefore, computers need only one common hardware circuit to handle both types of arithmetic. The user or programmer must interpret the results of such addition or subtraction differently depending on whether it is assumed that the numbers are signed or unsigned.

Overflow

When two numbers of n digits each are added and the sum occupies n+1 digits, we say that an overflow has occurred. When the addition is performed with paper and pencil, an overflow is not a problem since there is no limit to the width of the page to write down the sum. An overflow is a problem in digital computers because the width of registers is finite. A result that contains n+1 bits cannot be accommodated in a register with a standard length of n bits. For this reason, many computers detect the occurrence of an overflow, and when it occurs, a corresponding flip-flop is set which can then be checked by the user.

The detection of an overflow after the addition of two binary numbers depends on whether the numbers are considered to be signed or unsigned. When two unsigned numbers are added, an overflow is detected from the end carry out of the most significant position. In the case of singed numbers, the leftmost bit always represents the sign, and negative numbers are in 2's complement form. When two signed numbers are added, the sign bit is treated as part of the number and the end carry does not indicate an overflow.

An overflow cannot occur after an addition if one number is positive and the other is negative, since adding a positive number to a negative number produces a result that is smaller than the larger of the two original numbers. An overflow may occur if the two numbers added are both positive or both negative. To see how this can happen, consider the following example. Two signed binary numbers, +70 and +80, are stored in two 8-bit registers.

The range of numbers that each register can accommodate is from binary +127 to binary -128. Since the sum of the two numbers is +150, it exceeds the capacity of the 8-bit register. This is true if the numbers are both positive or both negative. The two additions in binary are shown below together with the last two carries.

carrie s: 0	1		carries: 1	0
+70	0	1000110	-70	1 0111010
+80	0	1010000	-80	1 0110000
-------		----------------	-------	------------- ---
+150	1	0010110	-150	0 1101010

Note that the 8-bit result that should have been positive has a negative sign bit and the 8-bit result that should have been negative has a positive sign bit. If, however, the carry out of the sign bit position is taken as the sign bit of the result, the 9-bit answer so obtained will be correct. Since the answer cannot be accommodated within 8 bits, we say that an overflow occurred. An overflow condition can be detected by observing the carry into the sign bit position and the carry out of the sign bit position. If these two carries are not equal, an overflow condition is produced. This is indicated in the examples where the two carries are explicitly shown. If the two carries are applied to an exclusive-OR gate, an over-flow will be detected when the output of the gate is equal to 1.

Decimal Fixed-Point Representation

The representation of decimal numbers in registers is a function of the binary code used to represent a decimal digit. A 4-bit decimal code requires four flip-flops for each decimal digit. The representation of 4385 in BCD requires 16 flip-flops, four flip-flops for each digit. The number will be represented in a register with 16 flip-flops as follows: 0100 0011 1000 0101

By representing numbers in decimal we are wasting a considerable amount of storage space since the number of bits needed to store a decimal number in a binary code is greater than the number of bits needed for its equivalent binary representation. Also, the circuits required to perform decimal arithmetic are more complex. However, there are some advantages in the use of decimal representation because computer input and output data are generated by people who use the decimal system. Some applications, such as business data processing, require small amounts of arithmetic computations compared to the amount required for input and output of decimal data.

For this reason, some computers and all electronic calculators perform arithmetic operations directly with the decimal data (in a binary code) and thus eliminate the need for conversion into binary and back to decimal. Some computer systems have hardware for arithmetic calculations with both binary and decimal data. The representation of signed decimal numbers in BCD is similar to the representation of signed numbers in binary. We can either use the familiar signed-magnitude system or the signed-complement system. The sign of a decimal number is usually represented with four bits to conform to the 4-bit code of the decimal digits. It is customary to designate a plus with four 0's and a minus with the BCD equivalent of 9, which is 1001.

The signed-magnitude system is difficult to use with computers. The signed-complement system can be either the 9's or the 10's complement, but the 10's complement is the one most often used. To obtain the 10's complement of a BCD number, we first take the 9's complement and then add one to the least significant digit. The 9's complement is calculated from the subtraction of each digit from 9. The procedures developed for the signed-2's complement system apply also to the signed-10's complement system for decimal numbers. Addition is done by adding all digits, including the sign digit, and discarding the end carry. Obviously, this assumes that all negative numbers are in 10's complement form. Consider the addition (+375) + (-240) = +135 done in the signed-10's complement system.

0 375	$(0000\ 0011\ 0111\ 0101)_{BCD}$
+9 760	$(1001\ 0111\ 0110\ 0000)_{BCD}$
0 135	$(0000\ 0001\ 0011\ 0101)_{BCD}$

The 9 in the leftmost position of the second number indicates that the number is negative. 9760 is the 10's complement of 0240. The two numbers are added and the end carry is discarded to obtain +135. Of course, the decimal numbers inside the computer must be in BCD, including the sign digits. The addition is done with BCD adders. The subtraction of decimal numbers either unsigned or in the signed-10's complement system is the same as in the binary case. Take the 10's complement of the subtrahend and add it to the minuend. Many computers have special hardware to perform arithmetic calculations directly with decimal numbers in BCD. The user of the computer can specify by programmed instructions that the arithmetic operations be performed with decimal numbers directly without having to convert them to binary.

Floating-Point Representation

The floating-point representation of a number has two parts. The first part represents a signed, fixed-point number called the ***mantissa***. The second part designates the position of the decimal (or binary) point and is called the ***exponent***. The fixed-point mantissa may be a fraction or an integer. For example, the decimal number +6132.789 is represented in floating-point with a fraction and an exponent as follows:

Fraction : +0.6132789 ; Exponent : +04

The value of the exponent indicates that the actual position of the decimal point is four positions to the right of the indicated decimal point in the fraction. This representation is equivalent to the scientific notation +0.6132789 x 10+4. Floating-point is always interpreted to represent a number in the following form:

$$m \times r^e$$

Only the mantissa m and the exponent e are physically represented in the register (including their signs). The radix r and the radix-point position of the mantissa are always assumed. The circuits that manipulate the floating-point numbers in registers conform with these two assumptions in order to provide the correct computational results. A floating-point binary number is represented in a similar manner except that it uses base 2 for the exponent. For example, the binary number +1001.11 is represented with an 8-bit fraction and 6-bit exponent as follows:

Fraction : 01001110 ; Exponent : 000100

The fraction has a 0 in the leftmost position to denote positive. The binary point of the fraction follows the sign bit but is not shown in the register. The exponent has the equivalent binary number +4. The floating-point number is equivalent to

$$m \times 2^e = +(.1001110)_2 \times 2^{+4}$$

A floating-point number is said to be ***normalized*** if the most significant digit of the mantissa is nonzero. For example, the decimal number 350 is normalized but 00035 is not. Regardless of where the position of the radix point is assumed to be in the mantissa, the number is normalized only if its leftmost digit is nonzero. For example, the 8-bit binary number 00011010 is not normalized because of the three leading 0s.

The number can be normalized by shifting it three positions to the left and discarding the leading 0s to obtain 11010000. The three shifts multiply the number by 23 = 8. To keep the same value for the floating-point number, the exponent must be subtracted by 3. Normalized numbers provide the maximum possible precision for the floating-point number. A zero cannot be normalized because it does not have a nonzero digit. It is usually represented in floating-point by all 0s in the mantissa and exponent.

Arithmetic operations with floating-point numbers are more complicated than arithmetic operations with fixed-point numbers and their execution takes longer and requires more complex hardware.
However, floating-point representation is a must for scientific computations because of the scaling problems involved with fixed-point computations. Many computers and all electronic calculators have the built-in capability of performing floating-point arithmetic operations. Computers that do not have hardware for floating-point computations have a set of subroutines to help the user program scientific problems with floating-point numbers.

Other Binary Codes

In previous sections we introduced the most common types of binary-coded data found in digital computers. Other binary codes for decimal numbers and alphanumeric characters are sometimes used. Digital computers also employ other binary codes for special applications. A few additional binary codes encountered in digital computers are presented in this section.

Gray Code

Digital systems can process data in discrete form only. Many physical systems supply continuous output data. The data must be converted into digital form before they can be used by a digital computer. Continuous, or analog, information is converted into digital form by means of an analog-to-digital converter. The reflected binary or ***Gray code***, shown in Table , is sometimes used for the converted digital data.

Binary code	*Decimal equivalent*	*Binary code*	*Decimal equivalent*
0000	0	1100	8
0001	1	1101	9
0011	2	1111	10
0010	3	1110	11
0110	4	1010	12
0111	5	1011	13
0101	6	1001	14
0100	7	1000	15

Table 9. 4-Bit Gray Code

Gray codes counters are sometimes used to provide the timing sequence that control the operations in a digital system. A Gray code counter is a counter whose flip-flops go through a sequence of states as specified in Table 1.5. Gray code counters remove the ambiguity during the change from one state of the counter to the next because only one bit can change during the state transition.

Other Decimal Codes

Binary codes for decimal digits require a minimum of four bits. Numerous different codes can be formulated by arranging four or more bits in 10 distinct possible combinations. A few possibilities are shown in Table .

Decimal digit	*BCD 8421*	*2421*	*Excess-3*	*Excess-3 gray*
0	0000	0000	0011	0010
1	0001	0001	0100	0110
2	0010	0010	0101	0111
3	0011	0011	0110	0101
4	0100	0100	0111	0100
5	0101	1011	1000	1100
6	0110	1100	1001	1101
7	0111	1101	1010	1111
8	1000	1110	1011	1110
9	1001	1111	1100	1010
Unused	1010	0101	0000	0000
bit	1011	0110	0001	0001
combinations	1100	0111	0010	0011
	1101	1000	1101	1000
	1110	1001	1110	1001
	1111	1010	1111	1011

Table 10. Different Binary Codes for the Decimal Digit

The BCD (binary-coded decimal) has been introduced before. It uses a straight assignment of the binary equivalent of the digit. The six unused bit combinations listed have no meaning when BCD is used, just as the letter H has no meaning when decimal digit symbols are written down. For example, saying that 1001 110 is a decimal number in BCD is like saying that 9H is a decimal number in the conventional symbol designation. Both cases contain an invalid symbol and therefore designate a meaningless number. One disadvantage of using BCD is the difficulty encountered when the 9's complement of the number is to be computed. On the other hand, the 9's complement is easily obtained with the 2421 and the excess-3 codes listed in Table .

These two codes have a ***self-complementing*** property which means that the 9's complement of a decimal number, when represented in one of these codes, is easily obtained by changing 1's to 0's and 0's to 1's. The property is useful when arithmetic operations are done in signed-complement representation. The 2421 is an example of a ***weighted code***. In a weighted code, the bits are multiplied by the weights indicated and the sum of the weighted bits gives the decimal digit. For example, the bit combination 1101, when weighted by the respective digits 2421, gives the decimal equivalent of 2 x 1 + 4 x 1 + 2 x 0 + 1 + 1 = 7. The BCD code can be assigned the weights 8421 and for this reason it is sometimes called the 8421 code.

The ***excess-3 code*** is a decimal code that has been used in older computers. This is an un weighted code. Its binary code assignment is obtained from the corresponding BCD equivalent binary number after the addition of binary 3 (0011). From Table 1.5 we note that the Gray code is not suited for a decimal code if we were to choose the first 10 entries in the table. This is because the transition from 9 back to 0 involves a change of three bits (from 1101 to 0000). To overcome this difficulty, we choose the 10 numbers starting from the third entry 0010 up to the twelfth entry 1010.

Now the transition from 1010 to 0010 involves a change of only one bit. Since the code has been shifted up three numbers, it is called the excess-3 Gray. This code is listed with the other decimal codes in Table .

Other Alphanumeric Codes

The ASCII code is the standard code commonly used for the transmission of binary information. Each character is represented by a 7-bit code and usually an eighth bit is inserted for parity. The code consists of 128 characters. Ninety-five characters represent *graphic symbols* that include upper- and lowercase letters, numerals zero to nine, punctuation marks, and special symbols. Twenty-three characters represent format effectors, which are functional characters for controlling the layout of printing or display devices such as carriage return, line feed, horizontal tabulation, and back space. The other 10 characters are used to direct the data communication flow and report its status.

Another alphanumeric (sometimes called alphanumeric code used in IBM equipment is the ***EB-CDIC (Extended BCD Interchange Code)***. It uses eight bits for each character (and a ninth bit for parity). EBCDIC has the same character symbols as ASCII but the bit assignment to characters is different. When alphanumeric characters are used internally in a computer for data processing (not for transmission purpose) it is more convenient to use a 6-bit code to represent 64-characters. A 6-bit code can specify the 26 uppercase letters of the alphabet, numerals zero to nine, and up to 28 special characters. This set of characters is usually sufficient for data-processing purposes. Using fewer bits to code characters has the advantage of reducing the memory space needed to store large quantities of alphanumeric data.

Register Transfer and Micro-operations

Introduction

A digital system is an interconnection of digital hardware modules that accomplish a specific information-processing task. Digital systems vary in size and complexity, from a few integrated circuits to a complex of interconnected and interacting digital computers. Digital system design invariably uses a modular approach. The modules are constructed from such digital components as registers, decoders, arithmetic elements, and control logic. The various modules are interconnected with common data and control paths to form a digital computer system.

Objectives:

After studying this unit, the learner will be able to

- Explain Register Transfer Language
- Understand bus selection techniques
- Explain arithmetic and logical circuits
- Understand the operation of arithmetic logic shift unit

Register Transfer Language

Digital modules are best defined by the registers they contain and the operations that are performed on the data stored in them. The operations executed on data stored in registers are called ***micro operations***. A micro-operation is an elementary operation performed on the information stored in one or more registers. The result of the operation may replace the previous binary information of a register or may be transferred to another register. Examples of micro-operations are shift, count, clear, and load.

The internal hardware organization of a digital computer is best defined by specifying:

1. *The set of registers it contains and their function.*
2. *The sequence of micro-operations performed on the binary information stored in the registers.*
3. *The control that initiates the sequence of micro-operations.*

It is possible to specify the sequence of micro-operations in a computer by explaining every operation in words, but this procedure usually involves a lengthy descriptive explanation. It is more convenient to adopt a suitable symbology to describe the sequence of transfers between registers and the various arithmetic and logic micro-operations associated with the transform. The use of symbols instead of a narrative explanation provides an organized and concise manner for listing the micro-operation sequences in registers and the control functions that initiate them.

The symbolic notation used to describe the micro-operation transfers among registers is called a ***register transfer language***. The term –register transfer‖ implies the availability of hardware logic circuits that can perform a stated Micro-operation and transfer the result of the operation to the same or another register. The word –language‖ is borrowed from programmers, who apply this term to programming languages. A programming language is a procedure for writing symbols to specify a given computational process. Similarly, a natural language such as English is a system for writing symbols and combining them into words and sentences for the purpose of communication between people.

A register transfer language is a system for expressing in symbolic form the micro-operation sequences among the registers of a digital module. It is a convenient tool for describing the internal organization of digital computers in concise and precise manner. It can also be used to facilitate the design process of digital systems. The register transfer language adopted here is believed to be as simple as possible, so it should not take very long to memorize.

We will proceed to define symbols for various types of micro-operations, and at the same time, describe associated hardware that can implement the stated micro-operations. The symbolic designation introduced in this chapter will be utilized in subsequent chapters to specify the register transfers, the micro-operations, and the control functions that describe the internal hardware organization of digital computers.

Register Transfer

Computer registers are designated by capital letters (sometimes followed by numerals) to denote the function of the register. For example, the register that holds an address for the memory unit is usually called a ***memory address register*** and is designated by the name ***MAR***. Other designations for registers are ***PC*** (for ***program counter***), ***IR*** (for ***instruction register***), and ***R1*** (for ***processor register***). The individual flip-flops in an *n-bit* register are numbers in sequence from *0* through *n-1*, starting from *0* in the rightmost position and increasing the numbers toward the left. Fig.11 shows the representation of registers in block diagram form. The most common way to represent a register is by a rectangular box with the name of the register inside, as in Fig.11 (a).

The individual bits can be distinguished as in (b). The numbering of bits in a 16-bit register can be marked on top of the box as shown in (c). A 16-bit register is partitioned into two parts in (d). Bits 0 through 7 are assigned the symbol *L* (for low byte) and bits 8 through 15 are assigned the symbol *H* (for high byte). The name of the 16-bit register is PC. The symbol ***PC (0-7)*** or ***PC (L)*** refers to the low-order byte and ***PC (8-15)*** or ***PC (H)*** to the high-order byte.

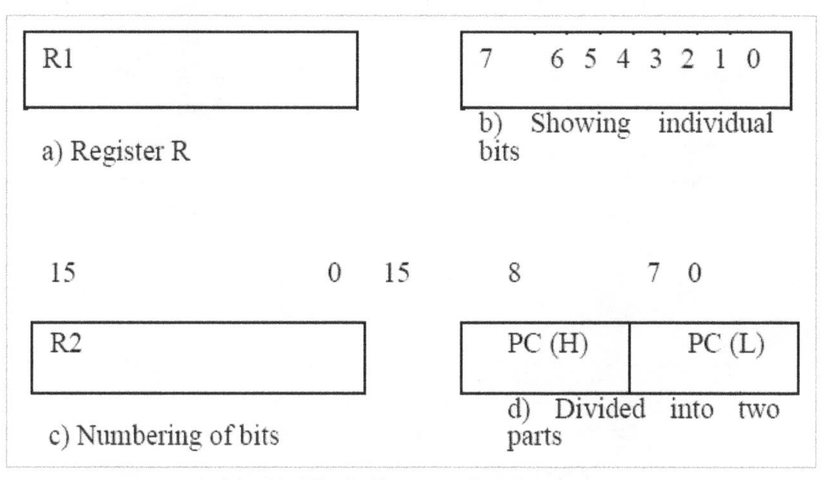

Fig 11. Block diagram of register

Information transfer from one register to another is designated in symbolic form by means of a replacement operator. The statement

R2 <-- R1

denotes a transfer of the content of register R1 into register R2. It designates a replacement of the content of R2 by the content of Rl. By definition, the content of the source register R1 does not change after the transfer.

A statement that specifies a register transfer implies that circuits are available from the outputs of the source register to the inputs of the destination register and that the destination register has a parallel load capability. Normally, we want the transfer to occur only under a predetermined control condition. This can be shown by means of an if-then statement.

control function:

where P is a control signal generated in the control section. It is sometimes convenient to separate the control variables from the register transfer operation by specifying a control function. A control function is a Boolean variable that is equal to 1 or 0. The control function is included in the statement as follows:

P: R2 <-- R1

The control condition is terminated with a colon. It symbolizes the requirement that the transfer operation be executed by the hardware only if P = 1. Every statement written in a register transfer notation implies a hardware construction for implementing the transfer. Figure 12 shows the block diagram that depicts the transfer from R1 to R2. The **n** outputs of register R1 are connected to the n inputs of register R2. The letter n will be used to indicate any number of bits for the register. It will be replaced by an actual number when the length of the register is known. Register R2 has a load input that is activated by the control variable P.

It is assumed that the control variable is synchronized with the same clock as the one applied to the register. As shown in the timing diagram, P is activated in the control section by the rising edge of a clock pulse at time t. The next positive transition of the clock at time t + 1 finds the load input active and the data inputs of R2 are then loaded into the register in parallel. P may go back to 0 at time t + 1; otherwise, the transfer will occur with every clock pulse transition while P remains active.

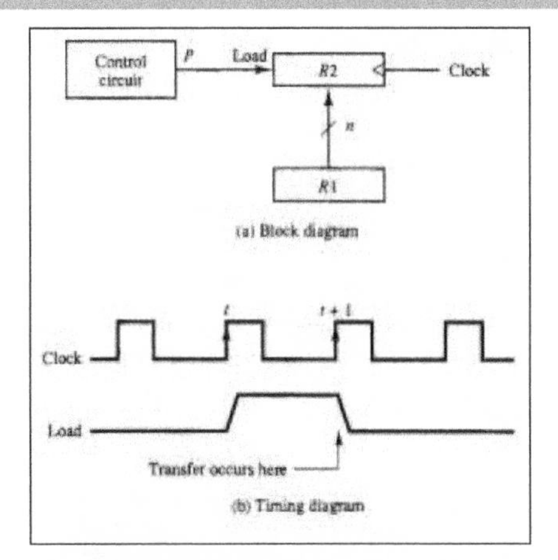

Fig. 12: Transfer from R1 to R2 when P = 1

Note that the clock is not included as a variable in the register transfer statements. It is assumed that all transfers occur during a clock edge transition. Even though the control condition such as P becomes active just after time t, the actual transfer does not occur until the register is triggered by the next positive transition of the clock at time t + 1.

Bus and Memory Transfers

A digital system composed of many registers, and paths must be provided to transfer information from one register to another. The number of wires connecting all of the registers will be excessive if separate lines are used between each register and all other registers in the system.

A bus structure, on the other hand, is more efficient for transferring information between registers in a multi-register configuration system. A bus consists of a set of common lines, one for each bit of register, through which binary information is transferred one at a time. Control signals determine which register is selected by the bus during a particular register transfer. A bus consists of a set of common lines, one for each bit of register, through which binary information is transferred one at a time. Control signals determine which register is selected by the bus during a particular register transfer.

We have used labels to make it more convenient for you to understand the input-output configuration of a Bus system for four registers. For instance, output 1 of register A is connected to input 0 of MUX1.

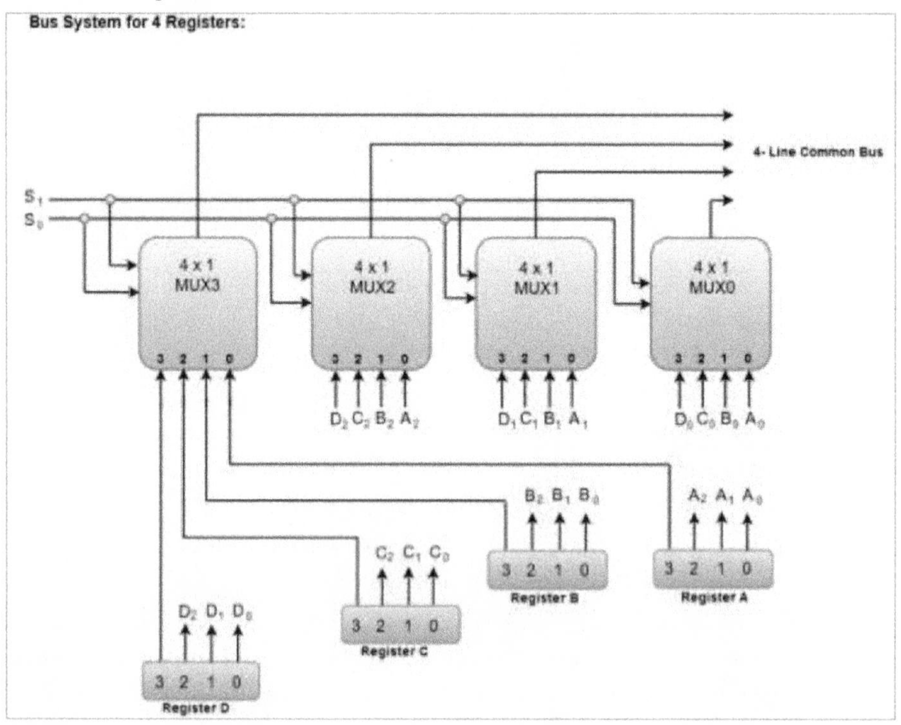

The two selection lines S1 and S2 are connected to the selection inputs of all four multiplexers. The selection lines choose the four bits of one register and transfer them into the four-line common bus.

When both of the select lines are at low logic, i.e. S1S0 = 00, the 0 data inputs of all four multiplexers are selected and applied to the outputs that forms the bus. This, in turn, causes the bus lines to receive the content of register A since the outputs of this register are connected to the 0 data inputs of the multiplexers.

Similarly, when S1S0 = 01, register B is selected, and the bus lines will receive the content provided by register B.

The following function table shows the register that is selected by the bus for each of the four possible binary values of the Selection lines.

S1	S0	Register Selected
0	0	A
0	1	B
1	0	C
1	1	D

A bus system can also be constructed using **three-state gates** instead of multiplexers.

The **three state gates** can be considered as a digital circuit that has three gates, two of which are signals equivalent to logic 1 and 0 as in a conventional gate. However, the third gate exhibits a high-impedance state.

The most commonly used three state gates in case of the bus system is a **buffer gate**.

The graphical symbol of a three-state buffer gate can be represented as:

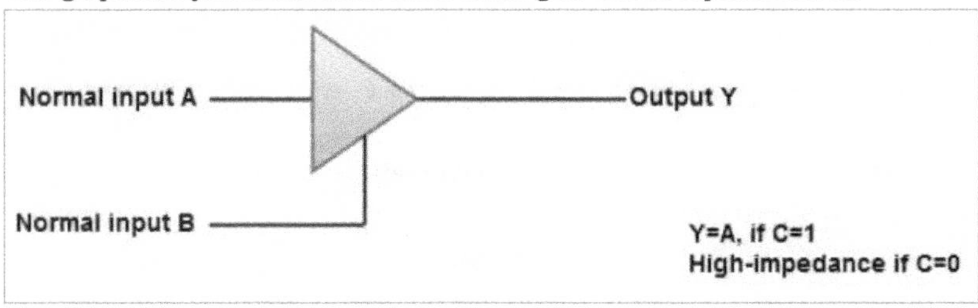

The following diagram demonstrates the construction of a bus system with three-state buffers.

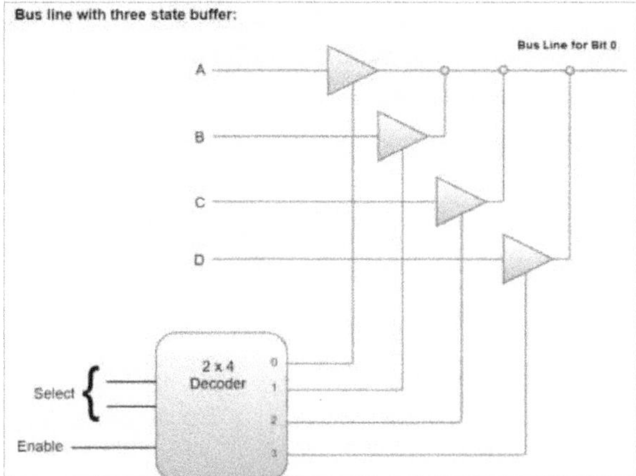

- The outputs generated by the four buffers are connected to form a single bus line.
- Only one buffer can be in active state at a given point of time.
- The control inputs to the buffers determine which of the four normal inputs will communicate with the bus line.

A 2 * 4 decoder ensures that no more than one control input is active at any given point of time.

Memory Transfer

Most of the standard notations used for specifying operations on memory transfer are stated below.

The transfer of information from a memory unit to the user end is called a **Read** operation.

The transfer of new information to be stored in the memory is called a **Write** operation.

A memory word is designated by the letter **M**.

We must specify the address of memory word while writing the memory transfer operations.

The **address register** is designated by **AR** and the **data register** by **DR**.

Thus, a read operation can be stated as:

Read: DR ← M [AR]

The **Read** statement causes a transfer of information into the data register (DR) from the memory word (M) selected by the address register (AR).

And the corresponding write operation can be stated as:

Write: M [AR] ← R1

The Write statement causes a transfer of information from register R1 into the memory word (M) selected by address register (AR).

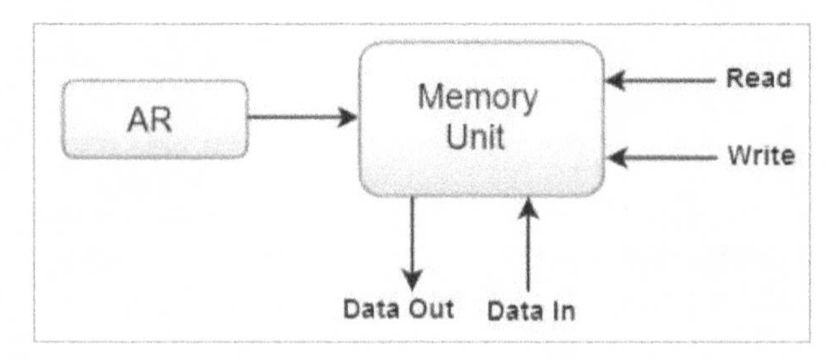

Arithmetic Micro-operations

In general, the Arithmetic Micro-operations deals with the operations performed on numeric data stored in the registers.

The basic Arithmetic Micro-operations are classified in the following categories:

1. **Addition**
2. **Subtraction**
3. **Increment**
4. **Decrement**
5. **Shift**

Some additional Arithmetic Micro-operations are classified as:

1. **Add with carry**
2. **Subtract with borrow**
3. **Transfer/Load, etc.**

The following table shows the symbolic representation of various Arithmetic Micro-operations.

Symbolic Representation	Description
R3 ← R1 + R2	The contents of R1 plus R2 are transferred to R3.
R3 ← R1 - R2	The contents of R1 minus R2 are transferred to R3.
R2 ← R2'	Complement the contents of R2 (1's complement)
R2 ← R2' + 1	2's complement the contents of R2 (negate)
R3 ← R1 + R2' + 1	R1 plus the 2's complement of R2 (subtraction)
R1 ← R1 + 1	Increment the contents of R1 by one
R1 ← R1 - 1	Decrement the contents of R1 by one

Note: The increment and decrement micro-operations are symbolized by '+ 1' and '? 1' respectively. Arithmetic operations like multiply and divide are not included in the basic set of micro-operations.

Binary Adder

The most basic arithmetic operation is addition. The circuit, which performs the addition of two binary numbers is known as **Binary adder**. First, let us implement an adder, which performs the addition of two bits.

Half Adder

Half adder is a combinational circuit, which performs the addition of two binary numbers A and B are of **single bit**. It produces two outputs sum, S & carry, C.

The **Truth table** of Half adder is shown below.

Inputs		Outputs	
A	B	C	S
0	0	0	0
0	1	0	1
1	0	0	1
1	1	1	0

When we do the addition of two bits, the resultant sum can have the values ranging from 0 to 2 in decimal. We can represent the decimal digits 0 and 1 with single bit in binary. But, we can't represent decimal digit 2 with single bit in binary. So, we require two bits for representing it in binary.

Let, sum, S is the Least significant bit and carry, C is the Most significant bit of the resultant sum. For first three combinations of inputs, carry, C is zero and the value of S will be either zero or one based on the **number of ones** present at the inputs. But, for last combination of inputs, carry, C is one and sum, S is zero, since the resultant sum is two.

From Truth table, we can directly write the **Boolean functions** for each output as

$$S=A\oplus B$$

$$C=AB$$

We can implement the above functions with 2-input Ex-OR gate & 2-input AND gate. The **circuit diagram** of Half adder is shown in the following figure.

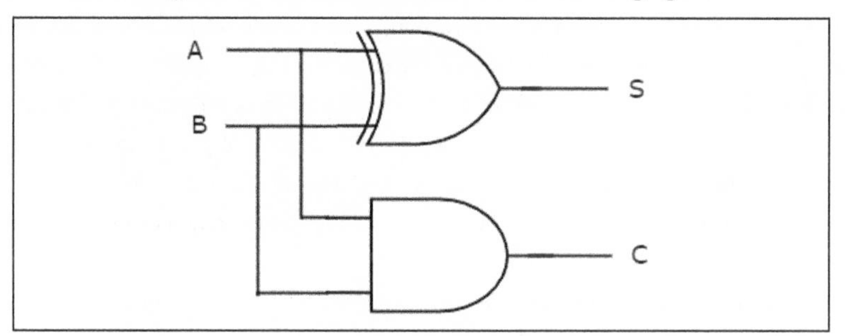

In the above circuit, a two input Ex-OR gate & two input AND gate produces sum, S & carry, C respectively. Therefore, Half-adder performs the addition of two bits.

Full Adder

Full adder is a combinational circuit, which performs the **addition of three bits** A, B and $\mathbf{C_{in}}$. Where, A & B are the two parallel significant bits and $\mathbf{C_{in}}$ is the carry bit, which is generated from previous stage. This Full adder also produces two outputs sum, S & carry, $\mathbf{C_{out}}$, which are similar to Half adder.

The **Truth table** of Full adder is shown below.

Inputs			Outputs	
A	B	C_{in}	C_{out}	S
0	0	0	0	0
0	0	1	0	1
0	1	0	0	1
0	1	1	1	0
1	0	0	0	1
1	0	1	1	0
1	1	0	1	0
1	1	1	1	1

When we do the addition of three bits, the resultant sum can have the values ranging from 0 to 3 in decimal. We can represent the decimal digits 0 and 1 with single bit in binary. But, we can't represent the decimal digits 2 and 3 with single bit in binary. So, we require two bits for representing those two decimal digits in binary.

Let, sum, S is the Least significant bit and carry, C_{out} is the Most significant bit of resultant sum. It is easy to fill the values of outputs for all combinations of inputs in the truth table. Just count the **number of ones** present at the inputs and write the equivalent binary number at outputs. If C_{in} is equal to zero, then Full adder truth table is same as that of Half adder truth table.

We will get the following **Boolean functions** for each output after simplification.

$$S = A \oplus B \oplus C_{in}$$

$$C_{out} = AB + (A \oplus B) c_{in}$$

The sum, S is equal to one, when odd number of ones present at the inputs. We know that Ex-OR gate produces an output, which is an odd function. So, we can use either two 2input Ex-OR gates or one 3-input Ex-OR gate in order to produce sum, S. We can implement carry, C_{out} using two 2-input AND gates & one OR gate. The **circuit diagram** of Full adder is shown in the following figure.

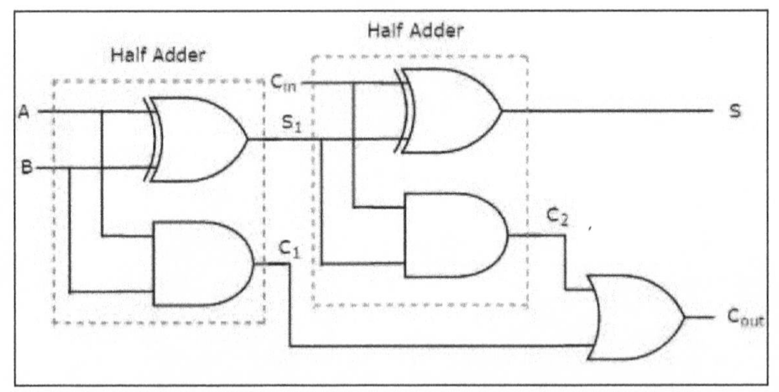

This adder is called as **Full adder** because for implementing one Full adder, we require two Half adders and one OR gate. If C_{in} is zero, then Full adder becomes Half adder. We can verify it easily from the above circuit diagram or from the Boolean functions of outputs of Full adder.

4-bit Binary Adder

The 4-bit binary adder performs the addition of two 4-bit numbers. Let the 4-bit binary numbers, $A=A_3A_2A_1A_0$ and $B=B_3B_2B_1B_0$. We can implement 4-bit binary adder in one of the two following ways.

Use one Half adder for doing the addition of two Least significant bits and three Full adders for doing the addition of three higher significant bits.

Use four Full adders for uniformity. Since, initial carry C_{in} is zero, the Full adder which is used for adding the least significant bits becomes Half adder.

For the time being, we considered second approach. The block diagram of 4-bit binary adder is shown in the following figure.

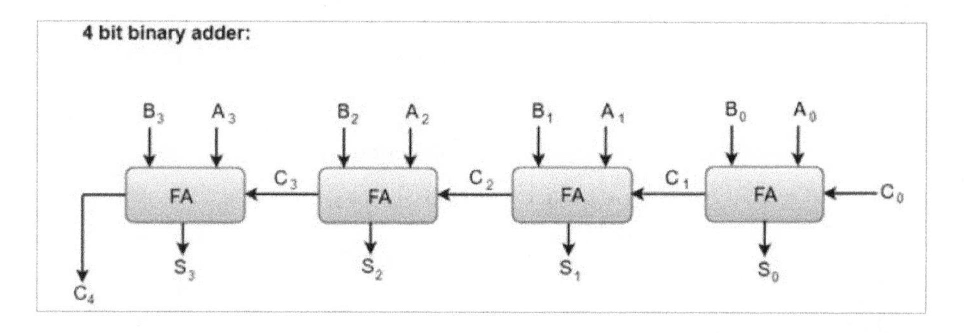

Here, the 4 Full adders are cascaded. Each Full adder is getting the respective bits of two parallel inputs A & B. The carry output of one Full adder will be the carry input of subsequent higher order Full adder. This 4-bit binary adder produces the resultant sum having at most 5 bits. So, carry out of last stage Full adder will be the MSB.

In this way, we can implement any higher order binary adder just by cascading the required number of Full adders. This binary adder is also called as ***ripple carry*** binary **adder** because the carry propagates ***ripples*** from one stage to the next stage.

Binary Subtractor

The circuit, which performs the subtraction of two binary numbers is known as **Binary subtractor**. We can implement Binary subtractor in following two methods.

- Cascade Full subtractors
- 2's complement method

In first method, we will get an n-bit binary subtractor by cascading 'n' Full subtractors. So, first you can implement Half subtractor and Full subtractor, similar to Half adder & Full adder. Then, you can implement an n-bit binary subtractor, by cascading 'n' Full subtractors. So, we will be having two separate circuits for binary addition and subtraction of two binary numbers.

In second method, we can use same binary adder for subtracting two binary numbers just by doing some modifications in the second input. So, internally binary addition operation takes place but, the output is resultant subtraction.

We know that the subtraction of two binary numbers A & B can be written as,

$$A-B = A + (\text{ }2\text{'scompliment of } B\text{ })$$

$$\Rightarrow A-B = A + (\text{ }1\text{'s compliment of } B\text{ }) + 1$$

4-bit Binary Subtractor

The 4-bit binary subtractor produces the **subtraction of two 4-bit numbers**. Let the 4bit binary numbers, $A = A_3 A_2 A_1 A_0$ and $B = B_3 B_2 B_1 B_0$. Internally, the operation of 4-bit Binary subtractor is similar to that of 4-bit Binary adder.

If the normal bits of binary number A, complemented bits of binary number B and initial carry borrow, C_{in} as one are applied to 4-bit Binary adder, then it becomes 4-bit Binary subtractor.

The **block diagram** of 4-bit binary subtractor is shown in the following figure.

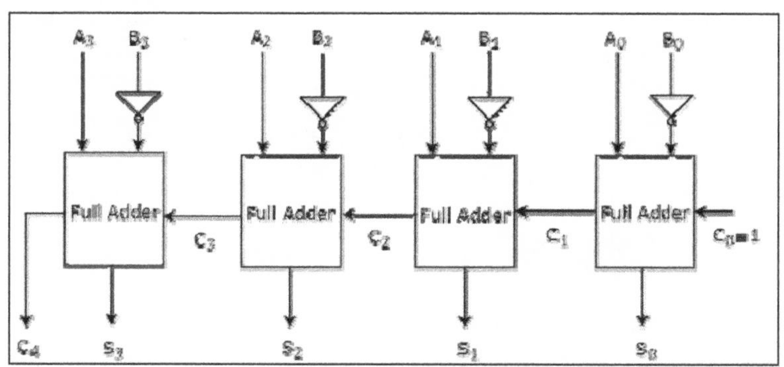

This 4-bit binary subtractor produces an output, which is having at most 5 bits. If Binary number A is greater than Binary number B, then MSB of the output is zero and the remaining bits hold the magnitude of A-B. If Binary number A is less than Binary number B, then MSB of the output is one. So, take the 2's complement of output in order to get the magnitude of A-B.

In this way, we can implement any higher order binary subtractor just by cascading the required number of Full adders with necessary modifications.

Binary Adder / Subtractor

The circuit, which can be used to perform either addition or subtraction of two binary numbers at any time is known as **Binary Adder / subtractor**. Both, Binary adder and Binary subtractor contain a set of Full adders, which are cascaded. The input bits of binary number A are directly applied in both Binary adder and Binary subtractor.

There are two differences in the inputs of Full adders that are present in Binary adder and Binary subtractor.

The input bits of binary number B are directly applied to Full adders in Binary adder, whereas the complemented bits of binary number B are applied to Full adders in Binary subtractor.

The initial carry, $C_0 = 0$ is applied in 4-bit Binary adder, whereas the initial carry borrow, $C_0 = 1$ is applied in 4-bit Binary subtractor.

We know that a **2-input Ex-OR gate** produces an output, which is same as that of first input when other input is zero. Similarly, it produces an output, which is complement of first input when other input is one.

Therefore, we can apply the input bits of binary number B, to 2-input Ex-OR gates. The other input to all these Ex-OR gates is C_0. So, based on the value of C_0, the Ex-OR gates produce either the normal or complemented bits of binary number B.

4-bit Binary Adder / Subtractor

The 4-bit binary adder / subtractor produces either the addition or the subtraction of two 4-bit numbers based on the value of initial carry or borrow, C_0. Let the 4-bit binary numbers, $A = A_3 A_2 A_1 A_0$ and $B = B_3 B_2 B_1 B_0$. The operation of 4-bit Binary adder / subtractor is similar to that of 4-bit Binary adder and 4-bit Binary subtractor.

Apply the normal bits of binary numbers A and B & initial carry or borrow, C_0 from externally to a 4-bit binary adder. The **block diagram** of 4-bit binary adder / subtractor is shown in the following figure.

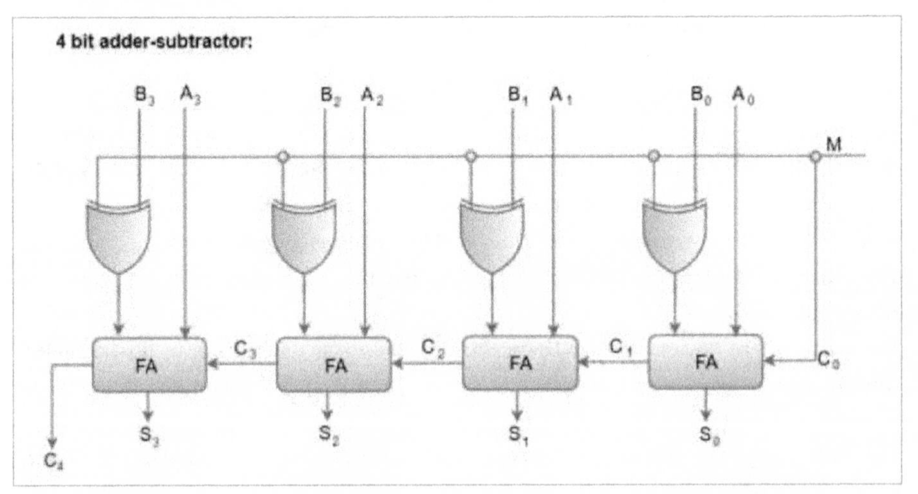

If initial carry, ***C_0*** is zero, then each full adder gets the normal bits of binary numbers A & B. So, the 4-bit binary adder / subtractor produces an output, which is the **addition of two binary numbers** A & B.

If initial borrow, ***C_0*** is one, then each full adder gets the normal bits of binary number A & complemented bits of binary number B. So, the 4-bit binary adder / subtractor produces an output, which is the **subtraction of two binary numbers** A & B.

Therefore, with the help of additional Ex-OR gates, the same circuit can be used for both addition and subtraction of two binary numbers.

Binary Incrementer

The increment microoperation adds one to a number in a register. For example, if a 4-bit register has a binary value 0110, it will go to 0111 after it is incremented. This microoperation is easily implemented with a binary counter. Every time the count enable is active, the clock pulse transition increments the content of the register by one. There may be occasions when the increment microoperation must be done with a combinational circuit independent of a particular register. This can be accomplished by means of half-adders connected in cascade.

The diagram of a 4-bit combinational circuit incrementer is shown in Fig. One of the inputs to the least significant half-adder (HA) is connected to logic-1 and the other input is connected to the least significant bit of the number to be incremented. The output carry from one half-adder is connected to one of the inputs of the next-higher-order half-adder.

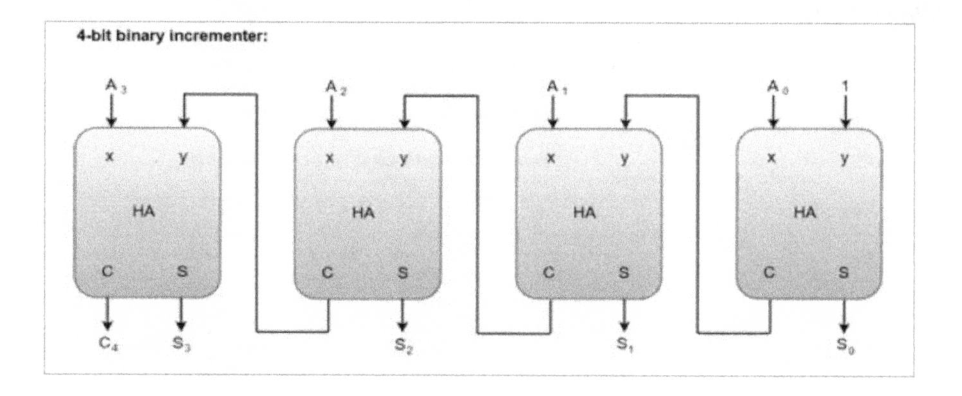

The circuit receives the four bits from A0 through A3, adds one to it, and generates the incremented output in S0 through S3. The output carry C4 will be 1 only after incrementing binary 1111. This also causes outputs S0 through S3 to go to 0.

The circuit of Fig. can be extended to an n-bit binary incrementer by extending the diagram to include n half-adders. The least significant bit must have one input connected to logic-1. The other inputs receive the number to be incremented or the carry from the previous stage.

Arithmetic Circuit

The arithmetic microoperations listed in Table can be implemented in one composite arithmetic circuit. The basic component of an arithmetic circuit is the parallel adder. By controlling the data inputs to the adder, it is possible to obtain different types of arithmetic operations.

The diagram of a 4-bit arithmetic circuit is shown in Fig.2.9. It has four full- adder circuits that constitute the 4-bit adder and four multiplexers for choosing different operations. There are two 4-bit inputs A and B and a 4-bit output D. The four inputs from A go directly to the X inputs of the binary adder. Each of the four inputs from B is connected to the data inputs of the multiplexers. The multiplexers data inputs also receive the complement of B. The other two data inputs are connected to logic-0 and logic-1. Logic-0 is a fixed voltage value (0 volts for TTL integrated circuits) and the logic-1 signal can be generated through an inverter whose input is 0.

Symbolic Representation	Description
R3 ← R1 + R2	The contents of R1 plus R2 are transferred to R3.
R3 ← R1 - R2	The contents of R1 minus R2 are transferred to R3.
R2 ← R2'	Complement the contents of R2 (1's complement)
R2 ← R2' + 1	2's complement the contents of R2 (negate)
R3 ← R1 + R2' + 1	R1 plus the 2's complement of R2 (subtraction)
R1 ← R1 + 1	Increment the contents of R1 by one
R1 ← R1 - 1	Decrement the contents of R1 by one

The four multiplexers are controlled by two selection inputs, S1 and S0. The input carry C_{in} goes to the carry input of the FA in the least significant position. The other carries are connected from one stage to the next.

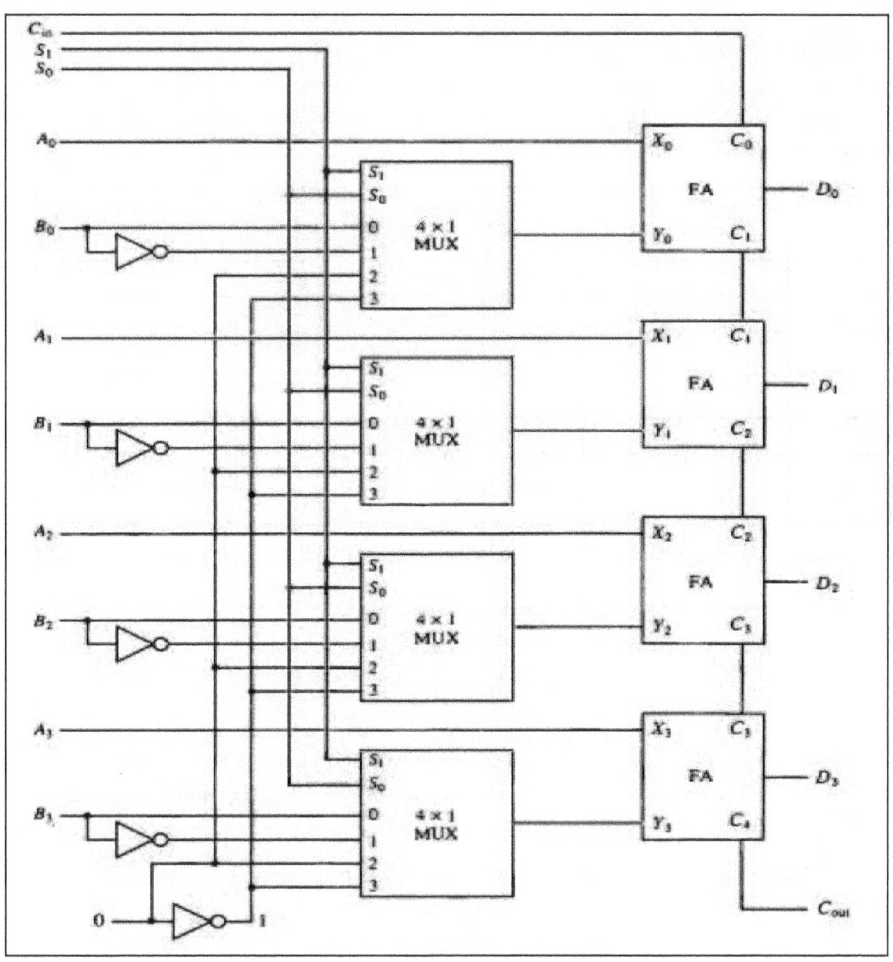

Fig. : 4-bit arithmetic circuit

The output of the binary adder is calculated from the following arithmetic sum:

$$D = A + Y + C_{in}$$

where A is the 4-bit binary number at the X inputs and Y is the 4-bit binary number at the Y inputs of the binary adder. C_{in} is the input carry, which can be equal to 0 or 1. Note that the symbol + in the equation above denotes an
arithmetic plus. By controlling the value of Y with the two selection inputs S1 and S0 and making C_{in} equal to 0 or 1, it is possible to generate the eight arithmetic microoperations listed in Table .

Select			*Input*	*Output*	*Microoperation*
S_1	S_0	C_{in}	*Y*	*D=A+Y+Cin*	
0	0	0	B	D=A+B	Add
0	0	1	B	D=A+B+1	Add with carry
0	1	0	$\overline{B}$	D=A+ $\overline{B}$	Subtract with borrow
0	1	1	$\overline{B}$	D=A+ $\overline{B}$ +1	Subtract
1	0	0	0	D=A	Transfer A
1	0	1	0	D=A+1	Increment A
1	1	0	1	D=A-1	Decrement A
1	1	1	1	D=A	Transfer A

Table : Arithmetic Circuit Function Table

When S_1S_0 = 00, the value of B is applied to the Y inputs of the adder.

If C_{in} = 0, the output D = A + B.

If C_{in} = 1, output D = A + B + 1.

Both cases perform the add microoperation with or without adding the input carry.
When S_1S_0 = 01, the complement of B is applied to the Y inputs of the adder.

If C_{in} = 1, then D = A + B + 1.

This produces A plus the 2's complement of B, which is equivalent to a subtraction of A – B.

When C_{in} = 0, then D = A + B .

This is equivalent to a subtract with borrow, that is, A – B – 1.

When S_1S_0 = 10, the inputs from B are neglected, and instead, all 0's are inserted into the Y inputs. The output becomes D = A + 0 + C_{in}. This gives D = A when C_{in} = 0 and D = A + 1 when C_{in} = 1. In the first case we have a direct transfer from input A to output D. In the second case, the value of A is incremented by 1.

When S_1S_0 = 11, all 1's are inserted into the Y inputs of the adder to produce the decrement operation D = A – 1 when C_{in} = 0. This is because a number with all 1's is equal to the 2's complement of 1 (the 2's complement of binary 0001 is 1111). Adding a number A to the 2's complement of 1 produces F = A + 2's complement of 1 = A – 1.

When C_{in} = 1, then D = A – 1 + 1 = A, which causes a direct transfer from input A to output D. Note that the microoperation D = A is generated twice, so there are only seven distinct microoperations in the arithmetic circuit.

Logic Microoperations

Logic microoperations specify binary operations for strings of bits stored in registers. These operations consider each bit of the register separately and treat them as binary variables. For example, the exclusive-OR microoperation with the contents of two registers R1 and R2 is symbolized by the statement

$$P: R_1 \leftarrow R_1 \oplus R_2$$

It specifies a logic microoperation to be executed on the individual bits of the registers provided that the control variable P = 1. As a numerical example, assume that each register has four bits. Let the content of R1 be 1010 and the content of R2 be 1100.
The exclusive-OR microoperation stated above symbolizes the following logic computation:

1010 Content of R1

1100 Content of R2

0110 Content of R1 after P = 1

The content of R1, after the execution of the microoperation, is equal to the bit-by-bit exclusive-OR operation on pairs of bits in R2 and previous values of R1.

The logic microoperations are seldom used in scientific computations, but they are very useful for bit manipulation of binary data and for making logical decisions.

Special symbols will be adopted for the logic microoperations OR, AND, and complement, to distinguish them from the corresponding symbols used to express Boolean functions. The symbol V will be used to denote an OR microoperation and the symbol $\wedge$ to denote an AND microoperation.

The complement microoperation is the same as the 1's complement and uses a bar on top of the symbol that denotes the register name. By using different symbols, it will be possible to differentiate between a logic microoperation and a control (or Boolean) function. Another reason for adopting two sets of symbols is to be able to distinguish the symbol +, when used to symbolize an arithmetic plus, from a logic OR operation.

Although the + symbol has two meanings, it will be possible to distinguish between them by noting where the symbol occurs. When the symbol + occurs in a microoperation, it will denote an arithmetic plus. When it occurs in a control (or Boolean) function, it will denote an OR operation. We will never use it to symbolize an OR microoperation. For example, in the statement

statement

$$P+Q: R_1 \leftarrow R_2 + R_3,\ R_4 \leftarrow R_5 \vee R_6$$

the + between P and Q is an OR operation between two binary variables of a control function. The + between R2 and R3 specifies an add microoperation. The OR microoperation is designated by the symbol V between registers R5 and R6.

List of Logic Microoperations

There are 16 different logic binary variables. They can operations that can be performed with two be determined from all possible truth tables obtained with two binary variables as shown in Table 2.5. In this table, each of the 16 columns F0 through F15 represents a truth table of one possible Boolean function for the two variables x and y. Note that the functions are determined from the 16 binary combinations that can be assigned to F.

x y	F_0	F_1	F_2	F_3	F_4	F_5	F_6	F_7	F_8	F_9	F_{10}	F_{11}	F_{12}	F_{13}	F_{14}	F_{15}
0 0	0	0	0	0	0	0	0	0	1	1	1	1	1	1	1	1
0 1	0	0	0	0	1	1	1	1	0	0	0	0	1	1	1	1
1 0	0	0	1	1	0	0	1	1	0	0	1	1	0	0	1	1
1 1	0	1	0	1	0	1	0	1	0	1	0	1	0	1	0	1

Table : Truth Tables for 16 Functions of Two Variables

The 16 Boolean functions of two variables x and y are expressed in algebraic form in the first column of Table 2.6. The 16 logic microoperations are derived from these functions by replacing variable x by the binary content of register A and variable y by the binary content of register B. It is important to realize that the Boolean functions listed in the first column of Table 2.6 represent a relationship between two binary variables x and y.

The logic microoperations listed in the second column represent a relationship between the binary content of two registers A and B. Each bit of the register is treated as a binary variable and the microoperation is performed on the string of bits stored in the registers.

Boolean Function	Microoperation	Name
$F_0 = 0$	$F \leftarrow 0$	Clear
$F_1 = xy$	$F \leftarrow A \wedge B$	AND
$F_2 = xy'$	$F \leftarrow A \wedge \overline{B}$	
$F_3 = x$	$F \leftarrow A$	Transfer A
$F_4 = x'y$	$F \leftarrow \overline{A} \wedge B$	
$F_5 = y$	$F \leftarrow B$	Transfer B
$F_6 = x \oplus y$	$F \leftarrow A \oplus B$	Exclusive-OR
$F_7 = x + y$	$F \leftarrow A \vee B$	OR

Boolean Function	Microoperation	Name
$F_8 = (x + y)'$	$F \leftarrow \overline{A \vee B}$	NOR
$F_9 = (x \oplus y)'$	$F \leftarrow \overline{A \oplus B}$	Exclusive-NOR
$F_{10} = y'$	$F \leftarrow \overline{B}$	Complement B
$F_{11} = x + y'$	$F \leftarrow A \vee \overline{B}$	
$F_{12} = x'$	$F \leftarrow \overline{A}$	Complement A
$F_{13} = x' + y$	$F \leftarrow \overline{A} \vee B$	
$F_{14} = (xy)'$	$F \leftarrow \overline{A \wedge B}$	NAND
$F_{15} = 1$	$F \leftarrow$ all 1's	Set to all 1's

Fig. Sixteen Logic Microoperations

Hardware Implementation

The hardware implementation of logic microoperations requires that logic gates be inserted for each bit or pair of bits in the registers to perform the required logic function. Although there are 16 logic microoperations, most computers use only four - **AND, OR, XOR (exclusive-OR)**, and complement–from which all others can be derived.

shows one stage of a circuit that generates the four basic logic microoperations. It consists of four gates and a multiplexer. Each of the four logic operations is generated through a gate that performs the required logic. The outputs of the gates are applied to the data inputs of the

multiplexer. The two selection inputs S1 and S0 choose one of the data inputs of the multiplexer and direct its value to the output. The diagram shows one typical stage with subscript i. For a logic circuit with n bits, the diagram must be repeated n times for I = 0, 1, 2, ..., n-1. The selection variables are applied to all stages. The function table in Fig.2.10 (b) lists the logic microoperations obtained for each combination of the selection variables.

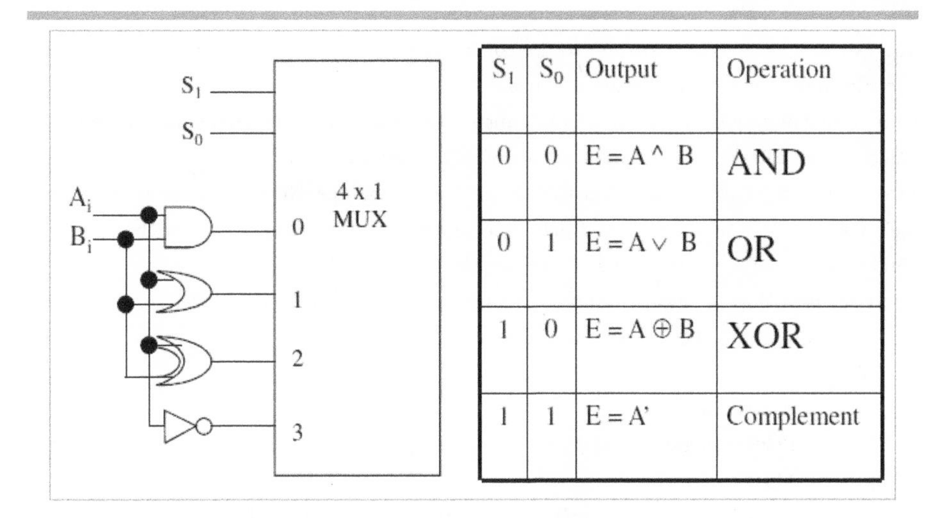

S_1	S_0	Output	Operation
0	0	$E = A \wedge B$	AND
0	1	$E = A \vee B$	OR
1	0	$E = A \oplus B$	XOR
1	1	$E = A'$	Complement

Fig. One stage of logic circuit

Some Applications

Logic microoperations are very useful for manipulating individual bits or a portion of a word stored in a register. They can be used to change bit values, delete a group of bits, or insert new bit values into a register. The following examples show how the bits of one register (designated by A) are manipulated by logic microoperations as a function of the bits of another register (designated by B). In a typical application, register A is a processor register and the bits of register B constitute a logic operand extracted from memory and placed in register B.

The selective-set operation sets to 1 the bits in register A where there are corresponding 1's in register B. It does not affect bit positions that have 0's in B. The following numerical example clarifies this operation:

1010 A before

1100 B (logic operand)

1110 A after

The two leftmost bits of B are 1's, so the corresponding bits of A are set to 1. One of these two bits was already set and the other has been changed from 0 to 1. The two bits of A with corresponding 0's in B remain unchanged. The example above serves as a truth table since it has all four possible combinations of two binary variables.

From the truth table we note that the bits of A after the operation are obtained from the logic-OR operation of bits in B and previous values of A. Therefore, the OR microoperation can be used to selectively set bits of a register.

The selective-complement operation complements bits in A where there are corresponding 1's in B. It does not affect bit positions that have 0's in B.

For example:

1010 A before

1100 B (logic operand)

0110 A after

Again the two leftmost bits of B are 1's, so the corresponding bits of A are complemented. This example again can serve as a truth table from which one can deduce that the selective-complement operation is just an exclusive-OR microoperation. Therefore, the exclusive -OR microoperation can be used to selectively complement bits of a register.

The selective-clear operation clears to 0 the bits in A only where there are corresponding 1's in B. For example:

1010 A before

1100 B (logic operand)

0010 A after

Again the two leftmost bits of B are 1's, so the corresponding bits of A are cleared to 0. One can deduce that the Boolean operation performed on the individual bits is AB'. The corresponding logic microoperation is

$$A \leftarrow A \wedge B$$

The mask operation is similar to the selective-clear operation except that the bits of A are cleared only where there are corresponding 0's in B.

The mask operation is an AND micro operation as seen from the following numerical example:

1010 A before

1100 B (logic operand)

1000 A after masking

The two rightmost bits of A are cleared because the corresponding bits of B are 0s. The two leftmost bits are left unchanged because the corresponding bits of B are 1s. The mask operation is more convenient to use than the selective-clear operation because most computers provide an AND instruction, and few provide an instruction that executes the microoperation for selective-clear.

The insert operation inserts a new value into a group of bits. This is done by first masking the bits and then ORing them with the required value. For example, suppose that an A register contains eight bits, 0110, 1010. To replace the four leftmost bits by the value 1001 we first mask the four unwanted bits:

0110 1010 A before

0000 1111 B (mask)

0000 1010 A after masking

and then insert the new value:

0000 1010 A before

1001 0000 B (insert)

1001 1010 A after insertion

The mask operation is an AND microoperation and the insert operation is an OR microoperation.

The clear operation compares the words in A and B and produces an all 0s result if the two numbers are equal. This operation is achieved by an exclusive-OR microoperation as shown by the following example:

1010 A

1010 B

0000 $A \leftarrow A \oplus B$

When A and B are equal, the two corresponding bits are either both 0 or both 1. In either case the exclusive-OR operation produces a 0. The all-0s result is then checked to determine if the two numbers were equal.

Shift Microoperations

Shift microoperations are used for serial transfer of data. They are also used in conjunction with arithmetic, logic, and other data-processing operations. The contents of a register can be shifted to the left or the right. At the same time that the bits are shifted, the first flip-flop receives its binary information from the serial input. During a shift-left operation the serial input transfers a bit into the rightmost position.

During a shift-right operation the serial input transfers a bit into the leftmost position. The information transferred through the serial input determines the type of shift. There are three types of shifts:
logical, circular, and arithmetic.
A logical shift is one that transfers 0 through the serial input. We will adopt the symbols shl and shr for logical shift-left and shift-right microoperations.
For example

R1 ← shl R1

R2 ← shr R2

are two microoperations that specify a 1-bit shift to the left of the content of register R1 and a 1-bit shift to the right of the content of register R2. The register symbol must be the same on both sides of the arrow. The bit transferred to the end position through the serial input is assumed to be 0 during a logical shift.
The circular shift (also known as a rotate operation) circulates the bits of the register around the two ends without loss of information. This is accomplished by connecting the serial output of the shift register to its serial input. We will use the symbols cil and cir for the circular shift left and right, respectively.

The symbolic notation for the shift microoperations is shown in Table

Symbolic Designation	Description
R ← shl R	Shift-left register R
R ← shr R	Shift-right register R
R ← cil R	Circular shift-left register R
R ← cir R	Circular shift-right register R
R ← ashl R	Arithmetic Shift-left register R
R ← ashr R	Arithmetic Shift-right register R

Table. Shift Micro-operations

An arithmetic shift is a microoperation that shifts a signed binary number to the left or right. An arithmetic shift-left multiplies a signed binary number by 2. An arithmetic shift-right divides the number by 2. Arithmetic shifts must leave the sign bit unchanged because the sign of the number remains the same when it is multiplied or divided by 2. The leftmost bit in a register holds the sign bit, and the remaining bits hold the number.

The sign bit is 0 for positive and 1 for negative. Negative numbers are in 2's complement form. Fig. shows a typical register of n bits. Bit R_{n-1} in the leftmost position holds the sign bit. R_{n-2} is the most significant bit of the number and R_0 is the least significant bit. The arithmetic shift-right leaves the sign bit unchanged and shifts the number (including the sign bit) to the right.

Thus R_{n-1} remains the same, R_{n-2} receives the bit from R_{n-1}, and so on for the other bits in the register. The bit in R_0 is lost.

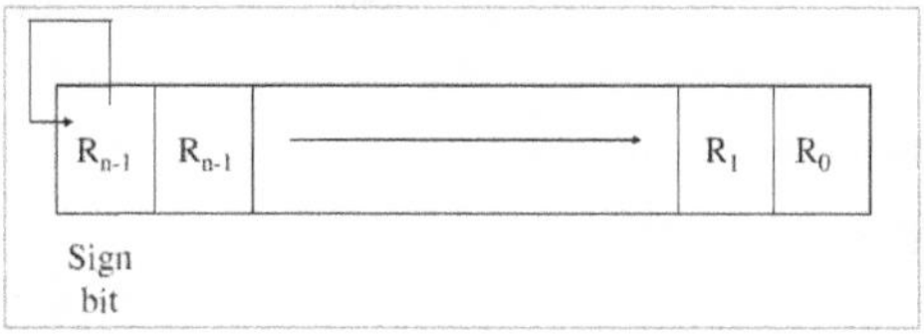

R_{n-1} R_{n-1} R_1 R_0

Sign bit

Fig. : Arithmetic shift right

The arithmetic shift-left inserts a 0 into R_0, and shifts all other bits to the left. The initial bit of R_{n-1} is lost and replaced by the bit from R_{n-2}. A sign reversal occurs if the bit in R_{n-1} changes in value after the shift. This happens if the multiplication by 2 causes an overflow. An overflow occurs after an arithmetic shift left if initially, before the shift, R_{n-1} is not equal to R_{n-2}. An overflow flip-flop Vs can be used to detect an arithmetic shift-left overflow.

$$V_s = R_{n-1} \oplus R_{n-2}$$

If Vs = 0, there is no overflow, but if Vs = 1, there is an overflow and a sign reversal after the shift. Vs must be transferred into the overflow flip-flop with the same clock pulse that shifts the register.

Hardware Implementation

A possible choice for a shift unit would be a bidirectional shift register with parallel load. Information can be transferred to the register in parallel and then shifted to the right or left. In this type of configuration, a clock pulse is needed for loading the data into the register, and another pulse is needed to initiate the shift. In a processor unit with many registers it is more efficient to implement the shift operation with a combinational circuit. In this way the content of a register that has to be shifted is first placed onto a common bus whose output is connected to the combinational shifter, and the shifted number is then loaded back into the register. This requires only one clock pulse for loading the shifted value into the register.

A combinational circuit shifter can be constructed with multiplexers as shown in Fig. The 4-bit shifter has four data inputs. A_0 through A_3, and four data outputs, H_0 through H_3. There are two serial inputs, one for shift left (IL) and the other for shift right (IR).

When the selection input S=0, the input data are shifted right (down in the diagram). When S=1, the input data are shifted left (up in the diagram). The function table in Fig. shows which input goes to each output after the shift. A shifter with n data inputs and outputs requires n multiplexers.

The two serial inputs can be controlled by another multiplexer to provide the three possible types of shifts.

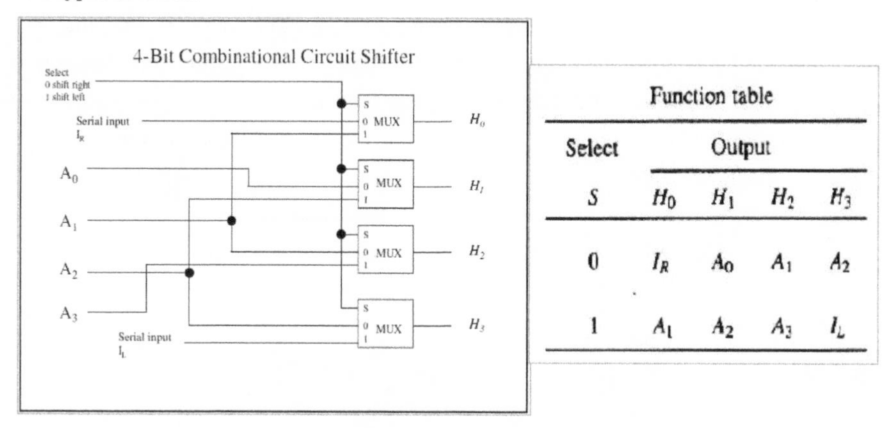

Function table

Select	Output			
S	H_0	H_1	H_2	H_3
0	I_R	A_0	A_1	A_2
1	A_1	A_2	A_3	I_L

4-bit combinational circuit shifter

Arithmetic Logic Shift Unit

Instead of having individual registers performing the microoperations directly, computer systems employ a number of storage registers connected to a common operational unit called an arithmetic logic unit, abbreviated ALU. To perform a microoperation, the contents of specified registers are placed in the inputs of the common ALU. The ALU performs an operation and the result of the operation is then transferred to a destination register.

The ALU is a combinational circuit so that the entire register transfer operation from the source registers through the ALU and into the destination register can be performed during one clock pulse period. The shift microoperations are often performed in a separate unit, but sometimes the shift unit is made part of the overall ALU.

The arithmetic, logic, and shift circuits introduced in previous sections can be combined into one ALU with common selection variables. One stage of an arithmetic logic shift unit is shown in Fig. The subscript I designates a typical stage. Inputs A_i and B_i are applied to both the arithmetic and logic

units. A particular microoperation is selected with inputs S_1 and S_0. A 4 x 1 multiplexer at the output chooses between an arithmetic output in E_i and a logic output in H_i .

The data in the multiplexer are selected with inputs S_3 and S_2. The other two data inputs to the multiplexer receive inputs A_{i-1} for the shift-right operation and A_{i+1} for the shift-left operation. Note that the diagram shows just one typical stage. The circuit of Fig. must be repeated n times for an n-bit ALU. The output carry C_{i+1} of a given arithmetic stage must be connected to the input carry C_i of the next stage in sequence.

The input carry to the first stage is the input carry C_{in}, which provides a selection variable for the arithmetic operations.

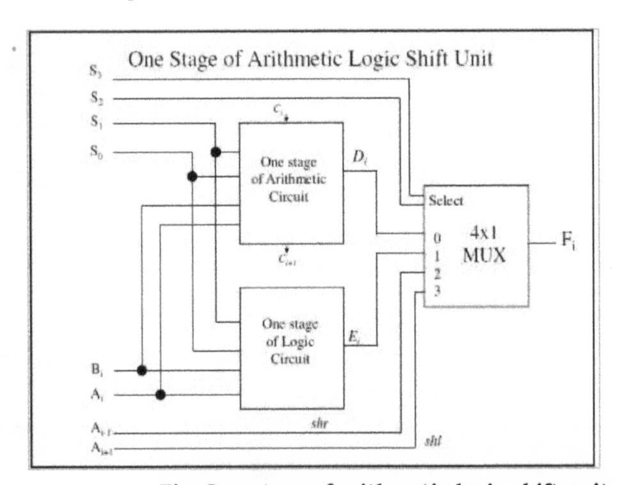

Fig. One stage of arithmetic logic shift unit

The circuit whose one stage is specified in Fig. provides eight arithmetic operation, four logic operations, and two shift operations. Each operation is selected with the five variables S_3, S_2, S_1, S_0, and C_{in}. The input carry C_{in} is used for selecting an arithmetic operation only.

Table lists the 14 operations of the ALU. The first eight are arithmetic operations and are selected with S_3S_2=00. The next four are logic operations and are selected with S_3S_2=01. The input carry has no effect during the logic operations and is marked with don't-care x's. The last two operations are shift operations and are selected with S_3S_2=10 and 11. The other three selection inputs have no effect on the shift.

Function Table for Arithmetic Logic Shift Unit

Operation Select

S_3	S_2	S_1	S_0	C_{in}	Operation	Function
0	0	0	0	0	F =A	Transfer A
0	0	0	0	1	F = A + 1	Increment A
0	0	0	1	0	F = A + B	Addition
0	0	0	1	1	F = A + B + 1	Add with Carry
0	0	1	0	0	$F = A + \overline{B}$	Subtract with Borrow
0	0	1	0	1	$F = A + \overline{B} + 1$	Subtraction
0	0	1	1	0	F = A – 1	Decrement A
0	0	1	1	1	F = A	Transfer A
S_3	S_2	S_1	S_0	C_{in}	Operation	Function
0	1	0	0	x	$F = A \wedge B$	AND
0	1	0	1	x	$F = A \vee B$	OR
0	1	1	0	x	$F = A \oplus B$	XOR
0	1	1	1	x	F = A	Complement A
1	0	x	x	x	F = shr A	Shift-Right A into F
1	1	x	x	x	F = shl A	Shift-Left A into F

Table . : Function Table for Arithmetic Logic Shift Unit

INSTRUCTION CODES

• Every different processor type has its own design (different registers, buses, microoperations, machine instructions, etc)

• Modern processor is a very complex device

– It contain Many registers

– Multiple arithmetic units, for both integer and floating point calculations

– The ability to pipeline several consecutive instructions to speed execution

Computer Instructions

Computer instructions are the basic components of a machine language program. They are also known as ***macrooperations****, since each one is comprised of a sequences of microoperations.* Each instruction initiates a sequence of microoperations that fetch operands from registers or memory, possibly perform arithmetic, logic, or shift operations, and store results in registers or memory.

Instructions are encoded as binary *instruction codes. Each instruction code contains of a operation code, or opcode, which designates the overall purpose of the instruction (e.g. add, subtract, move, input, etc.). The number of bits allocated for the opcode determined how many different instructions the architecture supports.*

In addition to the opcode, many instructions also contain one or more *operands, which indicate where in registers or memory the data required for the operation is located. For example, and add instruction requires two operands, and a not instruction requires one.*

```
 15    12 11         6 5          0
+----------------------------------+
| Opcode |  Operand   |  Operand   |
+----------------------------------+
```

The opcode and operands are most often encoded as unsigned binary numbers in order to minimize the number of bits used to store them. For example, a 4-bit opcode encoded as a binary number could represent up to 16 different operations.

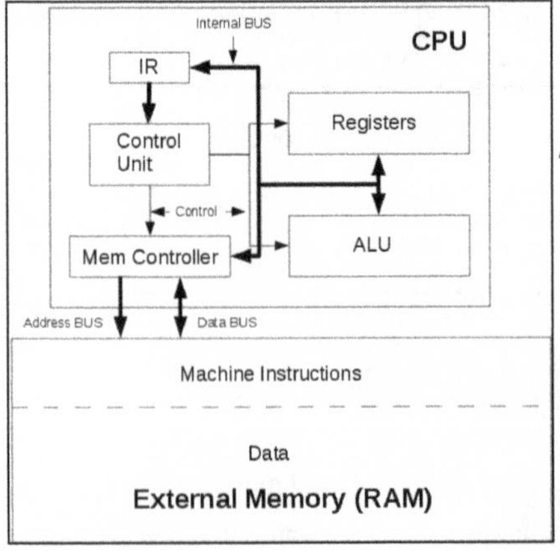

The *control unit is responsible for decoding the opcode and operand bits in the instruction register, and then generating the control signals necessary to drive all other hardware in the CPU to perform the sequence of microoperations that comprise the instruction.*

Figure . CPU Block Diagram

Operand-based Architecture Classification

Architectures are also classified according to how instructions access memory and process data:

Memory-to-memory: Most instructions can access memory for any operand. The VAX architecture from Digital Equipment Corporation is an example.

```
addl3   x, y, sum      # x, y, and sum are memory addresses
```

Register-memory: Instructions allow only one operand to be a memory address, while the other (s) must be CPU registers. The x86 architecture is an example.

```
movl    eax, x

addl    eax, y

movl    sum, eax
```

Load-store: Only load and store instructions can access memory. All others must use CPU registers for all operands. The MIPS processor, originally from Digital Equipment Corporation is an example.

```
lw      $t0, x

lw      $t1, y

add     $t0, $t0, $t1

sw      $t0, sum
```

Accumulator-based: One special register, called the accumulator (AC), is an implied operand for most operations. The Zylog Z80 is an example.

```
load    x   # AC ← x

add     y   # AC ← AC + y

store   sum # sum ←- AC
```

Designing an Instruction Code

Machine instruction codes may all be the same length (e.g. MIPS processor), or codes for different instructions may be different lengths (e.g. x86, VAX processors).

Suppose all instruction codes of a hypothetical accumulator-based CPU are exactly 16 bits.

A simple instruction code format could consist of a 4-bit operation code (opcode) and a 12-bit memory address.

```
 15     12 11             0
+------------------------+
| Opcode | Address        |
+------------------------+
```

This would allow for how many different instructions? How much memory?

Suppose a program contains two variables, x and y. The variable x represents address 0x010 and y represents address 0x012. A segment of the list file, which shows machine code and assembly code side-by-side, might appear as follows:

```
0 010    add     x

1 012    sub     y
```

We see that the opcode for add is 000 (0x0) and the opcode for sub is 001 (0x1).

The format above represents memory-reference instructions, which act on an operand from memory and the accumulator. Not all operations require a second operand, so some instructions could act on the accumulator alone. In this case, address bits can be used for other purposes. For example:

```
clr      # AC = 0

neg      # AC = -AC

not      # AC = AC'

inc      # AC = AC + 1
```

One or more patterns in the 4-bit opcode can be used to signify that the other 12 bits specify an operation instead of an address. This reduces the number of memory-reference instructions possible, but increases the overall instruction count.

```
0XXX     add XXX

1XXX     sub XXX

...

F000     clr

F001     neg

F002     not

F003     inc
```

suppose a load-store architecture computer has 2-operand instructions, 32 registers, 1 megabyte of byte-addressable memory, 4 addressing modes, 50 register-reference instructions, and 6 load-store instructions. What would the instruction code look like for register-reference instructions? What would the instruction code look like for memory-reference instructions?

Solution: Since there are 50 register-reference instructions, we will need 6 bits for the opcode. (6 bits allows for up to 2^6 unique opcodes.) With 32 registers, we will need 5 bits to specify each register, so the instruction code format will be 16 bits:

```
+--------------------------+
| opcode |  reg1  |  reg2  |
+--------------------------+
    6        5        5
```

For 6 load-store opcodes, we need 3 bits. 4 addressing modes requires 2 bits to go with the address. A possible instruction code format is as follows:

```
+--------------------------------+
| opcode | reg | mode | address |
+--------------------------------+
    3       5     4       20
```

As a third example, suppose a register-memory architecture has 8 registers, a 64k memory capacity, 100 instructions, and 6 addressing modes. Design an instruction code format for memory-reference instructions.

Solution: To represent 100 instructions, we will need 7 bits for the opcode. We'll need 16 bits for a memory address for 64k memory, 3 bits to represent one of 8 registers, and 3 bits to cover all 6 addressing modes for the memory operand. One possible instruction format is shown below. Since this adds up to 19 bits, we would likely use 24 bits for the instruction code to make it fit well into byte-addressable memory. The additional bits could be used to support more opcodes and/or addressing modes.

```
+--------------------------------+
| opcode | reg | mode | address |
+--------------------------------+
    7       3     3       16
```

Suppose a direct address in assembly language is represented by a label, as in x below, and an indirect address by a label in parentheses, as in (ptr) below.

```
mov     x, r3
add     (ptr), r3
```

If the opcode for mov is 00000001, add is 0000010, the mode bits for direct addressing are 100, and the bits for indirect addressing are 101, the address x is 0x00F0, and ptr is 0x00F2, the instruction codes for the two instructions above would be:

0000001 011 100 0000000011110000

0000010 011 101 0000000011110010

Design an instruction code format for a memory-to-memory architecture with 16 registers, a 4 gigabyte memory capacity, 250 instructions, and 16 addressing modes. Assume that there are anywhere from 0 to 3 operands per instruction, and each operand may be in a register or in memory.

Some Common Addressing Modes

- Direct: Instruction code contains address of operand

  `0 005    AC = AC + contents of address 5`

  *1 memory-reference beyond fetching instruction

- Immediate: Instruction code contains operand

  `1 005    AC = AC + 5`

  * No memory-reference after fetching instruction

- Indirect: Instruction code contains address of address of operand

  `2 005    AC = AC + contents of address stored at address 5`

Effective address = actual address of the data in memory.

Effective Address by Addressing Mode

Mode	**Effective Address**
Immediate——>	Address of the instruction itself
Direct——>	Address contained in the instruction code
Indirect——>	Address at the address in the instruction code

Basic Computer Instruction Format

The Basic Computer has a 16-bit instruction code similar to the examples described above. It supports direct and indirect addressing modes.

How many bits are required to specify the addressing mode?

```
15 14 12 11        0
+------------------+
| I | OP | ADDRESS |
+------------------+

I = 0: direct
I = 1: indirect
```

Computer Instructions

All Basic Computer instruction codes are 16 bits wide. There are 3 instruction code formats:

Memory-reference instructions take a single memory address as an operand, and have the format:

```
15   14 12 11       0
+-------------------+
| I | OP   | Address |
+-------------------+
```

If I = 0, the instruction uses direct addressing. If I = 1, addressing in indirect.

How many memory-reference instructions can exist?

Register-reference instructions operate solely on the AC register, and have the following format:

```
15   14 12 11      0
+------------------+
| 0 | 111 | OP     |
+------------------+
```

How many register-reference instructions can exist? How many memory-reference instructions can coexist with register-reference instructions?

Input/output instructions have the following format:

```
15   14 12 11      0
+------------------+
| 1 | 111 | OP     |
+------------------+
```

Instruction Cycle

The CPU performs a sequence of microoperations for each instruction. The sequence for each instruction of the Basic Computer can be refined into 4 abstract phases:

1. ***Fetch instruction***
2. ***Decode***
3. ***Fetch operand***
4. ***Execute***

Program execution can be represented as a top-down design:

Program execution

Instruction 1

- Fetch instruction
- Decode
- Fetch operand
- Execute

Instruction 2

- Fetch instruction
- Decode
- Fetch operand
- Execute

Instruction 3.......

Program execution begins with:

PC ← address of first instruction, SC ← 0

After this, the SC is incremented at each clock cycle until an instruction is completed, and then it is cleared to begin the next instruction. This process repeats until a HLT instruction is executed, or until the power is shut off.

Instruction Fetch and Decode:

The instruction fetch and decode phases are the same for all instructions, so the control functions and microoperations will be independent of the instruction code.

Everything that happens in this phase is driven entirely by timing variables T_0, T_1 and T_2. Hence, all control inputs in the CPU during fetch and decode are functions of these three variables alone.

```
T0: AR ← PC (S0S1S2=010, T0=1)
T1: IR ← M [AR], PC ← PC + 1  (S0S1S2=111, T1=1)
T2: D0, . . . , D7 ← Decode IR(12-14), AR ← IR(0-11), I ←  IR(15)
```

For every timing cycle, we assume SC ← SC + 1 unless it is stated that SC ← 0.

The operation $D_{0\text{-}7}$ ← decoded IR(12-14) is not a register transfer like most of our microoperations, but is actually an inevitable consequence of loading a value into the IR register. Since the IR outputs 12-14 are directly connected to a decoder, the outputs of that decoder will change as soon as the new values of IR(12-14) propagate through the decoder.

Note that incrementing the PC at time T_1 assumes that the next instruction is at the next address. This may not be the case if the current instruction is a branch instruction. However, performing the increment here will save time if the next instruction immediately follows, and will do no harm if it doesn't. The incremented PC value is simply overwritten by branch instructions.

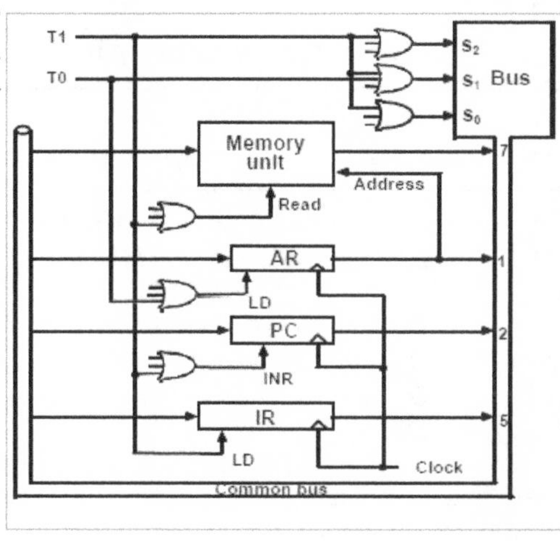

In hardware development, unlike serial software development, it is often advantageous to perform work that may not be necessary. Since we can perform multiple microoperations at the same time, we might was well do everything that *might be useful at the earliest possible time.*

Likewise, loading AR with the address field from IR at T_2 is only useful if the instruction is a memory-reference instruction. We won't know this until T_3, but there is no reason to wait since there is no harm in loading AR immediately.

Figure shows part of the implementation of the CPU for the first two clock pulses of the instruction cycle. Note that each control input for the bus, registers, and ALU is a Boolean function with multiple terms. Hence, the OR gates in the diagram.

The goal in control unit design is to determine the Boolean function needed for each control input of the registers, bus, and ALU.

Memory-Reference Instruction

In order to specify the microoperations needed for the execution of each instruction, it is necessary that the function that they are intended to perform be defined precisely. We will now show that the function of the memory-reference instructions can be defined precisely by means of register transfer notation. The given table lists the seven memory-reference instructions. The decoded output D_i for i = 0, 1, 2, 3, 4, 5, and 6 from the operation decoder that belongs to each instruction is included in the table.

TABLE Memory-Reference Instructions

Symbol	Operation decoder	Symbolic description
AND	D_0	$AC \leftarrow AC \wedge M[AR]$
ADD	D_1	$AC \leftarrow AC + M[AR], \quad E \leftarrow C_{out}$
LDA	D_2	$AC \leftarrow M[AR]$
STA	D_3	$M[AR] \leftarrow AC$
BUN	D_4	$PC \leftarrow AR$
BSA	D_5	$M[AR] \leftarrow PC, \quad PC \leftarrow AR + 1$
ISZ	D_6	$M[AR] \leftarrow M[AR] + 1$, If $M[AR] + 1 = 0$ then $PC \leftarrow PC + 1$

The effective address of the instruction is in the address register AR and was placed there during timing signal T_2 when I = 0, or during timing signal T_3 when I = 1. The execution of the memory-reference instructions starts with timing signal T_4. The symbolic description of each instruction is specified in the table in terms of register transfer notation.

The actual execution of the instruction in the bus system will require a sequence of microoperations. This is because data stored in memory cannot be processed directly.
The data must be read from memory to a register where they can be operated on with logic circuits. We now explain the operation of each instruction and list the control functions and microoperations needed for their execution.

AND to AC

- This is an instruction that performs the AND logic operation on pairs of bits in AC and the memory word specified by the effective address.
- The result of the operation is transferred to AC. The microoperations that execute this instruction are:

  $$D_0T_4: DR \leftarrow M[AR]$$
  $$D_0T_5: AC \leftarrow AC \wedge DR, SC \leftarrow 0$$

- The control function for this instruction uses the operation decoder D_0 since this output of the decoder is active when the instruction has an AND operation whose binary code value is 000. Two timing signals are needed to execute the instruction.
- The clock transition associated with timing signal T_4 transfers the operand from memory into DR.
- The clock transition associated with the next timing signal T_5 transfers to AC the result of the AND logic operation between the contents of DR and AC.
- The same clock transition clears SC to 0, transferring control to timing signal T_0 to start a new instruction cycle.

ADD to AC

- This instruction adds the content of the memory word specified by the effective address to the value of AC.
- The sum is transferred into AC and the output carry C_{out} is transferred to the E (extended accumulator) flip-flop.
- The microoperations needed to execute this instruction are

  D_1T_4: **DR ← M[AR]**

  D_1T_5: **AC ← AC + DR, E ←** C_{out}**, SC ← 0**

- The same two timing signals, T_4 and T_5, are used again but with operation decoder D_1 instead of D_0, which was used for the AND instruction.
- After the instruction is fetched from memory and decoded, only one output of the operation decoder will be active, and that output determines the sequence of rnicrooperations that the control follows during the execution of a memory-reference instruction.

LDA: Load to AC

- This instruction transfers the memory word specified by the effective address to AC.
- The microoperations needed to execute this instruction are

  D_2T_4: **DR ← M [AR]**

  D_2T_5: **AC ← DR, SC ← 0**

- Note that there is no direct path from the bus into AC (see figure under Common Bus System).
- The adder and logic circuit receive information from DR which can be transferred into AC.
- Therefore, it is necessary to read the memory word into DR first and then transfer the content of DR into AC.
- The reason for not connecting the bus to the inputs of AC is the delay encountered in the adder and logic circuit.
- It is assumed that the time it takes to read from memory and transfer the word through the bus as well as the adder and logic circuit is more than the time of one clock cycle.
- By not connecting the bus to the inputs of AC we can maintain one clock cycle per microoperation.

STA: Store AC

- This instruction stores the content of AC into the memory word specified by the effective address. Since the output of AC is applied to the bus and the data input of memory is connected to the bus, we can execute this instruction with one microoperation:

  $$D_3T_4: M[AR] \leftarrow AC, SC \leftarrow 0$$

BUN: Branch Unconditionally

- This instruction transfers the program to the instruction specified by the effective address.
- Remember that PC holds the address of the instruction to be read from memory in the next instruction cycle.
- PC is incremented at time T_1 to prepare it for the address of the next instruction in the program sequence.
- The BUN instruction allows the programmer to specify an instruction out of sequence and we say that the program branches (or jumps) unconditionally.
- The instruction is executed with one microoperation:

  $$D_4T_4: PC \leftarrow AR, SC \leftarrow 0$$

- The effective address from AR is transferred through the common bus to PC .
- Resetting SC to 0 transfers control to T_0. The next instruction is then fetched and executed from the memory address given by the new value in PC.

BSA: Branch and Save Return Address

- This instruction is useful for branching to a portion of the program called a subroutine or procedure.
- When executed, the BSA instruction stores the address of the next instruction in sequence (which is available in PC) into a memory location specified by the effective address.
- The effective address plus one is then transferred to PC to serve as the address of the first instruction in the subroutine.
- This operation was specified in Table above (see Memory-Reference Instructions) with the following register transfer:

  $$M[AR] \leftarrow PC, PC \leftarrow AR + 1$$

- A numerical example that demonstrates how this instruction is used with a subroutine is shown in Fig. below.
- The BSA instruction is assumed to be in memory at address 20. The I bit is 0 and the address part of the instruction has the binary equivalent of 135.
- After the fetch and decode phases, PC contains 21, which is the address of the next instruction in the program (referred to as the return address). AR holds the effective address 135.
- This is shown in part (a) of the figure. The BSA instruction performs the following numerical operation:

  M[135] ← 21, PC ← 135 + 1 = 136
- The result of this operation is shown in part (b) of the figure. The return address 21 is stored in memory location 135 and control continues with the subroutine program starting from address 136.

Figure Example of BSA instruction execution.

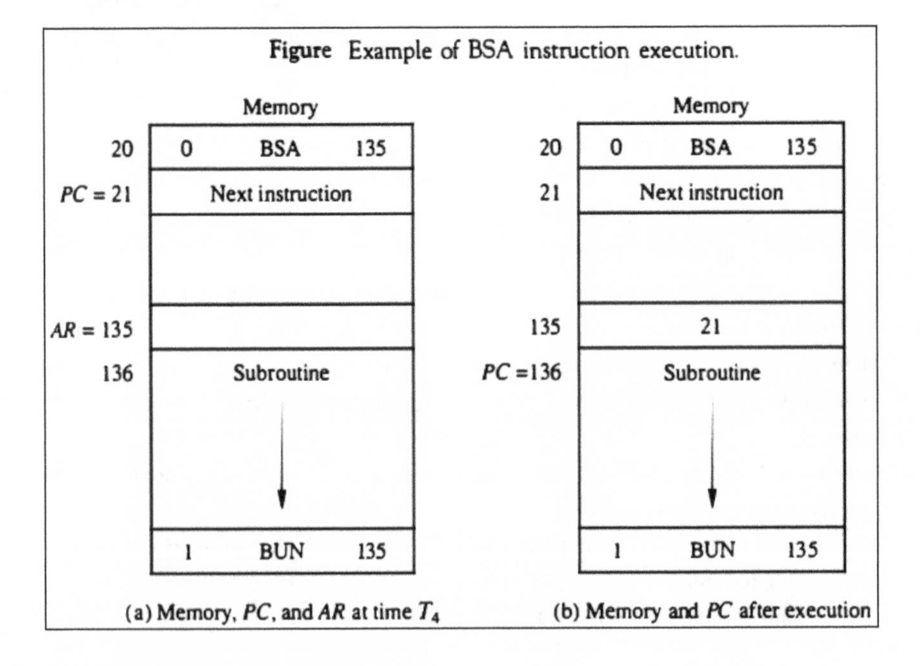

(a) Memory, PC, and AR at time T_4 (b) Memory and PC after execution

- The return to the original program (at address 21) is accomplished by means of an indirect BUN instruction placed at the end of the subroutine.
- When this instruction is executed, control goes to the indirect phase to read the effective address at location 135, where it finds the previously saved address 21.
- When the BUN instruction is executed, the effective address 21 is transferred to PC . The next instruction cycle finds PC with the value 21, so control continues to execute the instruction at the return address.
- The BSA instruction performs the function usually referred to as a subroutine call. The indirect BUN instruction at the end of the subroutine performs the function referred to as a subroutine return.
- In most commercial computers, the return address associated with a subroutine is stored in either a processor
- Register or in a portion of memory called a stack. It is not possible to perform the operation of the BSA instruction in one clock cycle when we use the bus system of the basic computer.
- To use the memory and the bus properly, the BSA instruction must be executed With a sequence of two microoperations:

$$\mathbf{D_5T_4: M[AR] \leftarrow PC, AR \leftarrow AR + 1}$$

$$\mathbf{D_5T_5: PC \leftarrow AR, SC \leftarrow 0}$$

- Timing signal T_4 initiates a memory write operation, places the content of PC onto the bus, and enables the INR input of AR .
- The memory write operation is completed and AR is incremented by the time the next clock transition occurs. The bus is used at T_5 to transfer the content of AR to PC .

ISZ: Increment and Skip if Zero

- This instruction increments the word specified by the effective address, and if the incremented value is equal to 0, PC is incremented by 1.
- The programmer usually stores a negative number (in 2's complement) in the memory word.
- As this negative number is repeatedly incremented by one, it eventually reaches the value of zero.
- gram.

- At that time PC is incremented by one in order to skip the next instruction in the program.
- Since it is not possible to increment a word inside the memory, it is necessary to read the word into DR, increment DR, and store the word back into memory.
- This is done with the following sequence of microoperations:

D_6T_4: DR ← M [AR]

D_6T_5: DR ← DR + 1

D_6T_6: M[AR] ← DR, if (DR = 0) then (PC ← PC + 1), SC ← 0

Control Flowchart

- A flowchart showing all microoperations for the execution of the seven memory-reference instructions is shown in Fig. below. The control functions are indicated on top of each box.

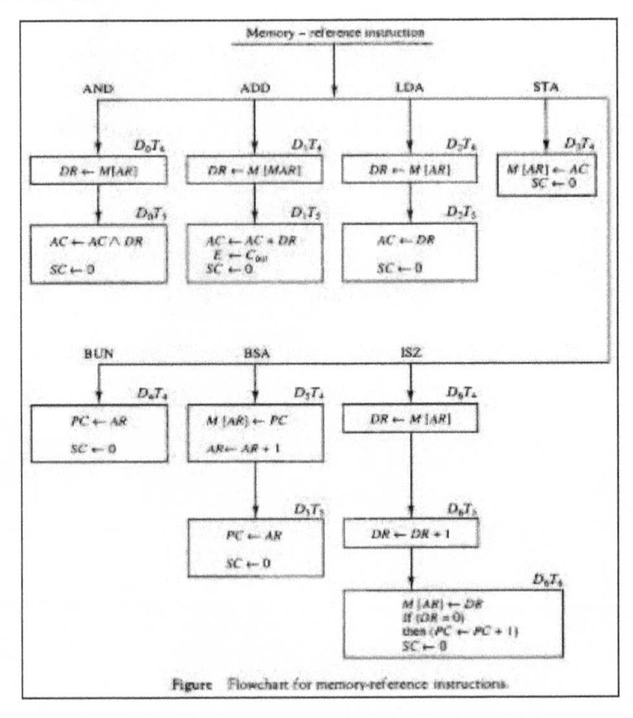

Figure Flowchart for memory-reference instructions.

- The microoperations that are performed during time T_4, T_5, or T_6 depend on the operation code value. This is indicated in the flowchart by six different paths, one of which the control takes after the instruction is decoded. The sequence counter SC is cleared to 0 with the last timing signal in each case.
- This causes a transfer of control to timing signal T_0 to start the next instruction cycle.
- Note that we need only seven timing signals to execute the longest instruction (ISZ).
- The computer can be designed with a 3-bit sequence counter. The reason for using a 4-bit counter for SC is to provide additional timing signals for other instructions that are presented in the problems section.

Input-Output and Interrupt

A computer can serve no useful purpose unless it communicates with the external environment. To demonstrate the most basic requirements for input and output communication, we will use as an illustration a terminal unit with a keyboard and printer.

Input-Output Configuration

1. The terminal sends and receives serial information. Each quantity of information has eight bits of an alphanumeric code.
2. The serial information from the keyboard is shifted into the input register INPR.
3. The serial information for the printer is stored in the output register OUTR.
4. These two registers communicate with a communication interface serially and with the AC in parallel. The input-output configuration is shown in Fig. below. The transmitter interface receives serial information from the keyboard and transmits it to INPR.
5. The receiver interface receives information from OUTR and sends it to the printer serially.
6. The input register INPR consists of eight bits and holds an alphanumeric input information. The 1-bit input flag FGI is a control flip-flop. The flag bit is set to 1 when new information is available in the input device and is cleared to 0 when the information is accepted by the computer.
7. The flag is needed to synchronize the timing rate difference between the input device and the computer.

8. The process of information transfer is as follows. Initially, the input flag FGI is cleared to 0. When a key is struck in the keyboard, an 8-bit alphanumeric code is shifted into INPR and the input flag FGI is set to 1.
9. As long as the flag is set, the information in INPR cannot be changed by striking another key. The computer checks the flag bit; if it is 1, the information from INPR is transferred in parallel into AC and FGI is cleared to 0. Once the flag is cleared, new information can be shifted into INPR by striking another key.

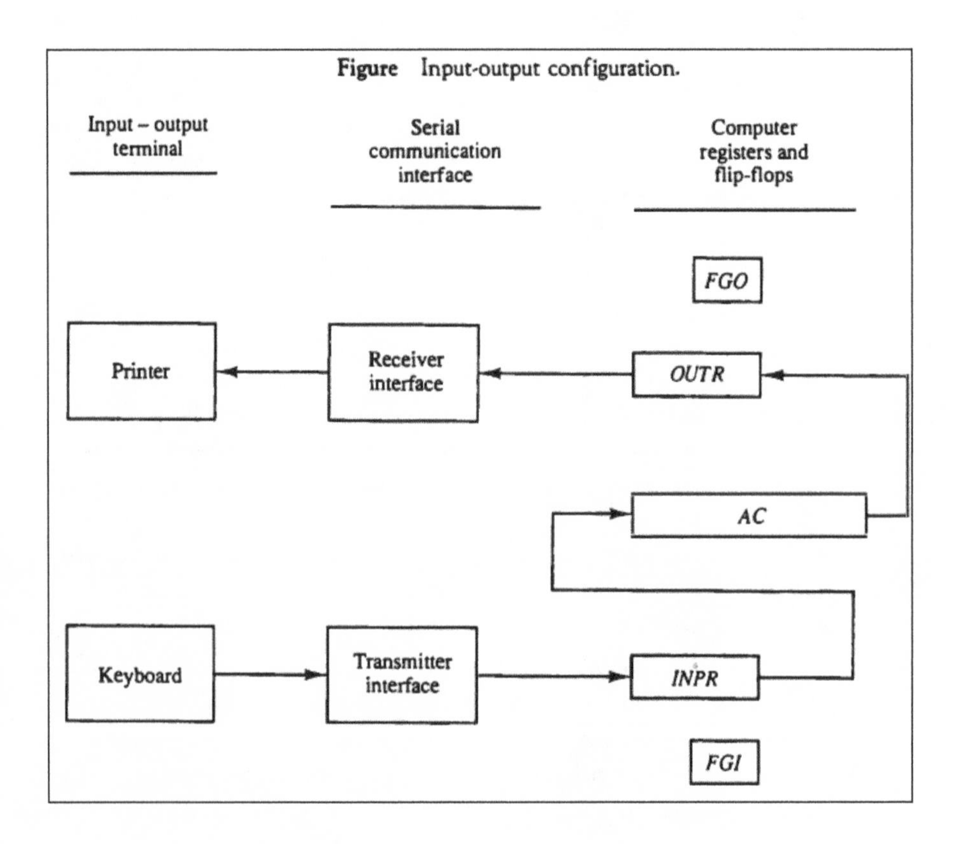

Figure Input-output configuration.

10. The output register OUTR works similarly but the direction of information flow is reversed. Initially, the output flag FGO is set to 1.
11. The computer checks the flag bit; if it is 1, the information from AC is transferred in parallel to OUTR and FGO is cleared to 0. The output device accepts the coded information, prints the corresponding character, and when the operation is completed, it sets FGO to 1.
12. The computer does not load a new character into OUTR when FGO is 0 because this condition indicates that the output device is in the process of printing the character.

Input-Output Instructions

1. Input and output instructions are needed for transferring information to and from AC register, for checking the flag bits, and for controlling the interrupt facility.
2. Input-output instructions have an operation code 1111 and are recognized by the control when $D_7 = 1$ and $I = 1$. The remaining bits of the instruction specify the particular operation.
3. The control functions and microoperations for the input-output instructions are listed in Table below. These instructions are executed with the clock transition associated with timing signal T_3. Each control function needs a Boolean relation D_7IT_3, which we designate for convenience by the symbol p. The control function is distinguished by one of the bits in IR(6-11).
4. By assigning the symbol B_i to bit i of IR, all control functions can be denoted by pB_i for i = 6 though 11. The sequence counter SC is cleared to 0 when $p = D_7IT_3 = 1$.
5. The INP instruction transfers the input information from INPR into the eight low-order bits of AC and also clears the input flag to 0.
6. The OUT instruction transfers the eight least significant bits of AC into the output register OUTR and clears the output flag to 0.
7. The next two instructions in Table above check the status of the flags and cause a skip of the next instruction if the flag is 1.
8. The instruction that is skipped will normally be a branch instruction to return and check the flag again.

9. The branch instruction is not skipped if the flag is 0. If the flag is 1, the branch instruction is skipped and an input or output instruction is executed.
10. The last two instructions set and clear an interrupt enable flip flop IEN. The purpose of IEN is explained in conjunction with the interrupt operation

Program Interrupt

- The process of communication just described is referred to as programmed control transfer. The computer keeps checking the flag bit, and when it finds it set, it initiates an information transfer.
- The difference of information flow rate between the computer and that of the input-output device makes this type of transfer inefficient. To see why this is inefficient, consider a computer that can go through an instruction cycle in 1 μs.
- Assume that the input-output device can transfer information at a maximum rate of 10 characters per second. This is equivalent to one character every 100,000 μs. Two instructions are executed when the computer checks the flag bit and decides not to transfer the information.
- This means that at the maximum rate, the computer will check the flag 50,000 times between each transfer. The computer is wasting time while checking the flag instead of doing some other useful processing task.
- An alternative to the programmed controlled procedure is to let the external device inform the computer when it is ready for the transfer. In the meantime the computer can be busy with other tasks. This type of transfer uses the interrupt facility.
- While the computer is running a program, it does not check the flags. However, when a flag is set, the computer is momentarily interrupted from proceeding with the current program and is informed of the fact that a flag has been set.
- The computer deviates momentarily from what it is doing to take care of the input or output transfer. It then returns to the current program to continue what it was doing before the interrupt.
- The interrupt enable flip-flop IEN can be set and cleared with two instructions. When IEN is cleared to 0 (with the IOF instruction), the flags cannot interrupt the computer. When IEN is set to 1 (with the ION instruction), the computer can be interrupted.

These two instructions provide the programmer with the capability of making a decision as to whether or not to use the interrupt facility.

TABLE Input-Output Instructions

$D_7IT_3 = p$ (common to all input–output instructions)
$IR(i) = B_i$ [bit in $IR(6–11)$ that specifies the instruction]

	p:	$SC \leftarrow 0$	Clear SC
INP	pB_{11}:	$AC(0–7) \leftarrow INPR, \quad FGI \leftarrow 0$	Input character
OUT	pB_{10}:	$OUTR \leftarrow AC(0–7), \quad FGO \leftarrow 0$	Output character
SKI	pB_9:	If $(FGI = 1)$ then $(PC \leftarrow PC + 1)$	Skip on input flag
SKO	pB_8:	If $(FGO = 1)$ then $(PC \leftarrow PC + 1)$	Skip on output flag
ION	pB_7:	$IEN \leftarrow 1$	Interrupt enable on
IOF	pB_6:	$IEN \leftarrow 0$	Interrupt enable off

The way that the interrupt is handled by the computer can be explained by means of the flowchart of Fig. above. An interrupt flip-flop R is included in the computer. When R = 0, the computer goes through an instruction cycle.

During the execute phase of the instruction cycle IEN is checked by the control. If it is 0, it indicates that the programmer does not want to use the interrupt, so control continues with the next instruction cycle. If IEN is 1, control checks the flag bits.

If both flags are 0, it indicates that neither the input nor the output registers are ready for transfer of information. In this case, control continues with the next instruction cycle. If either flag is set to 1 while IEN = 1, flip-flop R is set to 1.

At the end of the execute phase, control checks the value of R, and if it is equal to 1, it goes to an interrupt cycle instead of an instruction cycle. The interrupt cycle is a hardware implementation of a branch and save return address operation.

The return address available in PC is stored in a specific location where it can be found later when the program returns to the instruction at which it was interrupted.

This location may be a processor register, a memory stack, or a specific memory location. Here we choose the memory location at address 0 as the place for storing the return address. Control then inserts address 1 into PC and clears IEN and R so that no more interruptions can occur until the interrupt request from the flag has been serviced.

An example that shows what happens during the interrupt cycle is shown in Fig. below. Suppose that an interrupt occurs and R is set to 1 while the control is executing the instruction at address 255. At this time, the return address 256 is in PC .

The programmer has previously placed an input-output service program in memory starting from address 1120 and a BUN 1120 instruction at address 1. This is shown in Part (a) in Fig. below. When control reaches timing signal T_0 and finds that R = 1, it proceeds with the interrupt cycle.

The content of PC (256) is stored in memory location 0, PC is set to 1, and R is cleared to 0. At the beginning of the next instruction cycle, the instruction that is read from memory is in address 1 since this is the content of PC.

The branch instruction at address 1 causes the program to transfer to the input-output service program at address 1120. This program checks the flags, determines which flag is set, and then transfers the required input or output information.
Once this is done, the instruction ION is executed to set IEN to 1 (to enable further interrupts), and the program returns to the location where it was interrupted. This is shown in Part (b) in Fig. below.

The instruction that returns the computer to the original place in the main program is a branch indirect instruction with an address part of 0. This instruction is placed at the end of the UO service program.

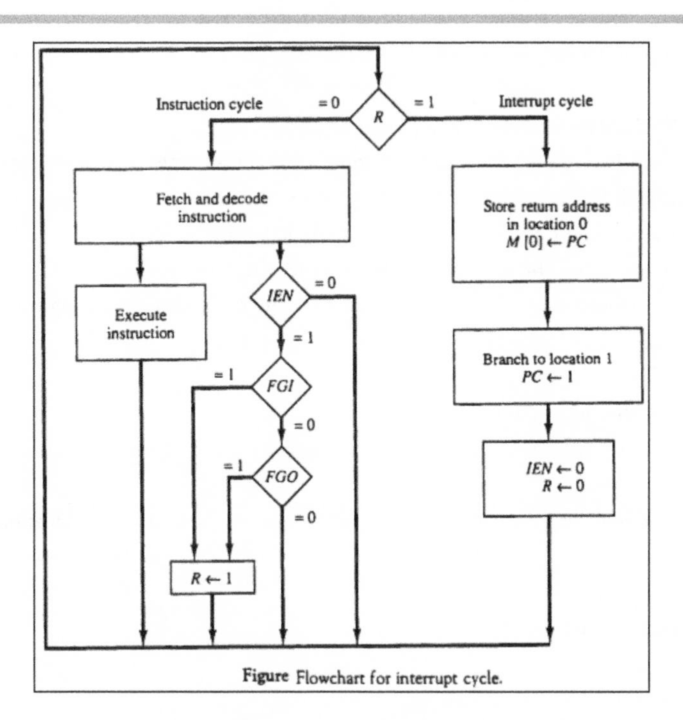

Figure Flowchart for interrupt cycle.

After this instruction is read from memory during the fetch phase, control goes to the indirect phase (because I = 1) to read the effective address.

The effective address is in location 0 and is the return address that was stored there during the previous interrupt cycle. The execution of the indirect BUN instruction results in placing into PC the return address from location 0.

Interrupt Cycle

The interrupt cycle is initiated after the last execute phase if the interrupt flip-flop R is equal to 1. This flip-flop is set to 1 if IEN = 1 and either FGI or FGO are equal to 1.
This can happen with any clock transition except when timing signals T_0, T_1 or T_2 are active.

The condition for setting flip-flop R to 1 can be expressed with the following register transfer statement:

$T'_0T'_1T'_2 (IEN) (FGI+FGO) : R \leftarrow 1$

The symbol + between FGI and FGO in the control function designates a logic OR operation. This is ANDed with IEN and T'0T'1T'2.

We now modify the fetch and decode phases of the instruction cycle. Instead of using only timing signals T_0, T_1 or T_2 (as shown in Figure in Section - Determine the Type of Instruction) we will AND the three timing signals with R' so that the fetch and decode phases will be recognized from the three control functions $R'T_0$, $R'T_1$ and $R'T_2$.

The reason for this is that after the instruction is executed and SC is cleared to 0, the control will go through a fetch phase only if R = 0. Otherwise, if R = 1, the control will go through an interrupt cycle.

The interrupt cycle stores the return address (available in PC) into memory location 0, branches to memory location 1, and clears IEN, R, and SC to 0. This can be done with the following sequence of microoperations:

RT_0: AR ← 0, TR ← PC

RT_1: M[AR] ← TR, PC ← 0

RT_2: PC ← PC + 1, IEN ← 0, R ← 0, SC ← 0

During the first timing signal AR is cleared to 0, and the content of PC is transferred to the temporary register TR.

With the second timing signal, the return address is stored in memory at location 0 and PC is cleared to 0. The third timing signal increments PC to 1, clears IEN and R, and control goes back to T_0 by clearing SC to 0.

The beginning of the next instruction cycle has the condition $R'T_0$ and the content of PC is equal to 1.

The control then goes through an instruction cycle that fetches and executes the BUN instruction in location 1.

INSTRUCTION FORMATS

The physical and logical structure of computers is normally described in reference manuals provided with the system. Such manuals explain the internal construction of the CPU, including the processor registers available and their logical capabilities. They list all hardware-implemented instructions, specify their binary code format, and provide a precise definition of each instruction. A computer will usually have a variety of instruction code formats. It is the function of the control unit within the CPU to interpret each instruction code and provide the necessary control functions needed to process the instruction.

The format of an instruction is usually depicted in a rectangular box symbolizing the bits of the instruction as they appear in memory words or in a control register. The bits of the instruction are divided into groups called fields. The most common fields found in instruction formats are:

1. An operation code field that specifies the operation to be performed.
2. An address field that designates a memory address or a processor registers.
3. A mode field that specifies the way the operand or the effective address is determined.

Other special fields are sometimes employed under certain circumstances, as for example a field that gives the number of shifts in a shift-type instruction.

The operation code field of an instruction is a group of bits that define various processor operations, such as add, subtract, complement, and shift. The bits that define the mode field of an instruction code specify a variety of alternatives for choosing the operands from the given address. The various addressing modes that have been formulated for digital computers are presented in coming Sec. In this section we are concerned with the address field of an instruction format and consider the effect of including multiple address fields is an instruction.

Operations specified by computer instructions are executed on some data stored in memory or processor registers, Operands residing in processor registers are specified with a register address. A register address is a binary number of k bits that defines one of 2k registers in the CPU. Thus a CPU with 16 processor registers R0 through R15 will have a register address field of four bits. The binary number 0101, for example, will designate register R5.

Computers may have instructions of several different lengths containing varying number of addresses. The number of address fields in the instruction format of a computer depends on the internal organization of its registers. Most computers fall into one of three types of CPU organizations:

1. **Single accumulator organization.**
2. **General register organization.**
3. **Stack organization.**

An example of an accumulator-type organization is the basic computer presented in Chap. 5. All operations are performed with an implied accumulator register. The instruction format in this type of computer uses one address field. For example, the instruction that specifies an arithmetic addition is defined by an assembly language instruction as ADD.

Where X is the address of the operand. The ADD instruction in this case results in the operation **AC ← AC + M[X].** AC is the accumulator register and M[X] symbolizes the memory word located at address X.

An example of a general register type of organization was presented in Fig. 7.1. The instruction format in this type of computer needs three register address fields. Thus the instruction for an arithmetic addition may be written in an assembly language as

ADD R1, R2, R3

To denote the operation **R1 ← R2 + R3**. The number of address fields in the instruction can be reduced from three to two if the destination register is the same as one of the source registers. Thus the instruction

ADD R1, R2

Would denote the operation **R1 ← R1 + R2.** Only register addresses for R1 and R2 need be specified in this instruction.

Computers with multiple processor registers use the move instruction with a mnemonic MOV to symbolize a transfer instruction. Thus the instruction

MOV R1, R2

Denotes the transfer **R1 ← R2 (or R2 ← R1**, depending on the particular computer). Thus transfer-type instructions need two address fields to specify the source and the destination.

General register-type computers employ two or three address fields in their instruction format. Each address field may specify a processor register or a memory word. An instruction symbolized by

ADD R1, X

Would specify the operation **R1 ← R + M [X].** It has two address fields, one for register R1 and the other for the memory address X.

The stack-organized CPU was presented in Fig. 8-4. Computers with stack organization would have PUSH and POP instructions which require an address field. Thus the instruction

PUSH X

Will push the word at address X to the top of the stack. The stack pointer is updated automatically. Operation-type instructions do not need an address field in stack-organized computers. This is because the operation is performed on the two items that are on top of the stack. The instruction

ADD

In a stack computer consists of an operation code only with no address field. This operation has the effect of popping the two top numbers from the stack, adding the numbers, and pushing the sum into the stack. There is no need to specify operands with an address field since all operands are implied to be in the stack.

Most computers fall into one of the three types of organizations that have just been described. Some computers combine features from more than one organization structure. For example, the Intel 808- microprocessor has seven CPU registers, one of which is an accumulator register As a consequence; the processor has some of the characteristics of a general register type and some of the characteristics of a accumulator type. All arithmetic and logic instruction, as well as the load and store instructions, use the accumulator register, so these instructions have only one address field. On the other hand, instructions that transfer data among the seven processor registers have a format that contains two register address fields.

Moreover, the Intel 8080 processor has a stack pointer and instructions to push and pop from a memory stack. The processor, however, does not have the zero-address-type instructions which are characteristic of a stack-organized CPU. To illustrate the influence of the number of addresses on computer programs, we will evaluate the arithmetic statement

$$X = (A + B) * (C + D).$$

Using zero, one, two, or three address instruction. We will use the symbols ADD, SUB, MUL, and DIV for the four arithmetic operations; MOV for the transfer-type operation; and LOAD and STORE for transfers to and from memory and AC register. We will assume that the operands are in memory addresses A, B, C, and D, and the result must be stored in memory at address X.

THREE-ADDRESS INSTRUCTIONS

Computers with three-address instruction formats can use each address field to specify either a processor register or a memory operand. The program in assembly language that evaluates X = (A + B) * (C + D) is shown below, together with comments that explain the register transfer operation of each instruction.

```
ADD  R1, A, B        R1 ← M [A] + M [B]
ADD  R2, C, D        R2 ← M [C] + M [D]
MUL  X, R1, R2       M [X] ← R1 * R2
```

It is assumed that the computer has two processor registers, R1 and R2. The symbol M [A] denotes the operand at memory address symbolized by A.

The advantage of the three-address format is that it results in short programs when evaluating arithmetic expressions. The disadvantage is that the binary-coded instructions require too many bits to specify three addresses. An example of a commercial computer that uses three-address instructions is the Cyber 170. The instruction formats in the Cyber computer are restricted to either three register address fields or two register address fields and one memory address field.

TWO-ADDRESS INSTRUCTIONS

Two address instructions are the most common in commercial computers. Here again each address field can specify either a processor register or a memory word. The program to evaluate X = (A + B) * (C + D) is as follows:

MOV R1, A	R1 ← M [A]
ADD R1, B	R1 ← R1 + M [B]
MOV R2, C	R2 ← M [C]
ADD R2, D	R2 ← R2 + M [D]
MUL R1, R2	R1 ← R1*R2
MOV X, R1	M [X] ← R1

The MOV instruction moves or transfers the operands to and from memory and processor registers. The first symbol listed in an instruction is assumed to be both a source and the destination where the result of the operation is transferred.

ONE-ADDRESS INSTRUCTIONS

One-address instructions use an implied accumulator (AC) register for all data manipulation. For multiplication and division there is a need for a second register. However, here we will neglect the second and assume that the AC contains the result of tall operations. The program to evaluate X = (A + B) * (C + D) is

LOAD	A	AC ← M [A]
ADD	B	AC ← A [C] + M [B]
STORE	T	M [T] ← AC
LOAD	C	AC ← M [C]
ADD	D	AC ← AC + M [D]
MUL	T	AC ← AC * M [T]
STORE	X	M [X] ← AC

All operations are done between the AC register and a memory operand. T is the address of a temporary memory location required for storing the intermediate result.

ZERO-ADDRESS INSTRUCTIONS

A stack-organized computer does not use an address field for the instructions ADD and MUL. The PUSH and POP instructions, however, need an address field to specify the operand that communicates with the stack.

The following program shows how X = (A + B) * (C + D) will be written for a stack organized computer. (TOS stands for top of stack)

PUSH	A	TOS ← A
PUSH	B	TOS ← B
ADD		TOS ← (A + B)
PUSH	C	TOS ← C
PUSH	D	TOS ← D
ADD		TOS ← (C + D)
MUL		TOS ← (C + D) * (A + B)
POP	X	M [X] ← TOS

To evaluate arithmetic expressions in a stack computer, it is necessary to convert the expression into reverse Polish notation. The name ―zero-address‖ is given to this type of computer because of the absence of an address field in the computational instructions.

ADDRESSING MODES

The operation field of an instruction specifies the operation to be performed. This operation must be executed on some data stored in computer registers or memory words. The way the operands are chosen during program execution in dependent on the addressing mode of the instruction. The addressing mode of the instruction. The addressing mode specifies a rule for interpreting or modifying the address field of the instruction before the operand is actually referenced. Computers use addressing mode techniques for the purpose of accommodating one or both of the following provisions:

1. To give programming versatility to the user by providing such facilities as pointers to Memory, counters for loop control, indexing of data, and program relocation
2. To reduce the number of bits in the addressing field of the instruction.

3. The availability of the addressing modes gives the experienced assembly language programmer flexibility for writing programs that are more efficient with respect to the number of instructions and execution time.

To understand the various addressing modes to be presented in this section, it is imperative that we understand the basic operation cycle of the computer. The control unit of a computer is designed to go through an instruction cycle that is divided into three major phases:

1. Fetch the instruction from memory
2. Decode the instruction.
3. Execute the instruction.

There is one register in the computer called the program counter of PC that keeps track of the instructions in the program stored in memory. PC holds the address of the instruction to be executed next and is incremented each time an instruction is fetched from memory. The decoding done in step 2 determines the operation to be performed, the addressing mode of the instruction and the location of the operands. The computer then executes the instruction and returns to step 1 to fetch the next instruction in sequence.

In some computers the addressing mode of the instruction is specified with a distinct binary code, just like the operation code is specified. Other computers use a single binary code that designates both the operation and the mode of the instruction. Instructions may be defined with a variety of addressing modes, and sometimes, two or more addressing modes are combined in one instruction.

An example of an instruction format with a distinct addressing mode field is shown in Fig. The operation code specified the operation to be performed. The mode field is sued to locate the operands needed for the operation. There may or may not be an address field in the instruction. If there is an address field, it may designate a memory address or a processor register. Moreover, as discussed in the preceding section, the instruction may have more than one address field, and each address field may be associated with its own particular addressing mode.

Although most addressing modes modify the address field of the instruction, there are two modes that need no address field at all. These are the implied and immediate modes.

1 Implied Mode: In this mode the operands are specified implicitly in the definition of the instruction. For example, the instruction ―complement accumulator‖ is an implied-mode instruction because the operand in the accumulator register is implied in the definition of the instruction. In fact, all register reference instructions that sue an accumulator are implied-mode instructions.

Op Code	Mode	Address

Figure 1: Instruction format with mode field

Zero-address instructions in a stack-organized computer are implied-mode instructions since the operands are implied to be on top of the stack.

2 Immediate Mode: In this mode the operand is specified in the instruction itself. Inother words, an immediate- mode instruction has an operand field rather than an address field. The operand field contains the actual operand to be used in conjunction with the operation specified in the instruction. Immediate-mode instructions are useful for initializing registers to a constant value.

It was mentioned previously that the address field of an instruction may specify either a memory word or a processor register. When the address field specifies a processor register, the instruction is said to be in the register mode.

3 Register Mode: In this mode the operands are in registers that reside within the CPU. The particular register is selected from a register field in the instruction. A k-bit field can specify any one of 2k registers.

4 Register Indirect Mode: In this mode the instruction specifies a register in the CPU whose contents give the address of the operand in memory. In other words, the selected register contains the address of the operand rather than the operand itself. Before using a register indirect mode instruction, the programmer must ensure that the memory address fo the operand is placed in the processor register with a previous instruction. A reference to the register is then equivalent to specifying a memory address. The advantage of a register indirect mode instruction is that the address field of the instruction sues fewer bits to select a register than would have been required to specify a memory address directly.

5 Auto increment or Auto decrement Mode: This is similar to the register indirect mode except that the register is incremented or decremented after (or before) its value is used to access memory. When the address stored in the register refers to a table of data in memory, it is necessary to increment or decrement the register after every access to the table. This can be achieved by using the increment or decrement instruction. However, because it is such a common requirement, some computers incorporate a special mode that automatically increments or decrements the content of the register after data access.

The address field of an instruction is used by the control unit in the CPU to obtain the operand from memory. Sometimes the value given in the address field is the address of the operand, but sometimes it is just an address from which the address of the operand is calculated. To differentiate among the various addressing modes it is necessary to distinguish between the address part of the instruction and the effective address used by the control when executing the instruction. The effective address is defined to be the memory address obtained from the computation dictated by the given addressing mode. The effective address is the address of the operand in a computational-type instruction. It is the address where control branches in response to a branch-type instruction. We have already defined two addressing modes in previous chapter.

6 Direct Address Mode: In this mode the effective address is equal to the address part of the instruction. The operand resides in memory and its address is given directly by the address field of the instruction. In a branch-type instruction the address field specifies the actual branch address.

7 Indirect Address Mode: In this mode the address field of the instruction gives the address where the effective address is stored in memory. Control fetches the instruction from memory and uses its address part to access memory again to read the effective address.

8 Relative Address Mode: In this mode the content of the program counter is added to the address part of the instruction in order to obtain the effective address. The address part of the instruction is usually a signed number (in 2's complement representation) which can be either positive or negative. When this number is added to the content of the program counter, the result produces an effective address whose position in memory is relative to the address of the next instruction. To clarify with an example, assume that the program counter contains the number 825 and the address part of the instruction contains the number 24. The instruction at location 825 is read from memory during the fetch phase and the program counter is then incremented by one to 826 + 24 = 850.

This is 24 memory locations forward from the address of the next instruction. Relative addressing is often used with branch-type instructions when the branch address is in the area surrounding the instruction word itself. It results in a shorter address field in the instruction format since the relative address can be specified with a smaller number of bits compared to the number of bits required to designate the entire memory address.

9 Indexed Addressing Mode: In this mode the content of an index register is added to the address part of the instruction to obtain the effective address. The index register is a special CPU register that contains an index value. The address field of the instruction defines the beginning address of a data array in memory. Each operand in the array is stored in memory relative to the beginning address. The distance between the beginning address and the address of the operand is the index value stores in the index register. Any operand in the array can be accessed with the same instruction provided that the index register contains the correct index value. The index register can be incremented to facilitate access to consecutive operands. Note that if an index-type instruction does not include an address field in its format, the instruction converts to the register indirect mode of operation. Some computers dedicate one CPU register to function solely as an index register. This register is involved implicitly when the index-mode instruction is used. In computers with many processor registers, any one of the CPU registers can contain the index number. In such a case the register must be specified explicitly in a register field within the instruction format.

10 Base Register Addressing Mode: In this mode the content of a base register is added to the address part of the instruction to obtain the effective address. This is similar to the indexed addressing mode except that the register is now called a base register instead of an index register. The difference between the two modes is in the way they are used rather than in the way that they are computed. An index register is assumed to hold an index number that is relative to the address part of the instruction. A base register is assumed to hold a base address and the address field of the instruction gives a displacement relative to this base address. The base register addressing mode is used in computers to facilitate the relocation of programs in memory. When programs and data are moved from one segment of memory to another, as required in multiprogramming systems, the address values of the base register requires updating to reflect the beginning of a new memory segment.

Numerical Example

To show the differences between the various modes, we will show the effect of the addressing modes on the instruction defined in Fig. The two-word instruction at address 200 and 201 is a "load to AC" instruction with an address field equal to 500. The first word of the instruction specifies the operation code and mode, and the second word specifies the address part.

PC has the value 200 for fetching this instruction. The content of processor register R1 is 400, and the content of an index register XR is 100. AC receives the operand after the instruction is executed. The figure lists a few pertinent addresses and shows the memory content at each of these addresses.

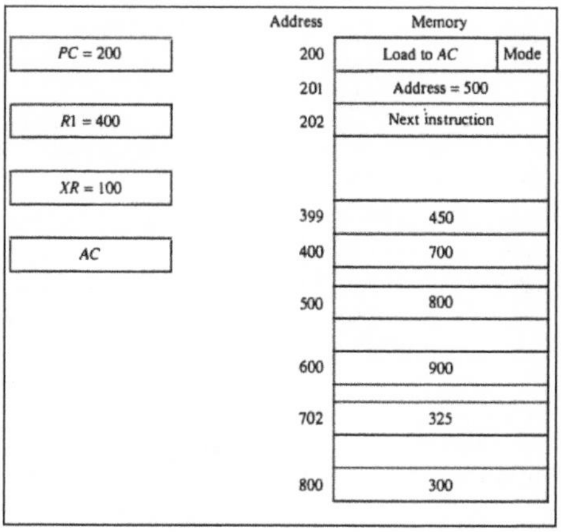

PC = 200

R1 = 400

XR = 100

AC

Address	Memory
200	Load to AC / Mode
201	Address = 500
202	Next instruction
399	450
400	700
500	800
600	900
702	325
800	300

The mode field of the instruction can specify any one of a number of modes. For each possible mode we calculate the effective address and the operand that must be loaded into AC.

In the direct address mode the effective address is the address part of the instruction 500 and the operand to be loaded into AC is 800. In the immediate mode the second word of the instruction is taken as the operand rather than an address, so 500 is loaded into AC.

(The effective address in this case is 201)

In the indirect mode the effective address is stored in memory at address 500. Therefore, the effective address is 800 and the operand is 300. In the relative mode the effective address is 500 + 202 = 702 and the operand is 325.

(Note that the value in PC after the fetch phase and during the execute phase is 202.) In the index mode the effective address is XR + 500 = 100 + 500 = 600 and the operand is 900. In the register mode the operand is in R1 and 400 is loaded into AC.

(There is no effective address in this case.) In the register indirect mode the effective address is 400, equal to the content of R1 and the operand loaded into AC is 700.

The auto-increment mode is the same as the register indirect mode except that R1 is incremented to 401 after the execution of the instruction. The auto-decrement mode decrements R1 to 399 prior to the execution of the instruction.

The operand loaded into AC is now 450. Table lists the values of the effective address and the operand loaded into AC for the nine addressing modes.

Addressing Mode	Effective Address	Content of *AC*
Direct address	500	800
Immediate operand	201	500
Indirect address	800	300
Relative address	702	325
Indexed address	600	900
Register	—	400
Register indirect	400	700
Autoincrement	400	700
Autodecrement	399	450

DATA Transfer and Manipulation

Most computer instructions can be classified into three categories:

1. Data transfer instructions
2. Data manipulation instructions
3. Program control instructions

Data transfer instructions cause transfer of data from one location to another without changing the binary information content. Data manipulation instructions are those that perform arithmetic, logic, and shift operations. Program control instructions provide decision-making capabilities and change the path taken by the program when executed in the computer. The instruction set of a particular computer determines the register transfer operations and control decisions that are available to the user.

Data Transfer and Manipulation

Data transfer instructions move data from one place in the computer to another without changing the data content. The most common transfers are between memory and processor registers, between processor registers and input or output, and between the processor registers themselves. Table gives a list of eight data transfer instructions used in many computers. Accompanying each instruction is a mnemonic symbol. It must be realized that different computers use different mnemonics for the same instruction name.

The load instruction has been used mostly to designate a transfer from memory to a processor register, usually an accumulator. The store instruction designates a transfer from a processor register into memory. The move instruction has been used in computers with multiple CPU registers to designate a transfer from one register to another. It has also been used for data transfers between CPU registers and memory or between two memory words. The exchange instruction swaps information between two registers or a register and a memory word. The input and output instructions transfer data among processor registers and input or output terminals.

The push and pop instructions transfer data between processor registers and a memory stack. It must be realized that the instructions listed in Table 8-5, as well as in subsequent tables in this section, are often associated with a variety of addressing modes. Some assembly language conventions modify the mnemonic symbol to differentiate between the different addressing modes.

Name	Mnemonic
Load	LD
Store	ST
Move	MOV
Exchange	XCH
Input	IN
Output	OUT
Push	PUSH
Pop	POP

TABLE . Typical Data Transfer Instructions

For example, the mnemonic for load immediate becomes LDI. Other assembly language conventions use a special character to designate the addressing mode. For example, the immediate mode is recognized from a pound sign # placed before the operand. In any case, the important thing is to realize that each instruction can occur with a variety of addressing modes. As an example, consider the load to accumulator instruction when used with eight different addressing modes.

Mode	Assembly Convention	Register Transfer
Direct address	LD ADR	$AC \leftarrow M[ADR]$
Indirect address	LD @ADR	$AC \leftarrow M[M[ADR]]$
Relative address	LD $ADR	$AC \leftarrow M[PC + ADR]$
Immediate operand	LD #NBR	$AC \leftarrow NBR$
Index addressing	LD ADR(X)	$AC \leftarrow M[ADR + XR]$
Register	LD R1	$AC \leftarrow R1$
Register indirect	LD (R1)	$AC \leftarrow M[R1]$
Autoincrement	LD (R1)+	$AC \leftarrow M[R1],\ R1 \leftarrow R1 + 1$

The above table shows the recommended assembly language convention and the actual transfer accomplished in each case. ADR stands for an address, NBR is a number or operand, X is an index register, Rl is a processor register, and AC is the accumulator register. The @ character symbolizes an indirect address. The $ character before an address makes the address relative to the program counter PC . The # character precedes the operand in an immediate-mode instruction. An indexed mode instruction is recognized by a register that is placed in parentheses after the symbolic address. The register mode is symbolized by giving the name of a processor register.

In the register indirect mode, the name of the register that holds the memory address is enclosed in parentheses. The autoincrement mode is distinguished from the register indirect mode by placing a plus after the parenthesized register. The autodecrement mode would use a minus instead. To be able to write assembly language programs for a computer, it is necessary to know the type of instructions available and also to be familiar with the addressing modes used in the particular computer.

Data Manipulation Instructions

Data manipulation instructions perform operations on data and provide the computational capabilities for the computer. The data manipulation instructions in a typical computer are usually divided into three basic types:

1. Arithmetic instructions
2. Logical and bit manipulation instructions
3. Shift instructions

Arithmetic Instructions

The four basic arithmetic operations are :

addition,
subtraction,
multiplication,
and division.

A list of typical arithmetic instructions is given in Table . The increment instruction adds 1 to the value stored in a register or memory word. One common characteristic of the increment operations when executed in processor registers is that a binary number of all 1' s when incremented produces a result of all 0' s. The decrement instruction subtracts 1 from a value stored in a register or memory word. A number with all D's, when decremented, produces a number with all 1's.

Name	Mnemonic
Increment	INC
Decrement	DEC
Add	ADD
Subtract	SUB
Multiply	MUL
Divide	DIV
Add with carry	ADDC
Subtract with borrow	SUBB
Negate (2's complement)	NEG

Logical and Bit Manipulation Instructions

Logical instructions perform binary operations on strings of bits stored in registers. They are useful for manipulating individual bits or a group of bits that represent binary-coded information. The logical instructions consider each bit of the operand separately and treat it as a Boolean variable. By proper application of the logical instructions it is possible to change bit values, to clear a group of bits, or to insert new bit values into operands stored in registers or memory words.

Some typical logical and bit manipulation instructions are listed in Table. The clear instruction causes the specified operand to be replaced by D's. The complement instruction produces the 1's complement by inverting all the bits of the operand. The AND, OR, and XOR instructions produce the corresponding logical operations on individual bits of the operands. Although they perform Boolean operations, when used in computer instructions, the logical instructions should be considered as performing bit manipulation operations. There are three bit manipulation operations possible: a selected bit can be cleared to 0, or can be set to 1, or can be complemented. The three logical instructions are usually applied to do just that.

Name	Mnemonic
Clear	CLR
Complement	COM
AND	AND
OR	OR
Exclusive-OR	XOR
Clear carry	CLRC
Set carry	SETC
Complement carry	COMC
Enable interrupt	EI
Disable interrupt	DI

The AND instruction is used to clear a bit or a selected group of bits of an operand. For any Boolean variable x, the relationships

$x\, b_0 = 0$ and $x\, b_1 = x$ dictate that a binary variable ANDed with a 0 produces a 0; but the variable does not change in value when ANDed with a 1. Therefore, the AND instruction can be used to clear bits of an operand selectively by ANDing the operand with another operand that has 0' s in the bit positions that must be cleared. The AND instruction is also called a mask because it masks or inserts 0' s in a selected portion of an operand.

The OR instruction is used to set a bit or a selected group of bits of an ope rand. For any Boolean variable x, the relationships x + 1 = 1 and x + 0 = x dictate that a binary variable ORed with a 1 produces a 1; but the variable does not change when ORed with a 0. There fore, the OR instruction can be used to selectively set bits of an operand by ORing it with another operand with 1' s in the bit positions that must be set to 1 .

Similarly, the XOR instruction i s used t o selectively complement bits of an operand. This is because of the Boolean relationships $x \oplus 1 = x'$ and $x \oplus 0 = x$. Thus a binary variable is complemented when XORed with a 1 but does not change in value when XORed with a 0

Shift Instructions

Instructions to shift the content of an operand are quite useful and are often provided in several variations. Shifts are operations in which the bits of a word are moved to the left or right. The bit shifted in at the end of the word determines the type of shift used. Shift instructions may specify either logical shifts, arithmetic shifts, or rotate-type operations. In either case the shift may be to the right or to the left.

Table : Typical Shift Instructions

Name	Mnemonic
Logical shift right	SHR
Logical shift left	SHL
Arithmetic shift right	SHRA
Arithmetic shift left	SHLA
Rotate right	ROR
Rotate left	ROL
Rotate right through carry	RORC
Rotate left through carry	ROLC

The Above table lists four types of shift instructions. The logical shift inserts 0 to the end bit position. The end position is the leftmost bit for shift right and the rightmost bit position for the shift left. Arithmetic shifts usually conform with the rules for signed-2' s complement numbers

The arithmetic shift-right instruction must preserve the sign bit in the leftmost position. The sign bit is shifted to the right together with the rest of the number, but the sign bit itself remains unchanged. This is a shift-right operation with the end bit remaining the same. The arithmetic shift-left instruction inserts 0 to the end position and is identical to the logical shift-left instruction. For this reason many computers do not provide a distinct arithmetic shift-left instruction when the logical shift-left instruction is already available.

The rotate instructions produce a circular shift. Bits shifted out at one end of the word are not lost as in a logical shift but are circulated back into the other end. The rotate through carry instruction treats a carry bit as an extension of the register whose word is being rotated. Thus a rotate-left through carry instruction transfers the carry bit into the rightmost bit position of the register, transfers the leftmost bit position into the carry, and at the same time, shifts the entire register to the left.

Some computers have a multiple-field format for the shift instructions. One field contains the operation code and the others specify the type of shift and the number of times that an operand is to be shifted. A possible instruction code format of a shift instruction may include five fields as follows:

OP REG TYPE RL COUNT

Here **OP** is the operation code field; **REG** is a register address that specifies the location of the operand; **TYPE** is a 2-bit field specifying the four different types of shifts; RL is a 1-bit field specifying a shift right or left; and **COUNT** is a k-bit field specifying up to $2^k - 1$ shifts . With such a format, it is possible to specify the type of shift, the direction, and the number of shifts, all in one instruction.

Program Control

Instructions are always stored in successive memory locations. When processed in the CPU, the instructions are fetched from consecutive memory locations and executed. Each time an instruction is fetched from memory, the program counter is incremented so that it contains the address of the next instruction in sequence. After the execution of a data transfer or data manipulation instruction, control returns to the fetch cycle with the program counter containing the address of the instruction next in sequence. On the other hand, a program control type of instruction, when executed, may change the address value in the program counter and cause the flow of control to be altered.

In other words, program control instructions specify conditions for altering the content of the program counter, while data transfer and manipulation instructions specify conditions for data-processing operations. The change in value of the program counter as a result of the execution of a program control instruction causes a break in the sequence of instruction execution. This is an important feature in digital computers, as it provides control over the flow of program execution and a capability for branching to different program segments.

TABLE Typical Progra Control Instructions

Name	Mnemonic
Branch	BR
Jump	JMP
Skip	SKP
Call	CALL
Return	RET
Compare (by subtraction)	CMP
Test (by ANDing)	TST

Some typical program control instructions are listed in above table . The branch and jump instructions are used interchangeably to mean the same thing, but sometimes they are used to denote different addressing modes. The branch is usually a one-address instruction. It is written in assembly language as BR ADR, where ADR is a symbolic name for an address.

When executed, the branch instruction causes a transfer of the value of ADR into the program counter. Since the program counter contains the address of the instruction to be executed, the next instruction will come from location ADR .

Branch and jump instructions may be conditional or unconditional. An unconditional branch instruction causes a branch to the specified address without any conditions. The conditional branch instruction specifies a condition such as branch if positive or branch if zero. If the condition is met, the program counter is loaded with the branch address and the next instruction is taken from this address. If the condition is not met, the program counter is not changed and the next instruction is taken from the next location in sequence.

The skip instruction does not need an address field and is therefore a zero-address instruction. A conditional skip instruction will skip the next instruction if the condition is met. This is accomplished by incrementing the program counter during the execute phase in addition to its being incremented during the fetch phase. If the condition is not met, control proceeds with the next instruction in sequence where the programmer inserts an unconditional branch instruction. Thus a skip-branch pair of instructions causes a branch if the condition is not met, while a single conditional branch instruction causes a branch if the condition is met.

The call and return instructions are used in conjunction with subroutines. Their performance and implementation are discussed later in this section. The compare and test instructions do not change the program sequence directly. They are listed in Table 8-10 because of their application in setting conditions for subsequent conditional branch instructions. The compare instruction performs a subtraction between two operands, but the result of the operation is not retained.

However, certain status bit conditions are set as a result of the operation. Similarly, the test instruction performs the logical AND of two operands and updates certain status bits without retaining the result or changing the operands. The status bits of interest are the carry bit, the sign bit, a zero indication, and an overflow condition. The generation of these status bits will be discussed first and then we will show how they are used in conditional branch instructions.

Status Bit Conditions

It is sometimes convenient to supplement the ALU circuit in the CPU with a status register where status bit conditions can be stored for further analysis. Status bits are also called condition-code bits or flag bits. Figure shows the block diagram of an 8-bit ALU with a 4-bit status register. The four status bits are symbolized by C. S, Z, and V. The bits are set or cleared as a result of an operation performed in the ALU.

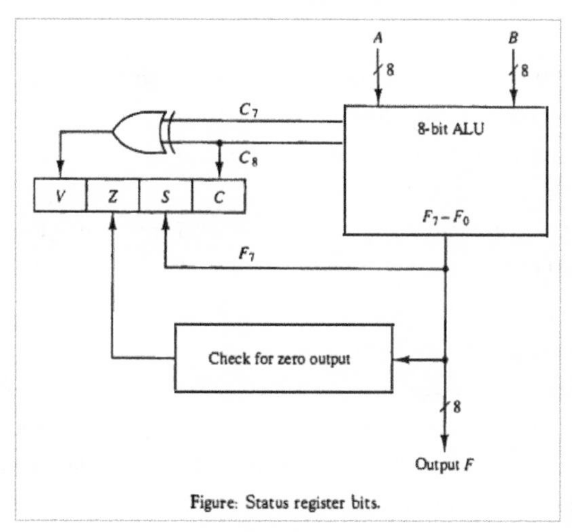

Figure: Status register bits.

1. Bit C (carry) is set to 1 if the end carry C8 is 1. It is cleared to 0 if the carry is 0.
2. Bit S (sign) is set to 1 if the highest-order bit F, is 1. It is set to 0 if the bit is 0.
3. Bit Z (zero) is set to 1 if the output of the ALU contains all O's. !t is cleared to 0 other wise. In other words, Z = 1 if the output is zero and Z = 0 if the output is not zero.
4. Bit V (overflow) is set to 1 if the exclusive-OR of the last two carries is equal to 1,and cleared to 0 otherwise. This is the condition for an overflow when negative numbers are in 2's complement. For the 8-bit ALU, V = 1 if the output is greater than + 127 or less than - 128.

The status bits can be checked after an ALU operation to determine certain relationships that exist between the values of A and B . If bit V is set after the addition of two signed numbers, it indicates an overflow condition. If Z is set after an exclusive-OR operation, it indicates that A = B . This is so because $x \oplus x = 0$, and the exclusive-OR of two equal operands gives an all-0' s result which sets the Z bit. A single bit in A can be checked to determine if it is 0 or 1 by masking all bits except the bit in question and then checking the Z status bit.

For example,

let A = 101x 1l00, where x is the bit to be checked. The AND operation of A with B = 00010000 produces a result 000x0000.

If x = 0, the Z status bit is set, but if x = 1, the Z bit is cleared since the result is not zero.

The AND operation can be generated with the TEST instruction listed in Table if the original content of A must be preserved.

Conditional Branch Instructions

The table in the next page gives a list of the most common branch instructions. Each mnemonic is constructed with the letter B (for branch) and an abbreviation of the condition name. When the opposite condition state is used, the letter N (for no) is inserted to define the 0 state. Thus BC is Branch on Carry, and BNC is Branch on No Carry. If the stated condition is true, program control is transferred to the address specified by the instruction. If not, control continues with the instruction that follows. The conditional instructions can be associated also with the jump, skip, call, or return type of program control instructions.

The zero status bit is used for testing if the result of an ALU operation is equal to zero or not. The carry bit is used to check if there is a carry out of the most significant bit position of the ALU. It is also used in conjunction with the rotate instructions to check the bit shifted from the end position of a register into the carry position.

The sign bit reflects the state of the most significant bit of the output from the ALU. S = 0 denotes a positive sign and S = 1, a negative sign. Therefore, a branch on plus checks for a sign bit of 0 and a branch on minus checks for a sign bit of 1.

Table: Conditional Branch Instrctions

Mnemonic	Branch condition	Tested condition
BZ	Branch if zero	$Z = 1$
BNZ	Branch if not zero	$Z = 0$
BC	Branch if carry	$C = 1$
BNC	Branch if no carry	$C = 0$
BP	Branch if plus	$S = 0$
BM	Branch if minus	$S = 1$
BV	Branch if overflow	$V = 1$
BNV	Branch if no overflow	$V = 0$
Unsigned compare conditions ($A - B$)		
BHI	Branch if higher	$A > B$
BHE	Branch if higher or equal	$A \geq B$
BLO	Branch if lower	$A < B$
BLOE	Branch if lower or equal	$A \leq B$
BE	Branch if equal	$A = B$
BNE	Branch if not equal	$A \neq B$
Signed compare conditions ($A - B$)		
BGT	Branch if greater than	$A > B$
BGE	Branch if greater or equal	$A \geq B$
BLT	Branch if less than	$A < B$
BLE	Branch if less or equal	$A \leq B$
BE	Branch if equal	$A = B$
BNE	Branch if not equal	$A \neq B$

It must be realized, however, that these two conditional branch instructions can be used to check the value of the most significant bit whether it represents a sign or not. The overflow bit is used in conjunction with arithmetic operations done on signed numbers in 2's complement representation. As stated previously, the compare instruction performs a subtraction of two operands, say A - B.

The result of the operation is not transferred into a destination register, but the status bits are affected The status register provides information about the relative magnitude of A and B. Some computers provide conditional branch instructions that can be applied right after the execution of a compare instruction.

The specific conditions to be tested depend on whether the two numbers A and B are considered to be unsigned or signed numbers. Table in this section gives a list of such conditional branch instructions. Note that we use the words higher and lower to denote the relations between unsigned numbers, and greater and less than for signed numbers. The relative magnitude shown under the tested condition column in the table seems to be the same for unsigned and signed numbers.

Example

Consider an 8-bit ALU as shown in Fig of this section . The largest unsigned number that can be accommodated in 8 bits is 255. The range of signed numbers is between + 127 and - 128. The subtraction of two numbers is the same whether they are unsigned or in signed -2's complement representation .

Let A = 11110000 and B = 00010100. To perform A - B, the ALU takes the 2's complement of B and adds it to A .

A :	1 1 1 1 0 0 0 0
$\bar{B}$+ 1:	+ 1 1 1 0 1 1 0 0
A - B:	1 1 0 1 1 1 0 0

$C = 1 \quad s = 1 \quad v = 0 \quad z = 0$

The compare instruction updates the status bits as shown. C = 1 because there is a carry out of the last stage. S = 1 because the leftmost bit is 1 . V = 0 because the last two carries are both equal to 1, and Z = 0 because the result is not equal to 0.

If we assume unsigned numbers, the decimal equivalent of A is 240 and that of B is 20. The subtraction in decimal is 240 - 20 = 220. The binary result 11011100 is indeed the equivalent of decimal 220. Since 240 > 20, we have that A > B and A ≠ B. These two relations can also be derived from the fact that status bit C is equal to 1 and bit Z is equal to 0. The instructions that will cause a branch after this comparison are BHI (branch if higher), BHE (branch if higher or equal), and BNE (branch if not equal). If we assume unsigned numbers, the decimal equivalent of A is 240 and that of B is 20. The subtraction in decimal is 240 - 20 = 220. The binary result 11011100 is indeed the equivalent of decimal 220. Since 240 > 20, we have that A > B and A ≠ B.

These two relations can also be derived from the fact that status bit C is equal to 1 and bit Z is equal to 0. The instructions that will cause a branch after this comparison are BHI (branch if higher), BHE (branch if higher or equal), and BNE (branch if not equal).

If we assume signed numbers, the decimal equivalent of A is - 16 . This is because the sign of A is negative and 11110000 is the 2's complement of 00010000, which is the decimal equivalent of + 16. The decimal equivalent of B is +20.

The subtraction in decimal is (-16) - (+ 20) = -36. The binary result 11011 100 (the 2' s complement of 001001 00) is indeed the equivalent of decimal -36.

Since (- 16) < (+ 20) we have that A < B and A ≠ B. These two relations can also be derived from the fact that status bits

S = 1 (negative),

V = 0 (no overflow),

and Z = 0 (not zero).

The instructions that will cause a branch after this comparison are BLT (branch if less than), BLE (branch if less or equal), and BNE (branch if not equal).

It should be noted that the instruction BNE and BNZ (branch if not zero) are identical. Similarly, the two instructions BE (branch if equal) and BZ (branch if zero) are also identical. Each is repeated three times in Table 8-11 for the purpose of clarity and completeness.

Subroutine Call and Return

- A subroutine is a self-contained sequence of instructions that performs a given computational task.
  - The instruction that transfers program control to a subroutine is known by different names. The most common names used are call subroutine, jump to subroutine, branch to subroutine, or branch and save address.
- The instruction is executed by performing two operations:
  - The address of the next instruction available in the program counter (the return address) is Stored in a temporary location so the subroutine knows where to return

- Control is transferred to the beginning of the subroutine.

  Different computers use a different temporary location for storing the return address.

  Some store the return address in the first memory location of the subroutine, some store it in a fixed location in memory, some store it in a processor register, and some store it in a memory stack. The most efficient way is to store the return address in a memory stack. The advantage of using a stack for the return address is that when a succession of subroutines is called, the sequential return addresses can be pushed into the stack. The return from subroutine instruction causes the stack to pop and the contents of the top of the stack are transferred to the program counter.

- A subroutine call is implemented with the following micro operations:

  SP ←SP - 1 *Decrement stack pointer*

  M [SP] ←PC *Push content of PC onto the stack*

  PC ← effective address *Transfer control to the subroutine*

- If another subroutine is called by the current subroutine, the new return address is pushed into The stack and so on. The instruction that returns from the last subroutine is implemented by the Micro operations:

  PC←M [SP] Pop stack and transfer to PC

  SP ←SP + 1 Increment stack pointer

By using a subroutine stack, all return addresses are automatically stored by the hardware in one unit. The programmer does not have to be concerned or remember where the return address was stored.

A recursive subroutine is a subroutine that calls itself. If only one register or memory location is used to store the return address, and the recursive subroutine calls itself, it destroys the previous return address.

Reduced Instruction Set Computer (RISC)

Instruction set or instruction set architecture is the structure of the computer that provides commands to the computer to guide the computer for processing data manipulation. Instruction set consists of instructions, addressing modes, native data types, registers, interrupt, exception handling and memory architecture. Instruction set can be emulated in software by using an interpreter or built into hardware of the processor.

Instruction Set Architecture can be considered as a boundary between the software and hardware. Classification of microcontrollers and microprocessors can be done based on the RISC and CISC instruction set architecture.

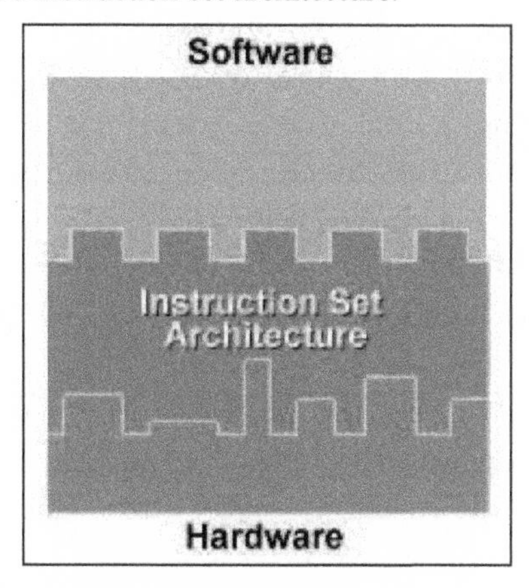

Instruction set specifies processor functionality including the operations supported by the processor, storage mechanisms of the processor, and the way of compiling the programs to the processor.

The microcontroller architecture that utilizes small and highly optimized set of instructions is termed as the Reduced Instruction Set Computer or simply called as RISC. It is also called as LOAD/STORE architecture.

In the late 1970s and early 1980s, RISC projects were primarily developed from Stanford, UC-Berkley and IBM. The John Coke of IBM research team developed RISC by reducing the number of instructions required for processing computations faster than the CISC. The RISC architecture is faster and the chips required for the manufacture of RISC architecture is also less expensive compared to the CISC architecture.

Typical Features of RISC Architecture

- Pipelining technique of RISC, executes multiple parts or stages of instructions simultaneously such that every instruction on the CPU is optimized. Hence, the RISC processors have Clock per Instruction of one cycle, and this is called as One Cycle Execution.
- It optimizes the usage of register with more number of registers in the RISC and more number of interactions within the memory can be prevented.
- Simple addressing modes, even complex addressing can be done by using arithmetic AND/ OR logical operations.
- It simplifies the compiler design by using identical general purpose registers which allows any register to be used in any context.
- For efficient usage of the registers and optimization of the pipelining uses, reduced instruction set is required.
- The number of bits used for the opcode is reduced.
- In general there are 32 or more registers in the RISC.
-

Advantages of RISC processor architecture

- Because of the small set of instructions of RISC, high-level language compilers can produce more efficient code.
- RISC allows freedom of using the space on microprocessors because of its simplicity.
- Instead of using Stack, many RISC processors use the registers for passing arguments and holding the local variables.

Small RISC Processor (SRP) Architecure

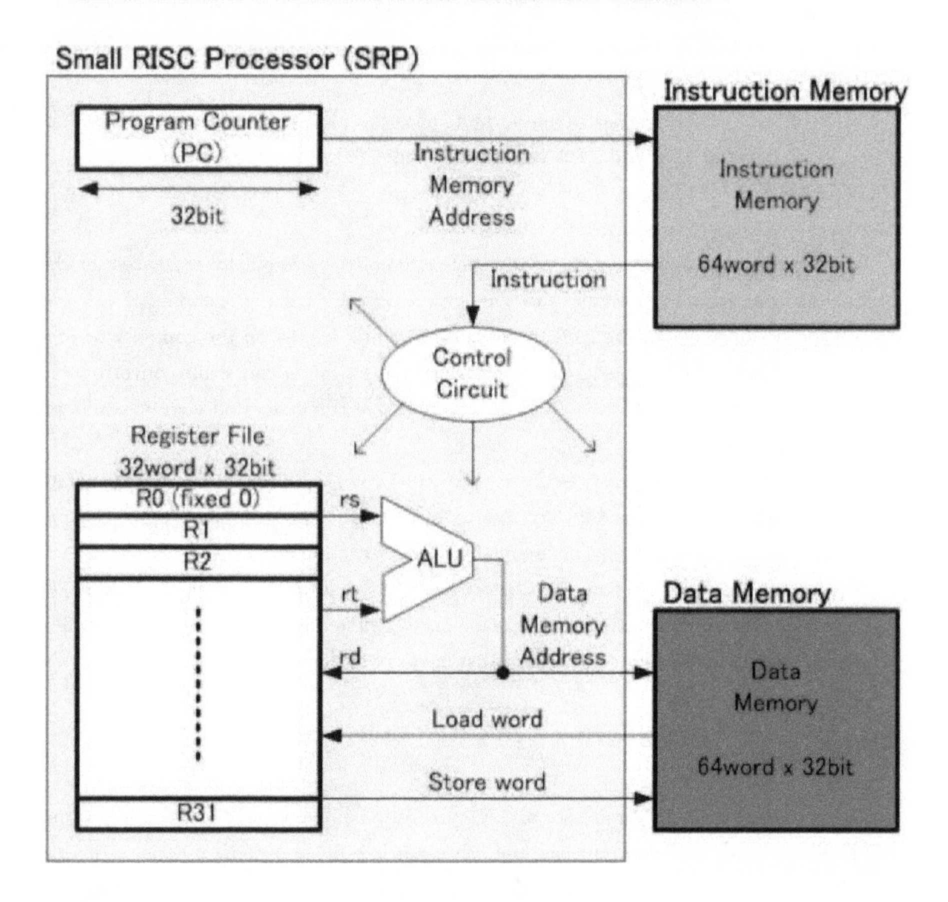

Figure: RISC Architecture

- RISC functions uses only a few parameters, and the RISC processors cannot use the call instructions, and therefore, use a fixed length instructions which are easy to pipeline.
- The speed of the operation can be maximized and the execution time can be minimized.
- Very less number of instruction formats (less than four), a few number of instructions (around 150) and a few addressing modes (less than four) are needed.

Drawbacks of RISC processor architecture

- With the increase in length of the instructions, the complexity increases for the RISC processors to execute due to its character cycle per instruction.
- The performance of the RISC processors depends mostly on the compiler or programmer as the knowledge of the compiler plays a major role while converting the CISC code to a RISC code; hence, the quality of the generated code depends on the compiler.
- While rescheduling the CISC code to a RISC code, termed as a code expansion, will increase the size. And, the quality of this code expansion will again depend on the compiler, and also on the machine's instruction set.
- The first level cache of the RISC processors is also a disadvantage of the RISC, in which these processors have large memory caches on the chip itself. For feeding the instructions, they require very fast memory systems.
-

CISC (Complex Instruction Set Computer) Architecture

The main intend of the CISC processor architecture is to complete task by using less number of assembly lines. For this purpose, the processor is built to execute a series of operations. Complex instruction is also termed as MULT, which operates memory banks of a computer directly without making the compiler to perform storing and loading functions.

Features of CISC Architecture

- To simplify the computer architecture, CISC supports microprogramming.
- CISC have more number of predefined instructions which makes high level languages easy to design and implement.
- CISC consists of less number of registers and more number of addressing modes, generally 5 to 20.
- CISC processor takes varying cycle time for execution of instructions – multi-clock cycles.
- Because of the complex instruction set of the CISC, the pipelining technique is very difficult.
- CISC consists of more number of instructions, generally from 100 to 250.
- Special instructions are used very rarely.
- Operands in memory are manipulated by instructions.

Advantages of CISC architecture

- Each machine language instruction is grouped into a microcode instruction and executed accordingly, and then are stored inbuilt in the memory of the main processor, termed as microcode implementation.
- As the microcode memory is faster than the main memory, the microcode instruction set can be implemented without considerable speed reduction over hard wired implementation.
- Entire new instruction set can be handled by modifying the micro program design.
- CISC, the number of instructions required to implement a program can be reduced by building rich instruction sets and can also be made to use slow main memory more efficiently.
- Because of the superset of instructions that consists of all earlier instructions, this makes micro coding easy.

Drawbacks of CISC

- The amount of clock time taken by different instructions will be different – due to this – the performance of the machine slows down.
- The instruction set complexity and the chip hardware increases as every new version of the processor consists of a subset of earlier generations.
- Only 20% of the existing instructions are used in a typical programming event, even though there are many specialized instructions in existence which are not even used frequently.
- The conditional codes are set by the CISC instructions as a side effect of each instruction which takes time for this setting – and, as the subsequent instruction changes the condition code bits – so, the compiler has to examine the condition code bits before this happens.

RISC vs. CISC

- The wasting cycles can be prevented by the programmer by removing the unnecessary code in the RISC, but, while using the CISC code leads to wasting cycles because of the inefficiency of the CISC.
- In RISC, each instruction is intended to perform a small task such that, to perform a complex task, multiple small instruction are used together, whereas only few instructions are required to do the same task using CISC – as it is capable of performing complex task as the instructions are similar to a high-language code.
- CISC is typically used for computers while RISC is used for smart phones, tablets and other electronic devices.

CHAPTER-2

Micro Programmed Control And The Memory System

What is microprogramming?

Microprogramming is a process of writing microcode for a microprocessor. Microcode is low-level code that defines how a microprocessor should function when it executes machine-language instructions. Typically, one machine language instruction translates into several microcode instruction, on some computers, the microcode is stored in ROM and can not be modified;

On some large computers, it is stored in EPRON and therefore can be replaced with newer versions.

Microprogrammed Control Unit:

- A control unit with its binary control values stored as words in memory is called as Microprogrammed control. Each word in the control memory contains micro-instruction that specifies one or more microoperations for the system. A sequence of microinstructions constitutes a micro program.
- Microprogrammed implementation is a software approach in contrast to the hardwired approach.
- It deals with various units of software but at the micro level i.e. micro-operation, micro-instruction, micro-program etc.
- Different key elements used for implementation of a control unit using Microprogrammed approach is shown in fig. below:

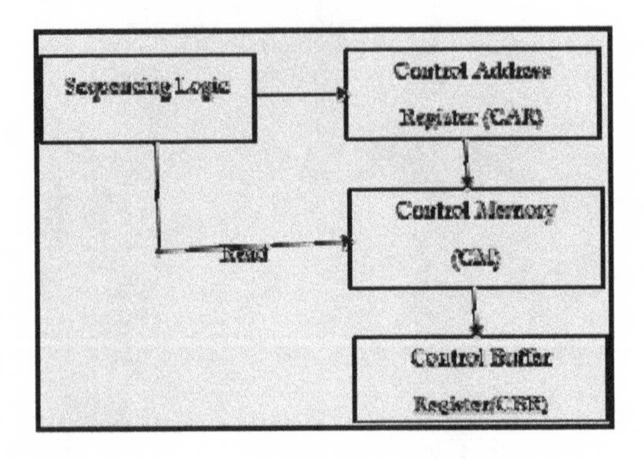

- **Control Memory:**

  The set of microinstruction is stored in control Memory (CM) also called as control store.

- **Control Address Register (CAR):**

  It contains the address of next microinstruction to be read. This is similar to the program counter (PC) which stores the address of the next instruction.

- **Control Buffer Register (CBR):**

  When microinstruction is read from the control memory, it is transferred to a control Buffer Register (CBR), which is similar to the instruction Register (IR) that stores the opcode of the instruction read from the memory.

- **Sequencing:**

  It loads the control Address register with the address of the next instruction to be read abd issues a read command to control memory.

We will now discuss the functioning of the Microprogrammed control unit with a single level control unit

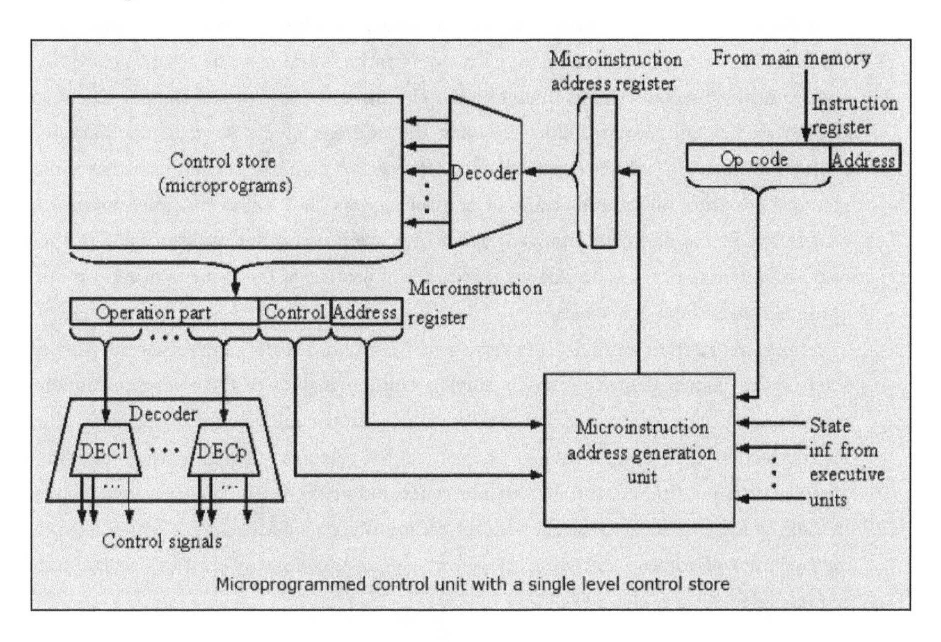

Microprogrammed control unit with a single level control store

The instruction op code from the instruction register is sent to the control store address register. Based on this address, the first microinstruction of a microprogram that interprets execution of this instruction is read to the microinstruction register. This microinstruction contains in its operation part encoded control signals, usually as several bit fields. The fields are decoded in a set microinstruction field decoders. Besides the encode control signal fields, the microinstruction contains the address of the next microinstruction of the given instruction microprogram and a control field used to control activities of the microinstruction address generator.

The last mentioned field determines the addressing mode (addressing operation) to be applied to the address embedded in the current

microinstruction. In microinstructions with the conditional addressing mode, this address is modified with the use of the processor condition flags that represent the status of computations in the current program. The last microinstruction in the microprogram of a given instruction is the microinstruction that fetches the next instruction from the main memory to the instruction register.

In a control unit with a two-level control store, besides the control memory for microinstructions, a nanoinstructions memory is included (see the figure below). In such control unit, microinstructions do not contain encoded control signals. The operation part of microinstructions contains the address of the word in the nanoinstructions memory, which contains encoded control signals. The nanoinstructions memory contains all combinations of control signals that appear in microprogram that interpret the complete instruction set of a given computer, written once in the form of nanoinstructions. In this way, redundant storing of the same operation parts of microinstructions is avoided.

The microinstruction word in this case can be much shorter than with the single level control store. It gives a much smaller volume in bits of the microinstruction memory and, as a result, a much smaller volume of the entire control memory. The microinstruction memory contains the control for selection of consecutive microinstructions, while that control signals are generated at the basis of nanoinstructions. In nanoinstructions, control signals are frequently encoded using 1 bit/ 1 signal method that eliminates decoding. However, signal encoding in multi-bit fields that requests decoding is also possible.

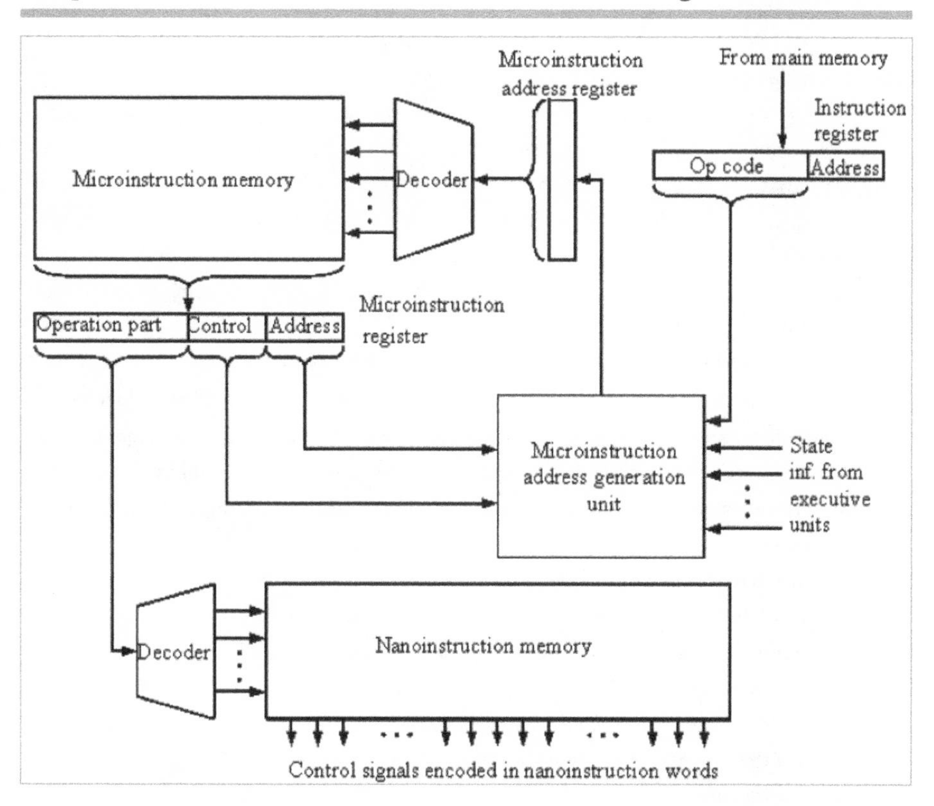

Microprogrammed control units are frequently applied in the design of contemporary microprocessors. Microprocessors of INTEL x86 series (USA), used in personal computers of the IBM PC type, have Microprogrammed control units with a single level control store. Microprocessors Motorola 68xxx series (USA), used for the design of Mackintosh personal computers of the Apple company, have Microprogrammed control units with two-level control stores. Microprocessors of the RISC type, designed by DECAlpha, Hewlett-Packard, Compaq, SUN companies, have hardwired control units.

Address Sequencing

Microinstructions are stored in control memory in groups, with each group specifying a routine. Each computer instruction has its own microprogram routine in control memory to generate the microoperations that execute the instruction. The hardware that controls the address sequencing of the control memory must be capable of sequencing the microinstructions within a routine and be able to branch from one routine to another. To appreciate the address sequencing in a microprogram control unit, let us enumerate the steps that the control must undergo during the execution of a single computer instruction.

An initial address is loaded into the control address register when power is turned on in the computer. This address is usually the address of the first microinstruction that activates the instruction fetch routine. The fetch routine may be sequenced by incrementing the control address register through the rest of its microinstructions. At the end of the fetch routine, the instruction is in the instruction register of the computer. The control memory next must go through the routine that determines the effective address of the operand. A machine instruction may have bits that specify various addressing modes, such as indirect address and index registers. The effective address computation routine in control memory can be reached through a branch microinstruction, which is conditioned on the status of the mode bits of the instruction. When the effective address computation routine is completed, the address of the operand is available in the memory
address register.

The next step is to generate the microoperations that execute the instruction fetched from memory. The microoperation steps to be generated in processor registers depend on the operation code part of the instruction. Each instruction has its own microprogram routine stored in a given location of control memory. The transformation from the instruction code bits to an address in control memory where the routine is located is referred to as a mapping process. A mapping procedure is a rule that transforms the instruction code into a control memory address. Once the required routine is reached, the microinstructions that execute the instruction may be sequenced by incrementing the control address register, but sometimes the sequence of microoperations will depend on values of certain status bits in processor registers . Microprogram that employ subroutines will require an external register for storing the return address. Return addresses cannot be stored in ROM because the unit has no writing capability.

When the execution of the instruction is completed, control must return to the fetch routine. This is accomplished by executing an unconditional branch microinstruction to the first address of the fetch routine. In summary, the address sequencing capabilities required in a control memory are:

1. Incrementing of the control address register.
2. Unconditional branch or conditional branch, depending on status bit conditions.
3. A mapping process from the bits of the instruction to an address for control memory.
4. A facility for subroutine call and return.

Figure shows a block diagram of a control memory and the associated hardware needed for selecting the next microinstruction address

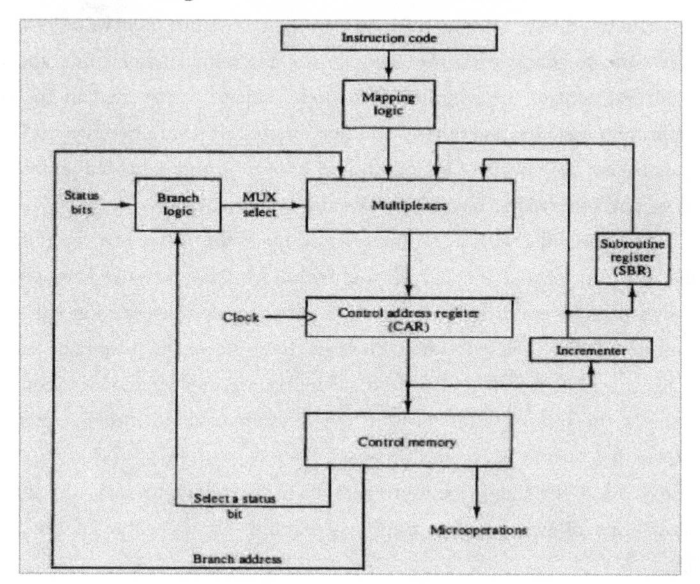

The microinstruction in control memory contains a set of bits to initiate microoperations in computer registers and other bits to specify the method by which the next address is obtained. The diagram shows four different paths from which the control address register (CAR) receives the address. The incrementer increments the content of the control address register by one, to select the next microinstruction in sequence. Branching is achieved by specifying the branch address in one of the fields of the microinstruction. Conditional branching is obtained by using part of the microinstruction to select a specific status bit in order to determine its condition. An external address is transferred into control memory via a mapping logic circuit. The return address for a subroutine is stored in a special register whose value is then used when the microprogram wishes to return from the subroutine.

Conditional Branching

The branch logic of Figure provides decision-making capabilities in the control unit. The status conditions are special bits in the system that provide parameter information such as the carry-out of an adder, the sign bit of a number, the mode bits of an instruction, and input or output status conditions. Information in these bits can be tested and actions initiated based on their condition: whether their value is 1 or 0.

The status bits, together with the field in the microinstruction that specifies a branch address, control the conditional branch decisions generated in the branch logic. The branch logic hardware may be implemented in a variety of ways. The simplest way is to test the specified condition and branch to the indicated address if the condition is met; otherwise, the address register is incremented.

This can be implemented with a multiplexer. Suppose that there are eight status bit conditions in the system. Three bits in the microinstruction are used to specify any one of eight status bit conditions. These three bits provide the selection variables for the multiplexer. If the selected status bit is in the 1 state, the output of the multiplexer is 1; otherwise, it is 0. A 1 output in the multiplexer generates a control signal to transfer the branch address from the microinstruction into the control address register. A 0 output in the multiplexer

causes the address register to be incremented. In this configuration, the microprogram follows one of two possible paths, depending on the value of the selected status bit.

An unconditional branch microinstruction can b e implemented b y loading the branch address from control memory into the control address register. This can be accomplished by fixing the value of one status bit at the input of the multiplexer, so it is always equal to 1. A reference to this bit by the status bit select lines from control memory causes the branch address to be loaded into the control address register unconditionally.

Mapping of Instruction

A special type of branch exists when a microinstruction specifies a branch to the first word in control memory where a microprogram routine for an instruction is located. The status bits for this type of branch are the bits in the operation code part of the instruction. For example, a computer with a simple instruction format as shown in Figure has an operation code of four bits which can specify up to 16 distinct instructions.

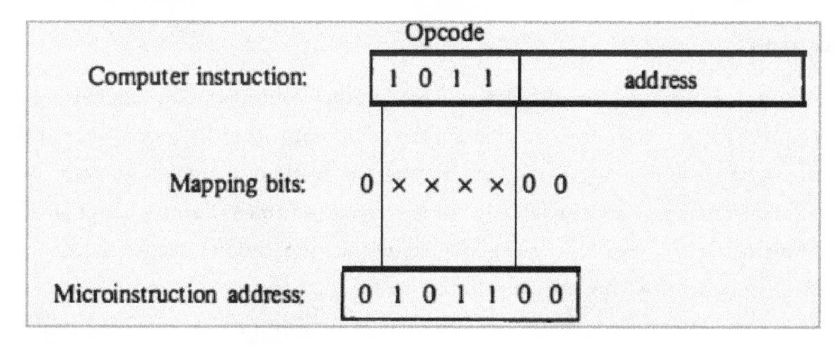

Assume further that the control memory has 128 words, requiring an address of seven bits. For each operation code there exists a microprogram routine in control memory that executes the instruction. One simple mapping process that converts the 4-bit operation code to a 7-bit address for control memory is shown in Figure This mapping consists of placing a 0 in the most significant bit of the address, transferring the four operation code bits, and clearing the two least significant bits of the control address register. This provides for each computer instruction a microprogram routine with a capacity of four microinstructions. If the routine needs more than four microinstructions, it can use addresses 1000000 through 1111111 .

If it uses fewer than four microinstructions, the unused memory locations would be available for other routines. One can extend this concept to a more general mapping rule by using a ROM to specify the mapping function. In this configuration, the bits of the instruction specify the address of a mapping ROM. The contents of the mapping ROM give the bits for the control address register. In this way the microprogram routine that executes the instruction can be placed in any desired location in control memory. The mapping concept provides flexibility for adding instructions for control memory as the need arises. The mapping function is sometimes implemented by means of an integrated circuit called programmable logic device or PLD. A PLD is similar to ROM in concept except that it uses AND and OR gates with internal electronic fuses. The interconnection between inputs, AND gates, OR gates, and outputs can be programmed as in ROM. A mapping function that can be expressed in terms of Boolean expressions can be implemented conveniently with a PLD.

Subroutines

Subroutines are programs that are used by other routines to accomplish a particular task. A subroutine can be called from any point within the main body of the microprogram. Frequently, many microprogram contain identical sections of code. Microinstructions can be saved by employing subroutines that use common sections of microcode. For example, the sequence of microoperations needed to generate the effective address of the operand for an instruction is common to all memory reference instructions. This sequence could be a subroutine that is called from within many other routines to execute the effective address computation. Microprogram that use subroutines must have a provision for storing the return address during a subroutine call and restoring the address during a subroutine return.

This may be accomplished by placing the incremented output from the control address register into a subroutine register and branching to the beginning of the subroutine. The subroutine register can then become the source for transferring the address for the return to the main routine. The best way to structure a register file that stores addresses for subroutines is to organize the registers in a last-in, first-out (LIFO) stack.

Microprogram Example

Once the configuration of a computer and its microprogrammed control unit is established, the designer's task is to generate the microcode for the control memory. This code generation is called microprogramming and is a process similar to conventional machine language programming.

Computer Configuration

The block diagram of the computer is shown in Fig. It consists of two memory units: a main memory for storing instructions and data, and a control memory for storing the microprogram. Four registers are associated with the processor unit and two with the control unit.

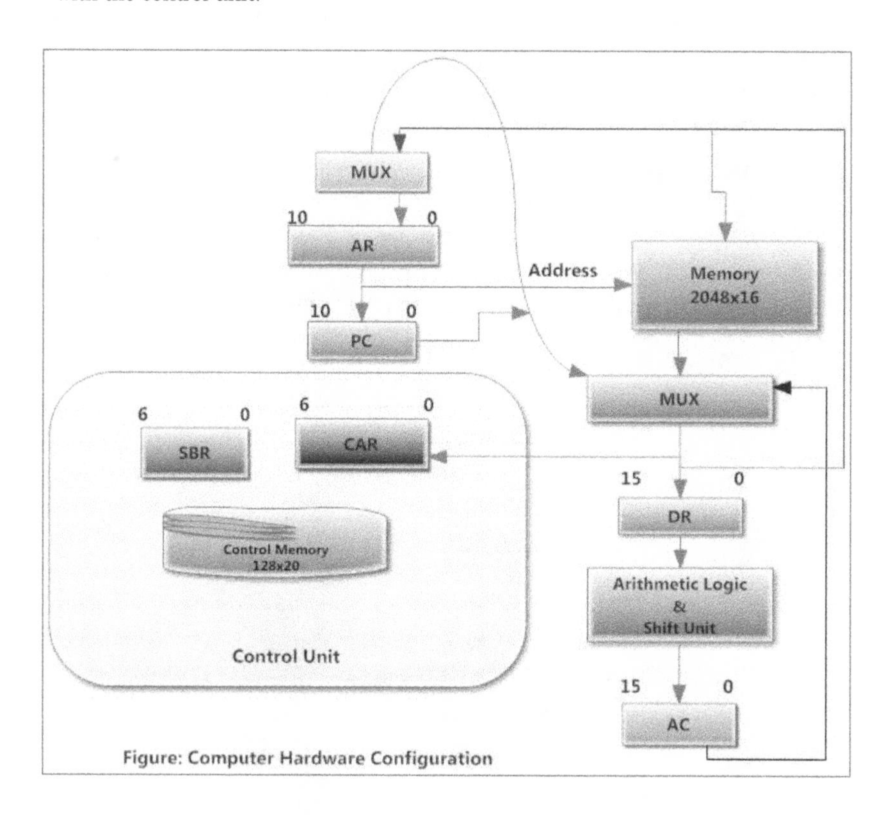

Figure: Computer Hardware Configuration

The processor registers are program counter PC, address register AR, data register DR, and accumulator register AC. The transfer of information among the registers in the processor is done through multiplexers rather than a common bus. DR can receive information from AC, PC, or memory. AR can receive information from PC or DR. PC can receive information only from AR. The arithmetic, logic, and shift unit per forms microoperations with data from AC and DR and places the result in AC . Note that memory receives its address from AR . Input data written to memory come from DR , and data read from memory can go only to DR.

Instruction format

The computer instruction consists of three fields: a 1-bit field for indirect addressing symbolized by I, a 4-bit operation code (opcode), and an 11-bit address field. Figure lists four of the 16 possible memory-reference instructions. The ADD instruction adds the content of the operand found in the effective address to the content of AC . The BRANCH instruction causes a branch to the effective address if the operand in AC is negative. The program proceeds with the next consecutive instruction if AC is not negative. The AC is negative if its sign bit (the bit in the leftmost position of the register) is a 1. The STORE instruction transfers the content of AC into the memory word specified by the effective address. The EXCHANGE instruction swaps the data between AC and the memory word specified by the effective address.

Figure Computer instructions

15	14 11	10 0
I	Opcode	Address

(a) Instruction format

Symbol	Opcode	Description
ADD	0000	$AC \leftarrow AC + M[EA]$
BRANCH	0001	If $(AC < 0)$ then $(PC \leftarrow EA)$
STORE	0010	$M[EA] \leftarrow AC$
EXCHANGE	0011	$AC \leftarrow M[EA], M[EA] \leftarrow AC$

EA is the effective address

Four computer instructions

It will be shown subsequently that each computer instruction must be Microprogrammed. In order not to complicate the microprogramming example, only four instructions are considered here. It should be realized that 12 other instructions can be included and each instruction must be Microprogrammed by the procedure outlined below.

Microinstruction Format

The microinstruction format for the control memory is shown in Figure. The 20 bits of the microinstruction are divided into four functional parts. The three fields F1, F2, and F3 specify microoperations for the computer. The CD field selects status bit conditions. The BR field specifies the type of branch to be used. The AD field contains a branch address. The address field is seven bits wide, since the control memory has 128 = 27 words.

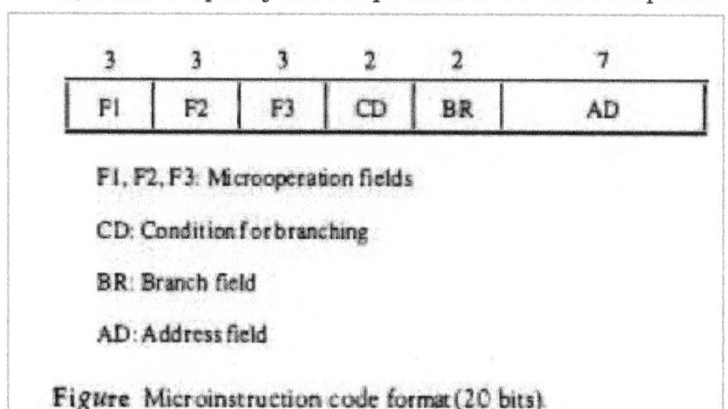

Figure Microinstruction code format (20 bits)

Microoperations:

The microoperations are subdivided into three fields of three bits each. The three bits in each field are encoded to specify seven distinct microoperations as listed in Table in the next page . This gives a total of 21 microoperations. No more than three microoperations can be chosen for a microinstruction, one from each field. If fewer than three microoperations are used, one or more of the fields will use the binary code 000 for no operation. As an illustration, a microinstruction can specify two simultaneous microoperations from F2 and F3 and none from Fl.

DR <- M [AR] **with F2 = 100**

and PC <- PC + 1 **with F3 = 101**

TABLE Symbols and Binary Code for Microinstruction Fields

F1	Microoperation	Symbol
000	None	NOP
001	$AC \leftarrow AC + DR$	ADD
010	$AC \leftarrow 0$	CLRAC
011	$AC \leftarrow AC + 1$	INCAC
100	$AC \leftarrow DR$	DRTAC
101	$AR \leftarrow DR(0\text{–}10)$	DRTAR
110	$AR \leftarrow PC$	PCTAR
111	$M[AR] \leftarrow DR$	WRITE

F2	Microoperation	Symbol
000	None	NOP
001	$AC \leftarrow AC - DR$	SUB
010	$AC \leftarrow AC \vee DR$	OR
011	$AC \leftarrow AC \wedge DR$	AND
100	$DR \leftarrow M[AR]$	READ
101	$DR \leftarrow AC$	ACTDR
110	$DR \leftarrow DR + 1$	INCDR
111	$DR(0\text{-}10) \leftarrow PC$	PCTDR

F3	Microoperation	Symbol
000	None	NOP
001	$AC \leftarrow AC \oplus DR$	XOR
010	$AC \leftarrow \overline{AC}$	COM
011	$AC \leftarrow \text{shl } AC$	SHL
100	$AC \leftarrow \text{shr } AC$	SHR
101	$PC \leftarrow PC + 1$	INCPC
110	$PC \leftarrow AR$	ARTPC
111	Reserved	

CD	Condition	Symbol	Comments
00	Always = 1	U	Unconditional branch
01	$DR(15)$	I	Indirect address bit
10	$AC(15)$	S	Sign bit of AC
11	$AC = 0$	Z	Zero value in AC

BR	Symbol	Function
00	JMP	$CAR \leftarrow AD$ if condition = 1 $CAR \leftarrow CAR + 1$ if condition = 0
01	CALL	$CAR \leftarrow AD$, $SBR \leftarrow CAR + 1$ if condition = 1 $CAR \leftarrow CAR + 1$ if condition = 0
10	RET	$CAR \leftarrow SBR$ (Return from subroutine)
11	MAP	$CAR(2\text{-}5) \leftarrow DR(11\text{-}14)$, $CAR(0,1,6) \leftarrow 0$

The nine bits of the microoperation fields will then be 000 100 101. It is important to realize that two or more conflicting microoperations cannot be specified simultaneously. For example, a microoperation field 010 001 000 has no meaning because it specifies the operations to clear AC to 0 and subtract DR from AC at the same time.

Each microoperation in Table is defined with a register transfer statement and is assigned a symbol for use in a symbolic microprogram. All transfer-type microoperations symbols use five letters. The first two letters designate the source register, the third letter is always a T, and the last two letters designate the destination register. For example, the microoperation that specifies the transfer AC <- DR (F1 = 100) has the symbol DRTAC, which stands for a transfer from DR to AC .

Condition field:

The CD (condition) field consists of two bits which are encoded to specify four status bit conditions as listed in Table . The first condition is always a 1, so that a reference to CD = 00 (or the symbol U) will always find the condition to be true. When this condition is used in conjunction with the BR (branch) field, it provides an unconditional branch operation. The indirect bit I is available from bit 15 of DR after an instruction is read from memory. The sign bit of AC provides the next status bit. The zero value, symbolized by Z, is a binary variable whose value is equal to 1 if all the bits in AC are equal to zero.

We will use the symbols U, I, S, and Z for the four status bits when we write microprograms in symbolic form.

Branch field:

The BR (branch) field consists of two bits. It is used, in conjunction with the address field AD, to choose the address of the next microinstruction. As shown in Table , when BR = 00, the control performs a jump GMP) operation (which is similar to a branch), and when BR = 01, it performs a call to subroutine (CALL) operation. The two operations are identical except that a call microinstruction stores the return address in the subroutine register SBR _ The jump and call operations depend on the value of the CD field. If the status bit condition specified in the CD field is equal to 1, the next address in the AD field is transferred to the control address register CAR _ Otherwise, CAR is incremented by 1 .

The return from subroutine i s accomplished with a B R field equal t o 10. This causes the transfer of the return address from SBR to CAR . The mapping from the operation code bits of the instruction to an address for CAR is accomplished when the BR field is equal to 11 . This mapping is as depicted in Figure. The bits of the operation code are in DR(ll-14) after an instruction is read from memory. Note that the last two conditions in the BR field are independent of the values in the CD and AD fields.

Symbolic Microinstructions:

The symbols defined in Table can be used to specify microinstructions in symbolic form. A symbolic microprogram can be translated into its binary equivalent by means of an assembler. The simplest and most straightforward way to formulate an assembly language for a microprogram is to define symbols for each field of the microinstruction and to give users the capability for defining their own symbolic addresses.

Each line of the assembly language microprogram defines a symbolic microinstruction. Each symbolic microinstruction is divided into five fields: label, microoperations, CD, BR, and AD. The fields specify the following information.

1. The label field may be empty or it may specify a symbolic address. A label is terminated with a colon (:).

2. The microoperations field consists of one, two, or three symbols, separated by commas, from those defined in Table . There may be no more than one symbol from each F field. The NOP symbol is used when the microinstruction has no microoperations. This will be translated by the assembler to nine zeros.

3. The CD field has one of the letters U, I, S, or Z.

4. The BR field contains one of the four symbols defined in Table 7-1 .

5. The A D field specifies a value for the address field o f the microinstruction in one of three possible ways:

    a. With a symbolic address, which must also appear as a label.

    b. b. With the symbol NEXT to designate the next address in sequence.

    c. When the BR field contains a RET or MAP symbol, the AD field is left empty and is converted to seven zeros by the assembler.

ORG

We will use also the pseudo instruction ORG to define the origin, or first address, of a microprogram routine. Thus the symbol ORG 64 informs the assembler to place the next microinstruction in control memory at decimal address 64, which is equivalent to the binary address 1000000.

The Fetch Routine

The control memory has 128 words, and each word contains 20 bits. To microprogram the control memory, it is necessary to determine the bit values of each of the 128 words. The first 64 words (addresses 0 to 63) are to be occupied by the routines for the 16 instructions. The last 64 words may be used for any other purpose. A convenient starting location for the fetch routine is address 64. The microinstructions needed for the fetch routine are

AR <- PC

DR <- M[AR], PC <- PC + 1

AR <- DR (0-10), CAR(2-5) <- DR (1 1-14), CAR(0, 1,6) <- 0

The address of the instruction is transferred from PC to AR and the instruction is then read from memory into DR . Since no instruction register is available, the instruction code remains in DR . The address part is transferred to AR and then control is transferred to one of 16 routines by mapping the operation code part of the instruction from DR into CAR .

fetch and decode:

The fetch routine needs three microinstructions, which are placed in control memory at addresses 64, 65, and 66. Using the assembly language conventions defined previously, we can write the symbolic microprogram for the fetch routine as follows:

FETCH :	ORG64			
	PCTAR	u	JMP	NEXT
	READ , INCPC	u	JMP	NEXT
	DRTAR	u	MAP	

The translation of the symbolic microprogram to binary produces the following binary microprogram. The bit values are obtained from Table.

Binary Address	F1	F2	F3	CD	BR	AD
1000000	110	000	000	00	00	1000001
1000001	000	100	101	00	00	1000010
1000010	101	000	000	00	11	0000000

The three microinstructions that constitute the fetch routine have been listed in three different representations. The register transfer representation shows the internal register transfer operations that each microinstruction implements. The symbolic representation is useful for writing microprograms in an assembly language format. The binary representation is the actual internal content that must be stored in control memory. It is customary to write microprograms in symbolic form and then use an assembler program to obtain a translation to binary.

The Memory System

Memory Hierarchy:

The memory unit Is an essential component in any digital computer since It Is needed for storing programs and data. A very small computer with limited application may be able to fulfill its intended task without the need of additional storage capacity. Most general purpose computers would run more efficiently if they were equipped with additional storage beyond the capacity of the main memory. There is just not enough space in one memory unit to accommodate all the programs used in a typical computer. Moreover, most computer users accumulate and continue to accumulate large amounts of data-processing software. Not all accumulated information is needed by the processor at the same time.

Auxiliary memory

Therefore, it is more economical to use low-cost storage devices to serve as a backup for storing the information that is not currently used by the CPU. The memory unit that communicates directly with the CPU is called the main memory. Devices that provide backup storage are called auxiliary memory. The most common auxiliary memory devices used in computer systems are magnetic disks and tapes. They are used for storing system programs, large data files, and other backup information. Only pro- grams and data currently needed by the processor reside in main memory. All other information Is stored in auxiliary memory and transferred to main memory when needed. The total memory capacity of a computer can be visualized as being a hierarchy of components. The memory hierarchy system consists of all storage devices employed in a computer system from the slow but high-capacity auxiliary memory to a relatively faster main memory, to an even smaller and faster cache memory accessible to the high-speed processing logic. Figure in the next page illustrates the components in a typical memory hierarchy. At the bottom of the hierarchy are the relatively slow magnetic tapes used to store removable files. Next are the magnetic disks used as backup storage. The main memory occupies a central position by being able to communicate directly with the CPU and with auxiliary memory devices through an UO processor. When programs not residing in main memory are needed by the CPU, they are brought in from auxiliary memory. Programs not currently needed in main memory are transferred into auxiliary memory to provide space for currently used programs and data .

A special very-high speed memory called a cache is sometimes used to increase the speed of processing by making current programs and data available to the CPU at a rapid rate. The cache memory is employed in computer systems to compensate for the speed differential between main memory access time and processor logic.

CPU logic is usually faster than main memory access time, with the result that processing speed is limited primarily by the speed of main memory. A technique used to compensate for the mismatch in operating speeds is to employ in extremely fast, small cache between the CPU and main memory whose access time is close to processor logic clock cycle time. The cache is used for storing segments of programs currently being executed in the CPU and temporary data frequently needed in the present calculations by

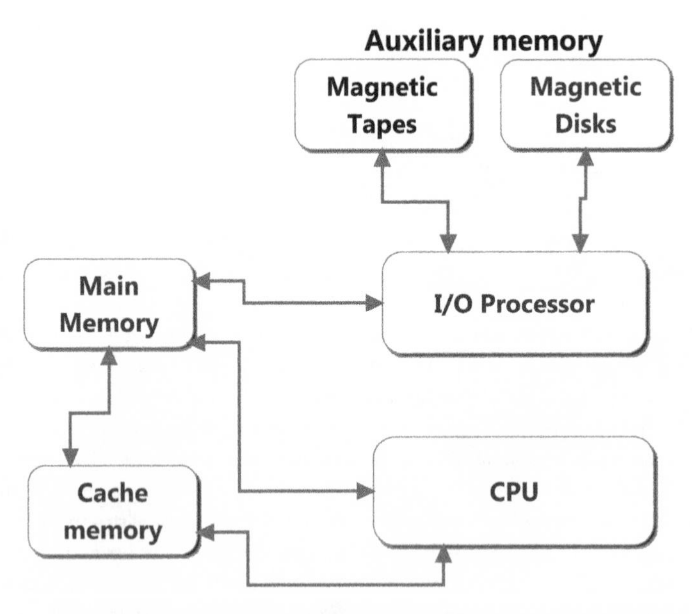

Figure - Memory hierarchy in a computer system.

Making programs and data available at a rapid rate, it is possible to increase the performance rate of the computer. While the I/O processor manages data transfers between auxiliary memory and main memory, the cache organization is concerned with the transfer of information between main memory and CPU. Thus each is involved with a different level in the memory hierarchy system. The reason for having two or three levels of memory hierarchy is economics. As the storage capacity of the memory increases, the cost per bit for storing binary information decreases and the access time of the memory becomes longer. The auxiliary memory has a large storage capacity, is relatively inexpensive, but has low access speed compared to main memory. The cache memory is very small, relatively expensive, and has very high access speed. Thus as the memory access speed increases, so does its relative cost. The overall goal of using a memory hierarchy is to obtain the highest-possible average access speed while minimizing the total cost of the entire memory system.

While the I/O processor manages data transfers between auxiliary memory and main memory, the cache organization is concerned with the transfer of information between main memory and CPU. Thus each is involved with a different level in the memory hierarchy system. The reason for having two or three levels of memory hierarchy is economics. As the storage capacity of the memory increases, the cost per bit for storing binary information decreases and the access time of the memory becomes longer. The auxiliary memory has a large storage capacity, is relatively inexpensive, but has low access speed compared to main memory. The cache memory is very small, relatively expensive, and has very high access speed. Thus as the memory access speed increases, so does its relative cost. The overall goal of using a memory hierarchy is to obtain the highest-possible average access speed while minimizing the total cost of the entire memory system.

Auxiliary and cache memories are used for different purposes. The cache holds those parts of the program and data that are most heavily used, while the auxiliary memory holds those parts that are not presently used by the CPU. Moreover, the CPU has direct access to both cache and main memory but not to auxiliary memory. The transfer from auxiliary to main memory is usually done by means of direct memory access of large blocks of data. The typical access time ratio between cache and main memory is about 1 to 7.

For example, a typical cache memory may have an access time of 100ns,while main memory access time may be 700ns. Auxiliary memory average access time is usually 1000 times that of main memory. Block size in auxiliary memory typically ranges from256 to 2048 words, while cache block size is typically from 1 to 16 words. Many operating systems are designed to enable the CPU to process a number of independent programs concurrently. This concept, called multiprogramming, refers to the existence of two or more programs indifferent parts of the memory hierarchy at the same time. In this way it is possible to keep all parts of the computer busy by working with several programs in sequence. For example, suppose that a program is being executed in the CPU and an I/O transfer is required. The CPU initiates the I/O processor to start executing the transfer. This leaves the CPU free to execute another program. In a multiprogramming system, when one program is waiting for input or output transfer, there is another program ready to utilize the CPU.

MAIN MEMORY

The main memory is the central storage unit in a computer system. It is a relatively large and fast memory used to store programs and data during the computer operation. The principal technology used for the main memory is based on semiconductor integrated circuits. Integrated circuit RAM chips are available in two possible operating modes, static and dynamic. The static RAM consists essentially of internal flip-flops that store the binary information. The stored information remains valid as long as power is applied to unit. The dynamic RAM stores the binary information in the form of electric charges that are applied to capacitors. The capacitors are provided inside the chip by MOS transistors. The stored charges on the capacitors tend to discharge with time and the capacitors must be periodically recharged by refreshing the dynamic memory. Refreshing is done by cycling through the words every few milliseconds to restore the decaying charge. The dynamic RAM offers reduced power consumption and larger storage capacity in a single memory chip. The static RAM is easier to use and has shorted read and write cycles.

Most of the main memory in a general-purpose computer is made up of RAM integrated circuit chips, but a portion of the memory may be constructed with ROM chips. Originally, RAM was used to refer to a random-access memory, but now it is used to designate a read/write memory to distinguish it from a read-only memory, although ROM is also random access.

RAM is used for storing the bulk of the programs and data that are subject to change. ROM is used for storing programs that are permanently resident in the computer and for tables of constants that do not change in value one the production of the computer is completed. Among other things, the ROM portion of main memory is needed for storing an initial program called a bootstrap loader. The bootstrap loader is a program whose function is to start the computer software operating when power is turned on. Since RAM is volatile, its contents are destroyed when power is turned off. The contents of ROM remain unchanged after power is turned off and on again. The startup of a computer consists of turning the power on and starting the execution of an initial program. Thus when power is turned on, the hardware of the computer sets the program counter to the first address of the bootstrap loader. The bootstrap program loads a portion of the operating system from disk to main memory and control is then transferred to the operating system, which prepares the computer from general use.

Basic Concepts of Semiconductor RAM Memories:

Semiconductor memory is used in any electronics assembly that uses computer processing technology. Semiconductor memory is the essential electronics component needed for any computer based PCB assembly. In addition to this, memory cards have become commonplace items for temporarily storing data - everything from the portable flash memory cards used for transferring files, to semiconductor memory cards used in cameras, mobile phones and the like. The use of semiconductor memory has grown, and the size of these memory cards has increased as the need for larger and larger amounts of storage is needed. To meet the growing needs for semiconductor memory, there are many types and technologies that are used.

As the demand grows new memory technologies are being introduced and the existing types and technologies are being further developed. A variety of different memory technologies are available - each one suited to different applications.. Names such as **ROM**, **RAM**, **EPROM**, **EEPROM**, Flash memory, **DRAM**, **SRAM**, **SDRAM**, as well as **F-RAM** and **MRAM** are available, and new types are being developed to enable improved performance. Terms like **DDR3**, **DDR4**, **DDR5** and many more are seen and these refer to different types of **SDRAM** semiconductor memory.

In addition to this the semiconductor devices are available in many forms - ICs for printed board assembly, USB memory cards, Compact Flash cards, SD memory cards and even solid state hard drives. Semiconductor memory is even incorporated into many microprocessor chips as on-board memory.

Semiconductor memory: main types

There are two main types or categories that can be used for semiconductor technology. These memory types or categories differentiate the memory to the way in which it operates:

RAM - Random Access Memory:

As the names suggest, the RAM or random access memory is a form of semiconductor memory technology that is used for reading and writing data in any order - in other words as it is required by the processor. It is used for such applications as the computer or processor memory where variables and other stored and are required on a random basis. Data is stored and read many times to and from this type of memory. Random access memory is used in huge quantities in computer applications as current day computing and processing technology requires large amounts of memory to enable them to handle the memory hungry applications used today. Many types of RAM including **SDRAM** with its **DDR3**, **DDR4**, and soon **DDR5** variants are used in huge quantities.

ROM - Read Only Memory:

A ROM is a form of semiconductor memory technology used where the data is written once and then not changed. In view of this it is used where data needs to be stored permanently, even when the power is removed - many memory technologies lose the data once the power is removed. As a result, this type of semiconductor memory technology is widely used for storing programs and data that must survive when a computer or processor is powered down. For example the BIOS of a computer will be stored in ROM. As the name implies, data cannot be easily written to ROM. Depending on the technology used in the ROM, writing the data into the ROM initially may require special hardware. Although it is often possible to change the data, this gain requires special hardware to erase the data ready for new data to be written in. As can be seen, these two types of memory are very different, and as a result they are used in very different ways.

Each of the semiconductor memory technologies outlined below falls into one of these two types of category. each technology offers its own advantages and is used in a particular way, or for a particular application.

Semiconductor memory technologies

There is a large variety of types of ROM and RAM that are available. Often the overall name for the memory technology includes the initials RAM or ROM and this gives a guide as to the overall type of format for the memory. With technology moving forwards apace, not only are the established technologies moving forwards with SDRAM technology moving from DDR3 to DDR4 and then to DDR5, but Flash memory used in memory cards is also developing as are the other technologies. In addition to this, new memory technologies are arriving on the scene and they are starting to make an impact in the market, enabling processor circuits to perform more effectively.

The different memory types or memory technologies are detailed below:

DRAM:

Dynamic RAM is a form of random access memory. DRAM uses a capacitor to store each bit of data, and the level of charge on each capacitor determines whether that bit is a logical 1 or 0. However these capacitors do not hold their charge indefinitely, and therefore the data needs to be refreshed periodically. As a result of this dynamic refreshing it gains its name of being a dynamic RAM. DRAM is the form of semiconductor memory that is often used in equipment including personal computers and workstations where it forms the main RAM for the computer. The semiconductor devices are normally available as integrated circuits for use in PCB assembly in the form of surface mount devices or less frequently now as leaded components.

EEPROM:

This is an Electrically Erasable Programmable Read Only Memory. Data can be written to these semiconductor devices and it can be erased using an electrical voltage. This is typically applied to an erase pin on the chip. Like other types of PROM, EEPROM retains the contents of the memory even when the power is turned off. Also like other types of ROM, EEPROM is not as fast as RAM.

EPROM:

This is an Erasable Programmable Read Only Memory. These semiconductor devices can be programmed and then erased at a later time. This is normally achieved by exposing the semiconductor device itself to ultraviolet light. To enable this to happen there is a circular window in the package of the EPROM to enable the light to reach the silicon of the device. When the PROM is in use, this window is normally covered by a label, especially when the data may need to be preserved for an extended period. The PROM stores its data as a charge on a capacitor. There is a charge storage capacitor for each cell and this can be read repeatedly as required. However it is found that after many years the charge may leak away and the data may be lost. Nevertheless, this type of semiconductor memory used to be widely used in applications where a form of ROM was required, but where the data needed to be changed periodically, as in a development environment, or where quantities were low.

Flash memory:

Flash memory may be considered as a development of EEPROM technology. Data can be written to it and it can be erased, although only in blocks, but data can be read on an individual cell basis. To erase and re-program areas of the chip, programming voltages at levels that are available within electronic equipment are used. It is also non-volatile, and this makes it particularly useful. As a result Flash memory is widely used in many applications including USB memory sticks, compact Flash memory cards, SD memory cards and also now solid state hard drives for computers and many other applications.

F-RAM:

Ferroelectric RAM is a random-access memory technology that has many similarities to the standard DRAM technology. The major difference is that it incorporates a ferroelectric layer instead of the more usual dielectric layer and this provides its non -volatile capability. As it offers a non-volatile capability, F-RAM is a direct competitor to Flash.

MRAM:

This is Magneto-resistive RAM, or Magnetic RAM. It is a non-volatile RAM memory technology that uses magnetic charges to store data instead of electric charges. Unlike technologies including DRAM, which require a constant flow of electricity to maintain the integrity of the data, MRAM retains data even when the power is removed. An additional advantage is that it only requires low power for active operation. As a result this technology could become a major player in the electronics industry now that production processes have been developed to enable it to be produced.

P-RAM / PCM:

This type of semiconductor memory is known as Phase change Random Access Memory, P-RAM or just Phase Change memory, PCM. It is based around a phenomenon where a form of chalcogenide glass changes is state or phase between an amorphous state (high resistance) and a polycrystalline state (low resistance). It is possible to detect the state of an individual cell and hence use this for data storage. Currently this type of memory has not been widely commercialized, but it is expected to be a competitor for flash memory.

PROM:

This stands for Programmable Read Only Memory. It is a semiconductor memory which can only have data written to it once - the data written to it is permanent. These memories are bought in a blank format and they are programmed using a special PROM programmer. Typically a PROM will consist of an array of fusible links some of which are "blown" during the programming process to provide the required data pattern.

SDRAM:

Synchronous DRAM. This form of semiconductor memory can run at faster speeds than conventional DRAM. It is synchronized to the clock of the processor and is capable of keeping two sets of memory addresses open simultaneously. By transferring data alternately from one set of addresses, and then the other, SDRAM cuts down on the delays associated with non-synchronous RAM, which must close one address bank before opening the next.

Within the SDRAM family there are several types of memory technologies that are seen. These are referred to by the letters DDR - Double Data Rate. DDR4 is currently the latest technology, but this is soon to be followed by DDR5 which will offer some significant improvements in performance.

SRAM:

Static Random Access Memory. This form of semiconductor memory gains its name from the fact that, unlike DRAM, the data does not need to be refreshed dynamically. These semiconductor devices are able to support faster read and write times than DRAM (typically 10 ns against 60 ns for DRAM), and in addition its cycle time is much shorter because it does not need to pause between accesses. However they consume more power, they are less dense and more expensive than DRAM. As a result of this SRAM is normally used for caches, while DRAM is used as the main semiconductor memory technology.

Semiconductor memory technology is developing at a fast rate to meet the ever growing needs of the electronics industry. Not only are the existing technologies themselves being developed, but considerable amounts of research are being invested in new types of semiconductor memory technology.

In terms of the memory technologies currently in use, SDRAM versions like DDR4 are being further developed to provide DDR5 which will offer significant performance improvements. In time, DDR5 will be developed to provide the next generation of SDRAM.

Other forms of memory are seen around the home in the form of USB memory sticks, Compact Flash, CF cards or SD memory cards for cameras and other applications as well as solid state hard drives for computers.

The semiconductor devices are available in a wide range of formats to meet the differing PCB assembly and other needs.

Architecture of RAM

Due to RAM architecture, the memory cells can be accessed for information from anywhere on the computer system.

This communication between different peripherals and RAM is achieved by data input and output lines, control lines which specify the direction of transfer, and address selection lines.

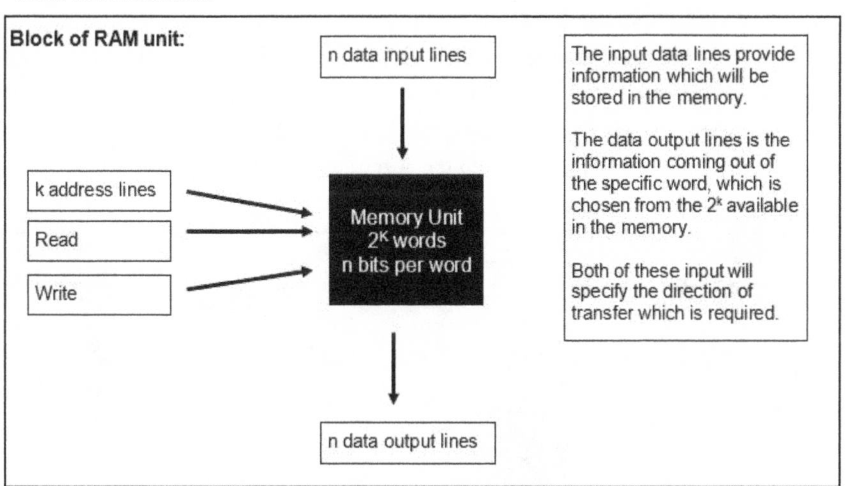

(A "word" is a unit that a machine uses when working with memory, i.e. 32bit machine, means the word is 32bits long), (A "bit" is the basic unit of information in computing)

Read and Write Operations

RAM can perform two operations, they are **read** and **write**.

Read: A signal transferring out

Write: A signal transferring in

Once the RAM accepts one of these control units, the internal circuits, which are situated inside the memory, provide the function, which is expected, from the user.

The process is:

- The binary address of the required word is applied into the address lines
- Apply the "data bits" that will be stored in memory into the data input lines
- The write input will be activated
- Once the steps above are complete, the memory unit will take the bits in the input data lines and will store them, specified by the address lines.

To transfer a stored word out of the memory unit the following occurs:

- The binary address of the required word is applied into the address lines
- Activate the read input (content of the word does not change after reading)

Lastly, the memory unit will take the "bits" from the "word" which was selected by the address, and apply them into the output data lines.

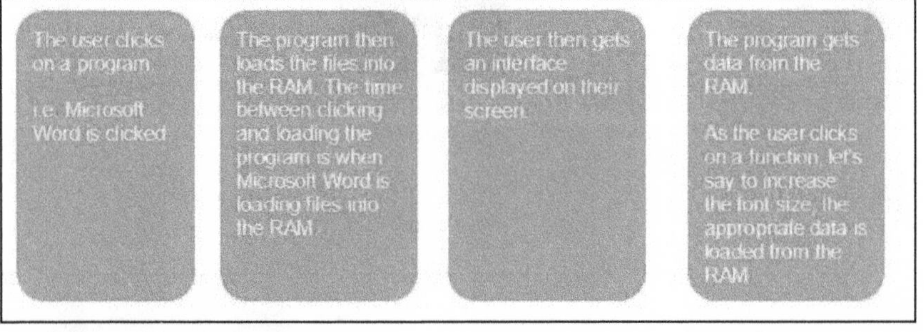

Advantages of having RAM

- Increases the computer system speed, essentially, the more RAM a system has the faster it will operate.
- RAM is a component that is a mandatory to have in a system to allow for the storage of data, which will be processed by the CPU.
- It's efficient. It's extremely fast compared to hard drive storage for a CPU to read data from.
- It can write and read operations.
- RAM is power efficient.
- Cost less than SSD's and operate faster than them.

Disadvantages of RAM:

- If CPU wants to read data only from the RAM, then the data access from the cache and the registers is slow in comparison to ROM.
- RAM is volatile, which means it is difficult to store data for a lengthy period of time. Unplanned circumstances like a power outage can result in data loss.
- It is expensive.

Read Only Memory

ROM stands for Read Only Memory. The memory from which we can only read but cannot write on it. This type of memory is non-volatile. The information is stored permanently in such memories during manufacture. A ROM stores such instructions that are required to start a computer. This operation is referred to as bootstrap. ROM chips are not only used in the computer but also in other electronic items like washing machine and microwave oven.

Let us now discuss the various types of ROMs and their characteristics.

MROM (Masked ROM)

The very first ROMs were hard-wired devices that contained a pre-programmed set of data or instructions. These kind of ROMs are known as masked ROMs, which are inexpensive.

PROM (Programmable Read Only Memory)

PROM is read-only memory that can be modified only once by a user. The user buys a blank PROM and enters the desired contents using a PROM program. Inside the PROM chip, there are small fuses which are burnt open during programming. It can be programmed only once and is not erasable.

EPROM (Erasable and Programmable Read Only Memory)

EPROM can be erased by exposing it to ultra-violet light for a duration of up to 40 minutes. Usually, an EPROM eraser achieves this function. During programming, an electrical charge is trapped in an insulated gate region. The charge is retained for more than 10 years because the charge has no leakage path. For erasing this charge, ultra-violet light is passed through a quartz crystal window (lid). This exposure to ultra-violet light dissipates the charge. During normal use, the quartz lid is sealed with a sticker.

EEPROM (Electrically Erasable and Programmable Read Only Memory)

EEPROM is programmed and erased electrically. It can be erased and reprogrammed about ten thousand times. Both erasing and programming take about 4 to 10 ms (millisecond). In EEPROM, any location can be selectively erased and programmed. EEPROMs can be erased one byte at a time, rather than erasing the entire chip. Hence, the process of reprogramming is flexible but slow.

Advantages of ROM

- The advantages of ROM are as follows –
- Non-volatile in nature
- Cannot be accidentally changed
- Cheaper than RAMs
- Easy to test
- More reliable than RAMs
- Static and do not require refreshing
- Contents are always known and can be verified

ROM integrated circuit

The primary component of the main memory is RAM integrated circuit chips, but a portion of memory may be constructed with ROM chips. A ROM memory is used for keeping programs and data that are permanently resident in the computer. Apart from the permanent storage of data, the ROM portion of main memory is needed for storing an initial program called a bootstrap loader.

The primary function of the **bootstrap** loader program is to start the computer software operating when power is turned on. ROM chips are also available in a variety of sizes and are also used as per the system requirement. The following block diagram demonstrates the chip interconnection in a 512 * 8 ROM chip.

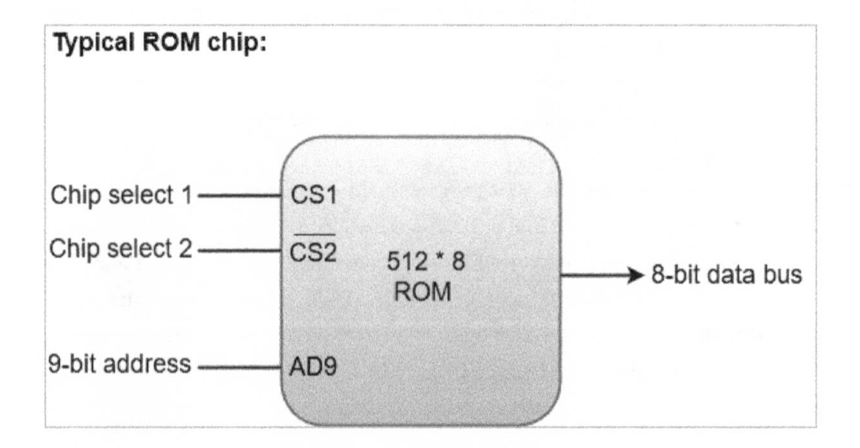

- A 128 * 8 ROM chip has a memory capacity of 128 words of eight bits (one byte) per word. This requires a 7-bit address and an 8-bit bidirectional data bus.
- The 8-bit bidirectional data bus allows the transfer of data either from memory to CPU during a read operation or from CPU to memory during a write operation.
- The read and write inputs specify the memory operation, and the two chip select (CS) control inputs are for enabling the chip only when the microprocessor selects it.
- The bidirectional data bus is constructed using three-state buffers.
- The output generated by three-state buffers can be placed in one of the three possible states which include a signal equivalent to logic 1, a signal equal to logic 0, or a high-impedance state.
- A ROM chip has a similar organization as a RAM chip. However, a ROM can only perform read operation; the data bus can only operate in an output mode.
- The 9-bit address lines in the ROM chip specify any one of the 512 bytes stored in it.
- The value for chip select 1 and chip select 2 must be 1 and 0 for the unit to operate. Otherwise, the data bus is said to be in a high-impedance state

Note: The logic 1 and 0 are standard digital signals whereas the high-impedance state behaves like an open circuit, which means that the output does not carry a signal and has no logic significance.

Memory Address Map

The designer of a computer system must calculate the amount of memory required for the particular application and assign it to either RAM or ROM. The interconnection between memory and processor is then established from knowledge of the size of memory needed and the type of RAM and ROM chips available. The addressing of memory can be established by means of a table that specifies the memory address assigned to each chip. The table, called a memory address map, is a pictorial representation of assigned address space for each chip in the system. To demonstrate with a particular example, assume that a computer system needs 512 bytes of RAM and 512 bytes of ROM. The RAM and ROM chips to be used are specified in Fig.

The memory address map for this configuration is shown in Table

TABLE ·1 Memory Address Map for Microprocomputer

Component	Hexadecimal address	Address bus									
		10	9	8	7	6	5	4	3	2	1
RAM 1	0000–007F	0	0	0	x	x	x	x	x	x	x
RAM 2	0080–00FF	0	0	1	x	x	x	x	x	x	x
RAM 3	0100–017F	0	1	0	x	x	x	x	x	x	x
RAM 4	0180–01FF	0	1	1	x	x	x	x	x	x	x
ROM	0200–03FF	1	x	x	x	x	x	x	x	x	x

The component column specifies whether a RAM or a ROM chip is used. The hexadecimal address column assigns a range of hexadecimal equivalent addresses for each chip. The address bus lines are listed in the third column. Although there are 16 lines in the address bus, the table shows only 10 lines because the other 6 are not used in this example and are assumed to be zero. The small x's under the address bus lines designate those lines that must be connected to the address inputs in each chip. The RAM chips have 128 bytes and need seven address lines. The ROM chip has 512 bytes and needs 9 address lines. The x's are always assigned to the low -order bus lines: lines 1 through 7 for the RAM and lines 1 through 9 for the ROM.

It is now necessary to distinguish between four RAM chips by assigning to each a different address. For this particular example we choose bus lines 8 and 9 to represent four distinct binary combinations. Note that any other pair of unused bus lines can be chosen for this purpose. The table clearly shows that the nine low-order bus lines constitute a memory space for RAM equal to 29 = 512 bytes. The distinction between a RAM and ROM address is done with another bus line. Here we choose line 10 for this purpose. When line 10 is 0, the CPU selects a RAM, and when this line is equal to 1, it selects the ROM.

The equivalent hexadecimal address for each chip is obtained from the information under the address bus assignment. The address bus lines are subdivided into groups of four bits each so that each group can be represented with a hexadecimal digit. The first hexadecimal digit represents lines 13 to 16 and is always 0. The next hexadecimal digit represents lines 9 to 12, but lines 11 and 12 are always 0. The range of hexadecimal addresses for each component is determined from the x's associated with it. These x's represent a binary number that can range from an all-0's to an all-1's value.

MEMORY CONNECTION TO CPU

RAM and ROM chips are connected to a CPU through the data and address buses. The low-order lines in the address bus select the byte within the chips and other lines in the address bus select a particular chip through its chip select inputs. The connection of memory chips to the CPU is shown in below Fig. This configuration gives a memory capacity of 512 bytes of RAM and 512 bytes of ROM. It implements the memory map of Table which is in the previous page. Each RAM receives the seven low-order bits of the address bus to select one of 128 possible bytes. The particular RAM chip selected is determined from lines 8 and 9 in the address bus. This is done through a 2 × 4 decoder whose outputs go to the SCI input in each RAM chip. Thus, when address lines 8 and 9 are equal to 00, the first RAM chip is selected. When 01, the second RAM chip is selected, and so on.

The RD and WR outputs from the microprocessor are applied to the inputs of each RAM chip. The selection between RAM and ROM is achieved through bus line 10. The RAMs are selected when the bit in this line is 0, and the ROM when the bit is 1. The other chip select input in the ROM is connected to the RD control line for the ROM chip to be enabled only during a read operation. Address bus lines 1 to 9 are applied to the input address of ROM without going through the decoder. This assigns addresses 0 to 511 to RAM and 512 to 1023 to ROM. The data bus of the ROM has only an output capability, whereas the data bus connected to the RAMs can transfer information in both directions.
The example just shown gives an indication of the interconnection complexity that can exist between memory chips and the CPU. The more chips that are connected, the more external decoders are required for selection among the chips. The designer must establish a memory map that assigns addresses to the various chips from which the required connections are determined.

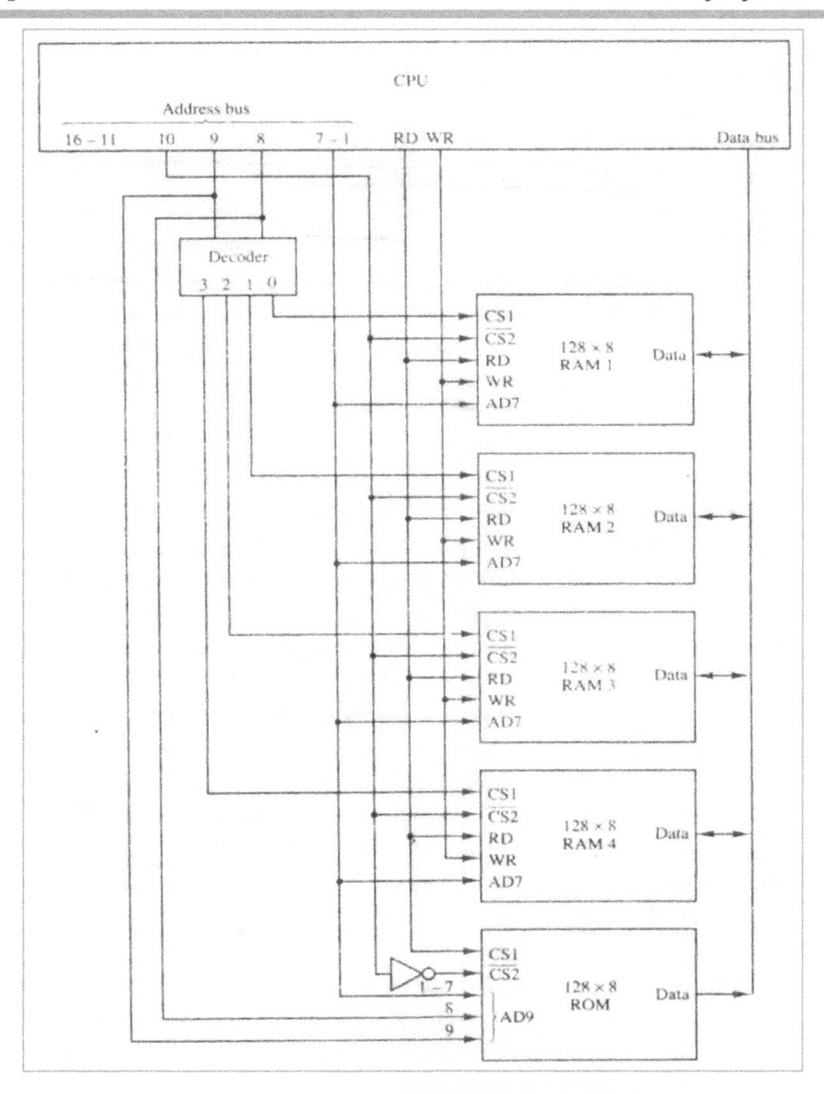

Figure -Memory connection to the CPU.

CACHE MEMORY

Analysis of a large number of typical programs has shown that the references, to memory at any given interval of time tend to be confined within a few localized areas in memory. The phenomenon is known as the property of locality of reference. The reason for this property may be understood considering that a typical computer program flows in a straight-line fashion with program loops and subroutine calls encountered frequently. When a program loop is executed, the CPU repeatedly refers to the set of instructions in memory that constitute the loop. Every time a given subroutine is called, its set of instructions is fetched from memory. Thus loops and subroutines tend to localize the references to memory for fetching instructions. To a lesser degree, memory references to data also tend to be localized.

Table-lookup procedures repeatedly refer to that portion in memory where the table is stored. Iterative procedures refer to common memory locations and array of numbers are confined within a local portion of memory. The result of all these observations is the locality of reference property, which states that over a short interval of time, the addresses generated by a typical program refer to a few localized areas of memory repeatedly, while the remainder of memory is accessed relatively frequently.

If the active portions of the program and data are placed in a fast small memory, the average memory access time can be reduced, thus reducing the total execution time of the program. Such a fast small memory is referred to as a cache memory. It is placed between the CPU and main memory as illustrated in below Fig. The cache memory access time is less than the access time of main memory by a factor of 5 to 10. The cache is the fastest component in the memory hierarchy and approaches the speed of CPU components.

The fundamental idea of cache organization is that by keeping the most frequently accessed instructions and data in the fast cache memory, the average memory access time will approach the access time of the cache. Although the cache is only a small fraction of the size of main memory, a large fraction of memory requests will be found in the fast cache memory because of the locality of reference property of programs.

The basic operation of the cache is as follows. When the CPU needs to access memory, the cache is examined. If the word is found in the cache, it is read from the fast memory. If the word addressed by the CPU is not found in the cache, the main memory is accessed to read the word. A block of words containing the one just accessed is then transferred from main memory to cache memory. The block size may vary from one word (the one just accessed) to about 16 words adjacent to the one just accessed. In this manner, some data are transferred to cache so that future references to memory find the required words in the fast cache memory.

The performance of cache memory is frequently measured in terms of a quantity called hit ratio. When the CPU refers to memory and finds the word in cache, it is said to produce a hit. If the word is not found in cache, it is in main memory and it counts as a miss. The ratio of the number of hits divided by the total CPU references to memory (hits plus misses) is the hit ratio. The hit ratio is best measured experimentally by running representative programs in the computer and measuring the number of hits and misses during a given interval of time. Hit ratios of 0.9 and higher have been reported. This high ratio verifies the validity of the locality of reference property.

The average memory access time of a computer system can be improved considerably by use of a cache. If the hit ratio is high enough so that most of the time the CPU accesses the cache instead of main memory, the average access time is closer to the access time of the fast cache memory. For example, a computer with cache access time of 100 ns, a main memory access time of 1000 ns, and a hit ratio of 0.9 produces an average access time of 200 ns. This is a considerable improvement over a similar computer without a cache memory, whose access time is 1000 ns.

The basic characteristic of cache memory is its fast access time. Therefore, very little or no time must be wasted when searching for words in the cache. The transformation of data from main memory to cache memory is referred to as a mapping process. Three types of mapping procedures are of practical interest when considering the organization of cache memory:

1. Associative mapping
2. Direct mapping
3. Set-associative mapping

To helping the discussion of these three mapping procedures we will use a specific example of a memory organization as shown in below Fig. The main memory can store 32K words of 12 bits each. The cache is capable of storing 512 of these words at any given time. For every word stored in cache, there is a duplicate copy in main memory.

The CPU communicates with both memories. It first sends a 15-bit address to cache. If there is a hit, the CPU accepts the 12 -bit data from cache. If there is a miss, the CPU reads the word from main memory and the word is then transferred to cache.

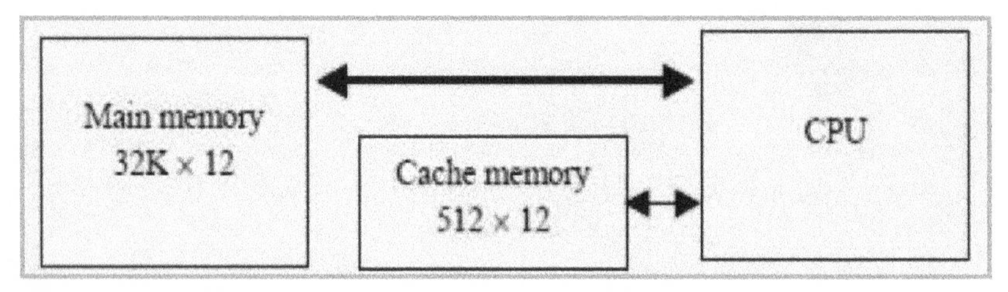

Figure - Example of cache memory

ASSOCIATIVE MAPPING

The fasters and most flexible cache organization use an associative memory. This organization is illustrated in below Fig. The associative memory stores both the address and content (data) of the memory word. This permits any location in cache to store any word from main memory. The diagram shows three words presently stored in the cache. The address value of 15 bits is shown as a five-digit octal number and its corresponding 12-bit word is shown as a four-digit octal number. A CPU address of 15 bits is placed in the argument register and the associative memory is searched for a matching address. If the address is found, the corresponding 12-bit data is read

And sent to the CPU. If no match occurs, the main memory is accessed for the word. The address-data pair is then transferred to the associative cache memory. If the cache is full, an address–data pair must be displaced to make room for a pair that is needed and not presently in the cache. The decision as to what pair is replaced is determined from the replacement algorithm that the designer chooses for the cache.

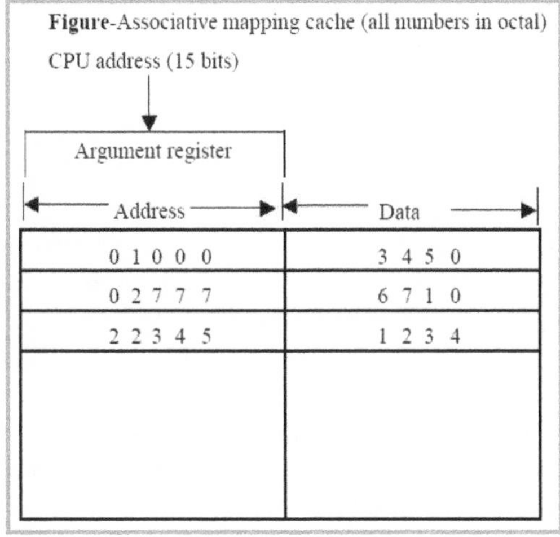

Figure-Associative mapping cache (all numbers in octal)

A simple procedure is to replace cells of the cache in round-robin order whenever a new word is requested from main memory. This constitutes a first-in first-out (FIFO) replacement policy.

DIRECT MAPPING

Associative memories are expensive compared to random-access memories because of the added logic associated with each cell. The possibility of using a random-access memory for the cache is investigated in Fig. The CPU address of 15 bits is divided into two fields. The nine least significant bits constitute the index field and the remaining six bits from the tag and the index bits. The number of bits in the index field is equal to the number of address bits required to access the cache memory.

In the general case, there are 2k words in cache memory and 2n words in main memory.

The n-bit memory address is divided into two fields: k bits for the index field and n – k bits for the tag field. The direct mapping cache organization uses the n-bit address to access the main memory and the k-bit index to access the cache. The internal organization of the words in the cache memory is as shown in Fig. (b). Each word in cache consists of the data word and its associated tag. When a new word is first brought into the cache, the tag bits are stored alongside the data bits. When the CPU generates a memory request, the index field is used for the address to access the cache.

The tag field of the CPU address is compared with the tag in the word read from the cache. If the two tags match, there is a hit and the desired data word is in cache. If the two tags match, there is a hit and the desired data word is in cache. If there is no match, there is a miss and the required word is read from main memory. It is then stored in the cache together with the new tag, replacing the previous value.

The disadvantage of direct mapping is that the hit ratio can droop considerably if two or more words whose addresses have the same index but different tags are accessed repeatedly. However, this possibility is minimized by the fact that such words are relatively far apart in the address range (multiples of 512 locations in this example).

To see how the direct-mapping organization operates, consider the numerical example shown in Fig. The word at address zero is presently stored in the cache (index = 000, tag = 00, data = 1220). Suppose that the CPU now wants to access the word at address 02000. The index address is 000, so it is sued to access the cache.

The two tags are then compared. The cache tag is 00 but the address tag is 02, which does not produce a match. Therefore, the main memory is accessed and the data word 5670 is transferred to the CPU. The cache word at index address 000 is then replaced with a tag of 02 and data of 5670.

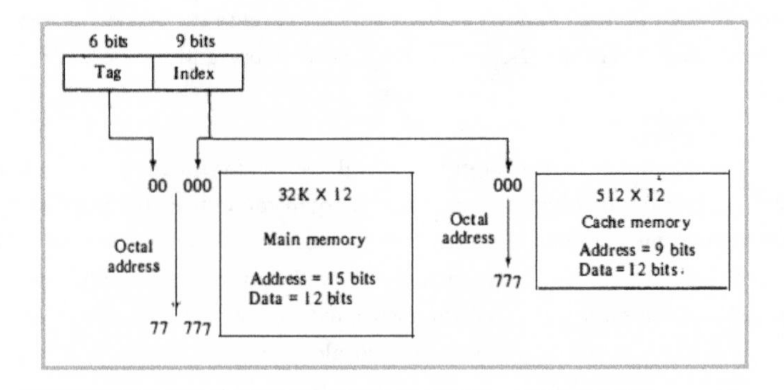

Figure : Addressing relationships between main and cache memories.

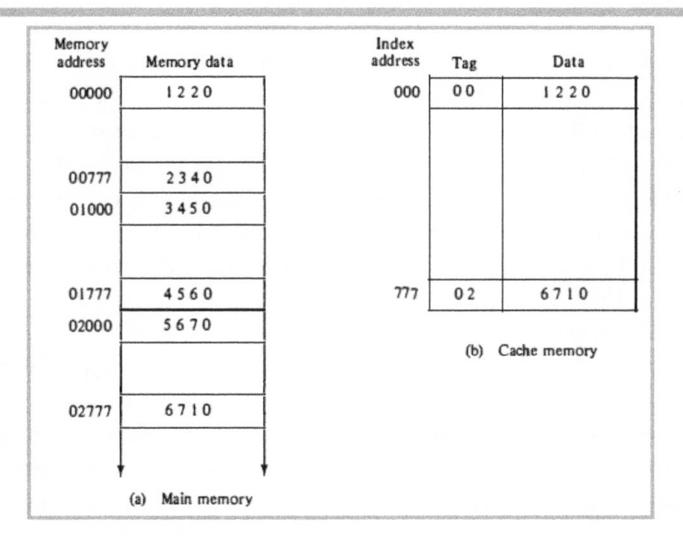

Figure Direct mapping cache organization.

The direct-mapping example just described uses a block size of one word. The same organization but using a block size of 8 words is shown in below Fig.

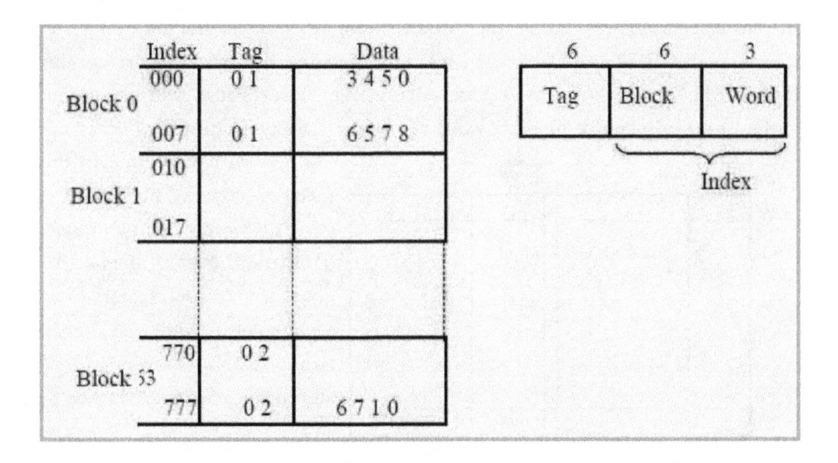

Field is now divided into two parts: the block field and the word field. In a 512-word cache there are 64 block of 8 words each, since 64 × 8 = 512. The block number is specified with a 6-bit field and the word within the block is specified with a 3-bit field. The tag field stored within the cache is common to all eight words of the same block. Every time a miss occurs, an entire block of eight words must be transferred from main memory to cache memory. Although this takes extra time, the hit ratio will most likely improve with a larger block size because of the sequential nature of computer programs.

SET-ASSOCIATIVE MAPPING

It was mentioned previously that the disadvantage of direct mapping is that two words with the same index in their address but with different tag values cannot reside in cache memory at the same time. A third type of cache organization, called set -associative mapping, is an improvement over the direct-mapping organization in that each word of cache can store two or more words of memory under the same index address. Each data word is stored together with its tag and the number of tag-data items in one word of cache is said to form a set. An example of a set-associative cache organization for a set size of two is shown in Fig. Each index address refers to two data words and their associated tags. Each tag requires six bits and each data word has 12 bits, so the word length is 2(6 + 12) = 36 bits. An index address of nine bits can accommodate 512 words. Thus the size of cache memory is 512 × 36. It can accommodate 1024 words of main memory since each word of cache contains two data words. In general, a set-associative cache of set size k will accommodate k words of main memory in each word of cache. The octal numbers listed in above Fig. are with reference to the main memory content illustrated in Fig. (a). The words stored at addresses 01000 and 02000 of main memory are stored in cache memory at index address 000. Similarly, the words at addresses 02777 and 00777 are stored in cache at index address 777.

Index	Tag	Data	Tag	Data
000	01	3450	02	5670
777		6710	00	2340

Figure- Two-way set-associative mapping cache.

When the CPU generates a memory request, the index value of the address is used to access the cache. The tag field of the CPU address is then compared with both tags in the cache to determine if a catch occurs. The comparison logic is done by an associative search of the tags in the set similar to an associative memory search: thus the name ―set-associative‖. The hit ratio will improve as the set size increases because more words with the same index but different tag can reside in cache. However, an increase in the set size increases the number of bit s in words of cache and requires more complex comparison logic.

When a miss occurs in a set-associative cache and the set is full, it is necessary to replace one of the tag-data items with a new value. The most common replacement algorithms used are: random replacement, first-in, first out (FIFO), and least recently used (LRU). With the random replacement policy the control chooses one tag-data item for replacement at random. The FIFO procedure selects for replacement the item that has been in the set the longest. The LRU algorithm selects for replacement the item that has been least recently used by the CPU. Both FIFO and LRU can be implemented by adding a few extra bits in each word of cache.

WRITING INTO CACHE

An important aspect of cache organization is concerned with memory write requests. When the CPU finds a word in cache during read operation, the main memory is not involved in the transfer. However, if the operation is a write, there are two ways that the system can proceed. The simplest and most commonly used procedure is to up data main memory with every memory write operation, with cache memory being updated in parallel if it contains the word at the specified address. This is called the write-through method. This method has the advantage that main memory always contains the same data as the cache,.

This characteristic is important in systems with direct memory access transfers. It ensures that the data residing in main memory are valid at tall times so that an I/O device communicating through DMA would receive the most recent updated data. The second procedure is called the write-back method. In this method only the cache location is updated during a write operation. The location is then marked by a flag so that later when the words are removed from the cache it is copied into main memory.

The reason for the write-back method is that during the time a word resides in the cache, it may be updated several times; however, as long as the word remains in the cache, it does not matter whether the copy in main memory is out of date, since requests from the word are filled from the cache. It is only when the word is displaced from the cache that an accurate copy need be rewritten into main memory. Analytical results indicate that the number of memory writes in a typical program ranges between 10 and 30 percent of the total references to memory.

CACHE INITIALIZATION

One more aspect of cache organization that must be taken into consideration is the problem of initialization. The cache is initialized when power is applied to the computer or when the main memory is loaded with a complete set of programs from auxiliary memory. After initialization the cache is considered to be empty, built in effect it contains some non-valid data. It is customary to include with each word in cache a valid bit to indicate whether or not the word contains valid data.

The cache is initialized by clearing all the valid bits to 0. The valid bit of a particular cache word is set to 1 the first time this word is loaded from main memory and stays set unless the cache has to be initialized again. The introduction of the valid bit means that a word in cache is not replaced by another word unless the valid bit is set to 1 and a mismatch of tags occurs. If the valid bit happens to be 0, the new word automatically replaces the invalid data. Thus the initialization condition has the effect of forcing misses from the cache until it fills with valid data.

VIRTUAL MEMORY

In a memory hierarchy system, programs and data are brought into main memory as they are needed by the CPU. Virtual memory is a concept used in some large computer systems that permit the user to construct programs as though a large memory space were available, equal to the totality of auxiliary memory. Each address that is referenced by the CPU goes through an address mapping from the so-called virtual address to a physical address in main memory. Virtual memory is used to give programmers the illusion that they have a very large memory at their disposal, even though the computer actually has a relatively small main memory. A virtual memory system provides a mechanism for translating program-generated addresses into correct main memory locations. This is done dynamically, while programs are being executed in the CPU. The translation or mapping is handled automatically by the hardware by means of a mapping table.

ADDRESS SPACE AND MEMORY SPACE

An address used by a programmer will be called a virtual address, and the set of such addresses the address space. An address in main memory is called a location or physical address. The set of such locations is called the memory space. Thus the address space is the set of addresses generated by programs as they reference instructions and data; the memory space consists of the actual main memory locations directly addressable for processing. In most computers the address and memory spaces are identical. The address space is allowed to be larger than the memory space in computers with virtual memory. As an illustration, consider a computer with a main -memory capacity of 32 K words (K = 1024). Fifteen bits are needed to specify a physical address in memory since 32 K = 2^{15} Suppose that the computer has available auxiliary memory for storing 2^{20} = 1024 K words. Thus auxiliary memory has a capacity for storing information equivalent to the capacity of 32 main memories. Denoting the address space by N and the memory space by M, we then have for this example N = 1024 K and M = 32 K.

In a multiprogramming computer system, programs and data are transferred to and from auxiliary memory and main memory based on demands imposed by the CPU. Suppose that program 1 is currently being executed in the CPU. Program 1 and a portion of its associated data re moved from auxiliary memory into main memory

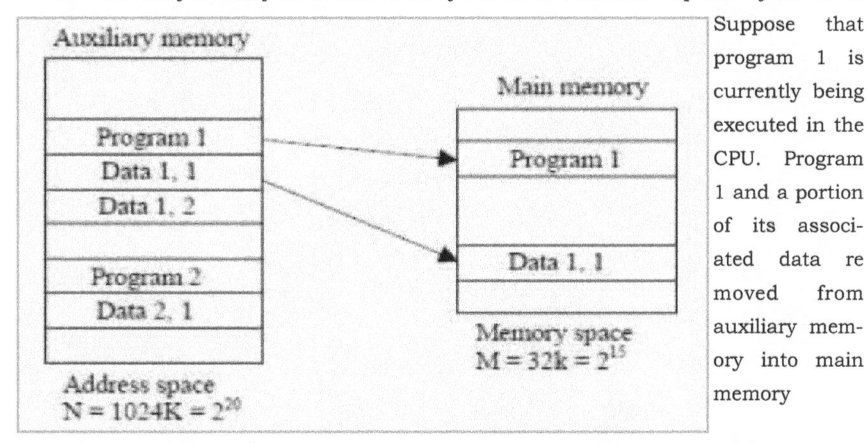

Fig-Relation between address and memory space in a virtual memory system

as shown in Fig. Portions of programs and data need not be in contiguous locations in memory since information is being moved in and out, and empty spaces may be available in scattered locations in memory.

In a virtual memory system, programmers are told that they have the total address space at their disposal. Moreover, the address field of the instruction code has a sufficient number of bits to specify all virtual addresses. In our example, the address field of an instruction code will consist of 20 bits but physical memory addresses must be specified with only 15 bits. Thus CPU will reference instructions and data with a 20-bit address, but the information at this address must be taken from physical memory because access to auxiliary storage for individual words will be prohibitively long. (Remember That for efficient transfers, auxiliary storage moves an entire record to the main memory).

That for efficient transfers, auxiliary storage moves an entire record to the main memory). A table is then needed, as shown in Fig, to map a virtual address of 20 bits to a physical address of 15 bits. The mapping is a dynamic operation, which means that every address is translated immediately as a word is referenced by CPU. The mapping table may be stored in a separate memory as shown in Fig. or in main memory. In the first case, an additional memory unit is required as well as one extra memory access time. In the second case, the table Takes space from main memory and two accesses to memory are required with the program running at half speed. A third alternative is to use an associative memory as explained below.

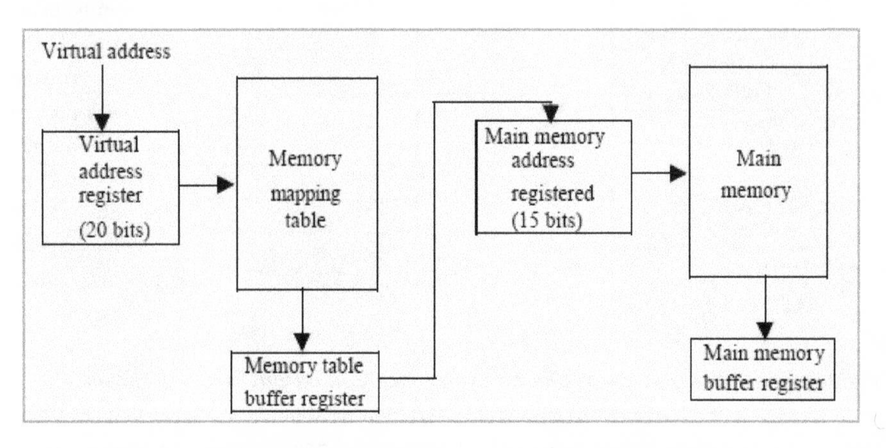

Figure - Memory table for mapping a virtual address.

ADDRESS MAPPING USING PAGES

The table implementation of the address mapping is simplified if the information in the address space and the memory space are each divided into groups of fixed size. The physical memory is broken down into groups of equal size called blocks, which may range from 64 to 4096 words each. The term page refers to groups of address space of the same size. For example, if a page or block consists of 1K words, then, using the previous example, address space is divided into 1024 pages and main memory is divided into 32 blocks. Although both a page and a block are split into groups of 1K words, a page refers to the organization of address space, while a block refers to the organization of memory space. The programs are also considered to be split into pages. Portions of programs are moved from auxiliary memory to main memory in records equal to the size of a page. The term "page frame" is sometimes used to denote a block.

Consider a computer with an address space of 8K and a memory space of 4K. If we split each into groups of 1K words we obtain eight pages and four blocks as shown in Fig. At any given time, up to four pages of address space may reside in main memory in any one of the four blocks. The mapping from address space to memory space is facilitated if each virtual address is considered to be represented by two numbers: a page number address and a line within the page. In a computer with 2^p words per page, p bits are used to specify a line address and the remaining high-order bits of the virtual address specify the page number. In the example of Fig, a virtual address has 13 bits. Since each page consists of 2^{10} = 1024 words, the high-order three bits of a virtual address will specify one of the eight pages and the low-order 10 bits give the line address within the page.

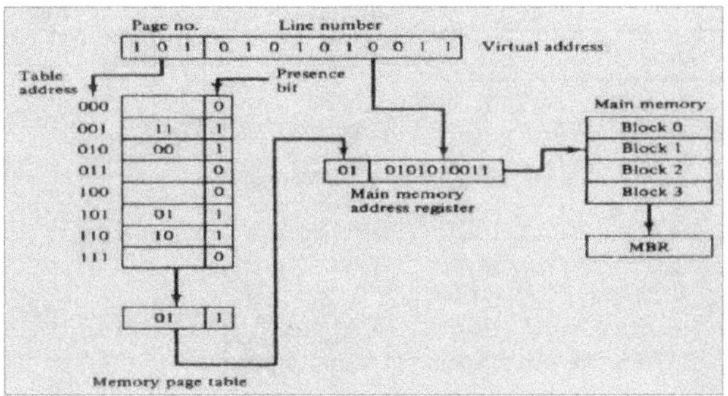

The word to the main memory buffer register ready to be used by the CPU. If the presence bit in the word read from the page table is 0, it signifies that the content of the word referenced by the virtual address does not reside in main memory. A call to the operating system is then generated to fetch the required page from auxiliary memory and place it into main memory before resuming computation.

ASSOCIATIVE MEMORY PAGE TABLE

A random-access memory page table is inefficient with respect to storage utilization. In the example of below Fig. we observe that eight words of memory are needed, one for each page, but at least four words will always be marked empty because main memory cannot accommodate more than four blocks. In general, system with n pages and m blocks would require a memory-page table of n locations of which up to m blocks will be marked with block numbers and all others will be empty. As a second numerical example, consider an address space of 1024K words and memory space of 32K words. If each page or block contains 1K words, the number of pages is 1024 and the number of blocks 32. The capacity of the memory-page table must be 1024 words and only 32 locations may have a presence bit equal to 1.

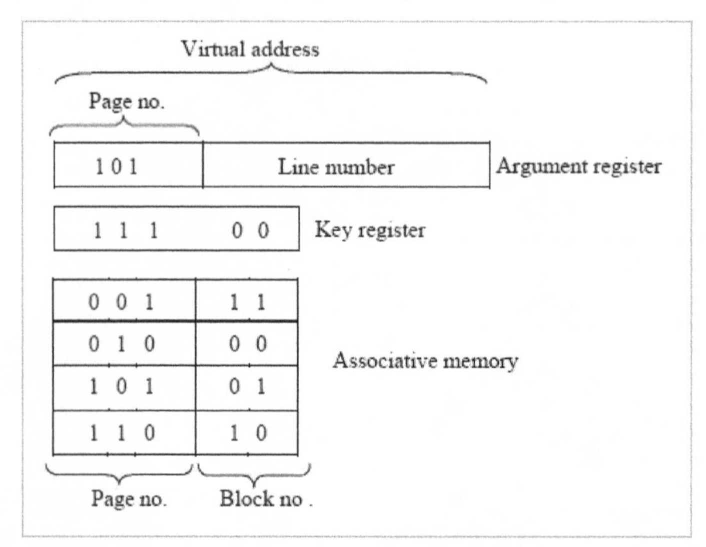

Figure -An associative memory page table.

At any given time, at least 992 locations will be empty and not in use. A more efficient way to organize the page table would be to construct it with a number of words equal to the number of blocks in main memory. In this way the size of the memory is reduced and each location is fully utilized. This method can be implemented by means of an associative memory with each word in memory containing a page number together with its corresponding block number The page field in each word is compared with the page number in the virtual address. If a match occurs, the word is read from memory and its corresponding block number is extracted.

Consider again the case of eight pages and four blocks as in the example of Fig. We replace the random access memory-page table with an associative memory of four words as shown in Fig. Each entry in the associative memory array consists of two fields. The first three bits specify a field from storing the page number. The last two bits constitute a field for storing the block number. The virtual address is placed in the argument register. The page number bits in the argument are compared with all page numbers in the page field of the associative memory. If the page number is found, the 5-bit word is read out from memory. The corresponding block number, being in the same word, is transferred to the main memory address register. If no match occurs, a call to the operating system is generated to bring the required page from auxiliary memory.

PAGE REPLACEMENT

A virtual memory system is a combination of hardware and software techniques. The memory management software system handles all the software operations for the efficient utilization of memory space. It must decide (1) which page in main memory ought to be removed to make room for a new page, (2) when a new page is to be transferred from auxiliary memory to main memory, and (3) where the page is to be placed in main memory. The hardware mapping mechanism and the memory management software together constitute the architecture of a virtual memory.

When a program starts execution, one or more pages are transferred into main memory and the page table is set to indicate their position. The program is executed from main memory until it attempts to reference a page that is still in auxiliary memory. This condition is called page fault. When page fault occurs, the execution of the present program is suspended until the required page is brought into main memory.

Since loading a page from auxiliary memory to main memory is basically an I/O operation, the operating system assigns this task to the I/O processor. In the meantime, controls transferred to the next program in memory that is waiting to be processed in the CPU. Later, when the memory block has been assigned and the transfer completed, the original program can resume its operation.

When a page fault occurs in a virtual memory system, it signifies that the page referenced by the CPU is not in main memory. A new page is then transferred from auxiliary memory to main memory. If main memory is full, it would be necessary to remove a page from a memory block to make room for the new page. The policy for choosing pages to remove is determined from the replacement algorithm that is used. The goal of a replacement policy is to try to remove the page least likely to be referenced in the immediate future.

Two of the most common replacement algorithms used are the first-in first-out (FIFO) and the least recently used (LRU). The FIFO algorithm selects for replacement the page the has been in memory the longest time. Each time a page is loaded into memory, its identification number is pushed into a FIFO stack. FIFO will be full whenever memory has no more empty blocks. When a new page must be loaded, the page least recently brought in is removed. The page to be removed is easily determined because its identification number is at the top of the FIFO stack. The FIFO replacement policy has the advantage of being easy to implement. It has the disadvantages that under certain circum-stances pages are removed and loaded form memory too frequently.

The LRU policy is more difficult to implement but has been more attractive on the assumption that the least recently used page is a better candidate for removal than the least recently loaded pages in FIFO. The LRU algorithm can be implemented by associating a counter with every page that is in main memory. When a page is referenced, its associated counter is set to zero. At fixed intervals of time, the counters associated with all pages presently in memory are incremented by 1. The least recently used page is the page with the highest count. The counters are often called aging registers, as their count indicates their age, that is, how long ago their associated pages have been reference.

Redundant Array of Inexpensive Disk (RAID)

RAID (redundant array of independent disks; originally redundant array of inexpensive disks) is a way of storing the same data in different places (thus, redundantly) on multiple hard disks. By placing data on multiple disks, I/O (input/output) operations can overlap in a balanced way, improving performance.

Since multiple disks increases the mean time between failures (MTBF), storing data redundantly also increases fault tolerance. A RAID appears to the operating system to be a single logical hard disk. RAID employs the technique of disk striping, which involves partitioning each drive's storage space into units ranging from a sector (512 bytes) up to several megabytes. The stripes of all the disks are interleaved and addressed in order. In a multi-user system, better performance requires establishing a stripe wide enough to hold the typical or maximum size record. This allows overlapped disk I/O across drives.

There are at least nine types of RAID plus a non-redundant array (RAID-0):

- **RAID-0:** This technique has striping, but no redundancy of data. It offers the best performance, but no fault-tolerance.

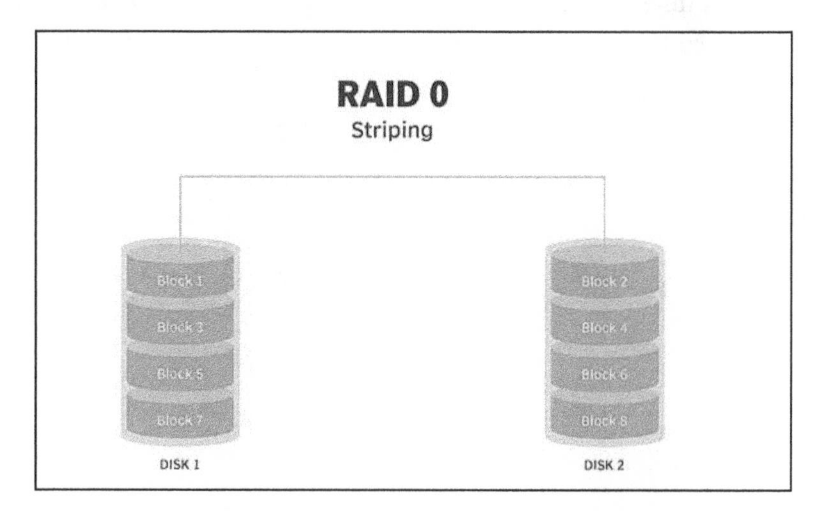

- **RAID-1:** This type is also known as disk mirroring and consists of at least two drives that duplicate the storage of data. There is no striping. Read performance is improved since either disk can be read at the same time

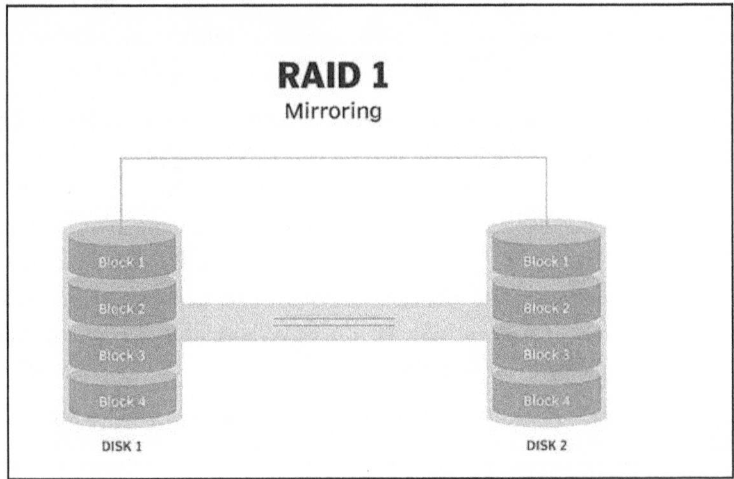

- **RAID-2:** This type uses striping across disks with some disks storing error checking and correcting (ECC) information. It has no advantage over.

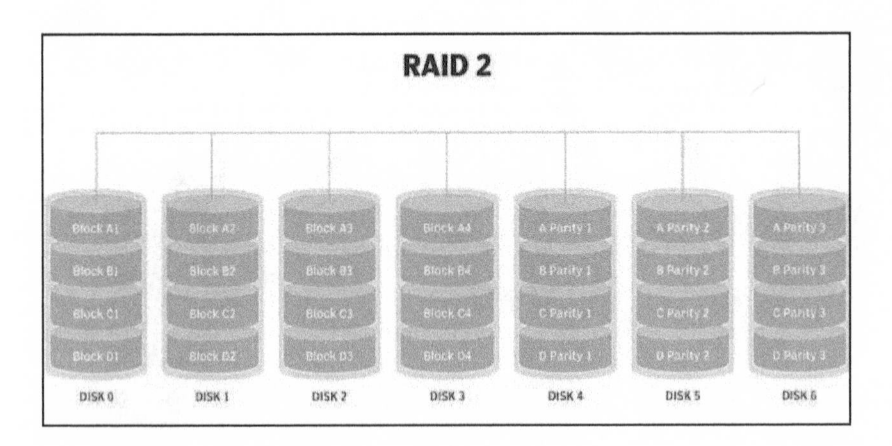

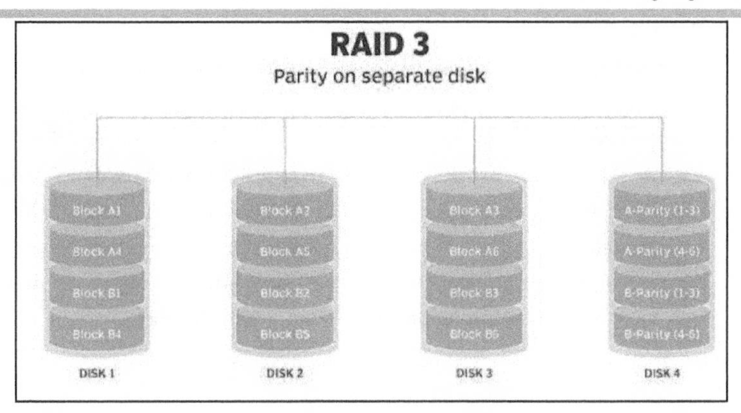

- **RAID-3:** This type uses striping and dedicates one drive to storing parity information. The embedded error checking (ECC) information is used to detect errors. Data recovery is accomplished by calculating the exclusive OR (XOR) of the information recorded on the other drives.

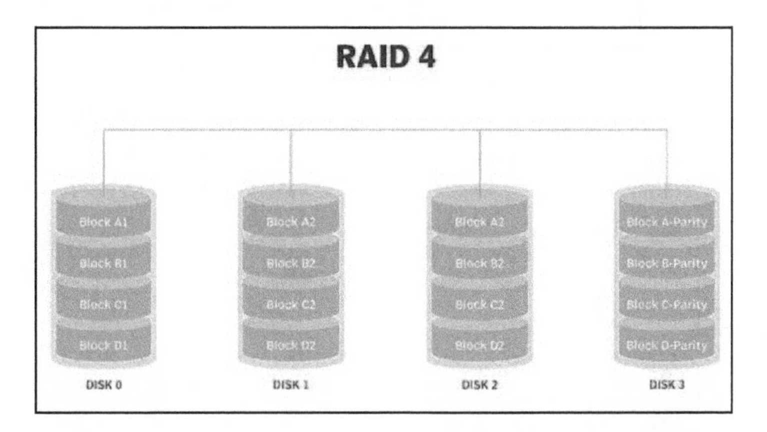

- **RAID-4:** This type uses large stripes, which means you can read records from any single drive.

- **RAID 5.** This level is based on parity block-level striping. The parity information is striped across each drive, enabling the array to function even if one drive were to fail. The array's architecture allows read and write operations to span multiple drives -- resulting in performance better than that of a single drive, but not as high as that of a RAID 0 array. RAID 5 requires at least three disks, but it is often recommended to use at least five disks for performance reasons. RAID 5 arrays are generally considered to be a poor choice for use on write-intensive systems because of the performance impact associated with writing parity data. When a disk fails, it can take a long time to rebuild a RAID 5 array.

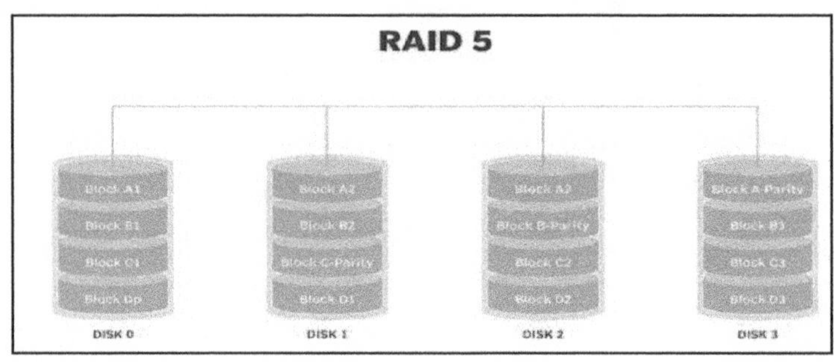

- **RAID 6.** This technique is similar to RAID 5, but it includes a second parity scheme distributed across the drives in the array. The use of additional parity enables the array to continue to function even if two disks fail simultaneously. However, this extra protection comes at a cost. RAID 6 arrays often have slower write performance than RAID 5 arrays.

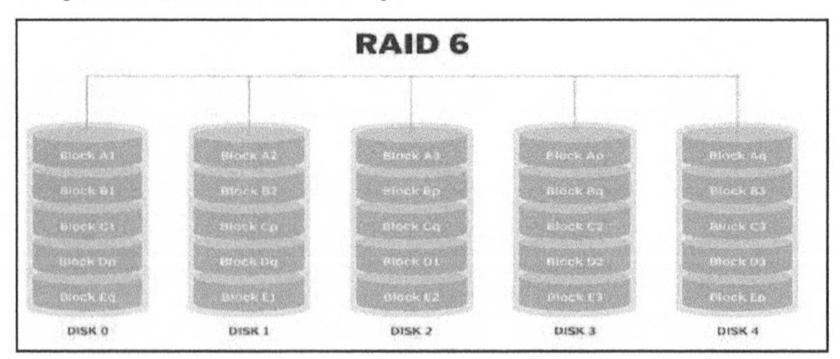

- **RAID-7:** This type includes a real-time embedded operating system as a controller, caching via a high-speed bus, and other characteristics of a stand-alone computer. One vendor offers this system.
- **RAID-10**: Combining RAID-0 and RAID-1 is often referred to as RAID-10, which offers higher performance than RAID-1 but at much higher cost. There are two subtypes: In RAID-0+1, data is organized as stripes across multiple disks, and then the striped disk sets are mirrored. In RAID-1+0, the data is mirrored and the mirrors are striped.
- **RAID-50 (or RAID-5+0):** This type consists of a series of RAID-5 groups and striped in RAID-0 fashion to improve RAID-5 performance without reducing data protection.
- **RAID-53 (or RAID-5+3):** This type uses striping (in RAID-0 style) for RAID-3's virtual disk blocks. This offers higher performance than RAID-3 but at much higher cost.
- **RAID-S (also known as Parity RAID):** This is an alternate, proprietary method for striped parity RAID from EMC Symmetric that is no longer in use on current equipment. It appears to be similar to RAID-5 with some performance enhancements as well as the enhancements that come from having a high-speed disk cache on the disk.

@@@@@@@@@@@@@@

&&&&&&&&&&&&&&&

CHAPTER-3

Input-Output Organization

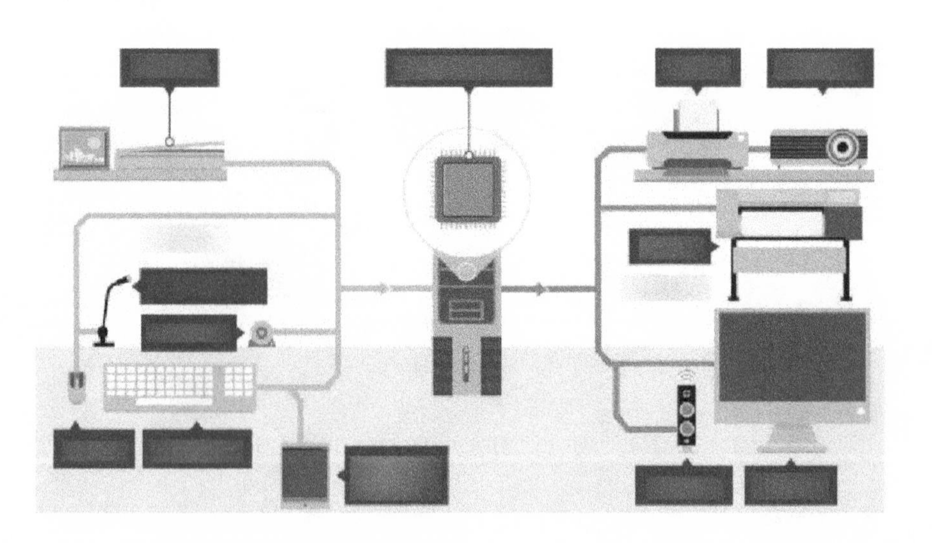

Input/output Subsystem

The I/O subsystem of a computer provides an efficient mode of communication between the central system and the outside environment. It handles all the input-output operations of the computer system.

Peripheral Devices

Input or output devices that are connected to computer are called **peripheral devices**. These devices are designed to read information into or out of the memory unit upon command from the CPU and are considered to be the part of computer system. These devices are also called **peripherals.**

For example: Keyboards, display units and printers are common peripheral devices.

There are three types of peripherals:

- **Input peripherals** : Allows user input, from the outside world to the computer. Example: Keyboard, Mouse etc.
- **Output peripherals**: Allows information output, from the computer to the outside world. Example: Printer, Monitor etc
- **Input-Output peripherals:** Allows both input (from outside world to computer) as well as, output (from computer to the outside world). Example: Touch screen etc.

Interfaces

Interface is a shared boundary between two separate components of the computer system which can be used to attach two or more components to the system for communication purposes.

There are two types of interface:

- CPU Interface
- I/O Interface

Let's understand the I/O Interface in details,

Input-Output Interface

Peripherals connected to a computer need special communication links for interfacing with CPU. In computer system, there are special hardware components between the CPU and peripherals to control or manage the input-output transfers. These components are called input-output interface units because they provide communication links between processor bus and peripherals. They provide a method for transferring information between internal system and input-output devices.

Modes of I/O Data Transfer

Data transfer between the central unit and I/O devices can be handled in generally three types of modes which are given below:

- Programmed I/O
- Interrupt Initiated I/O
- Direct Memory Access

Programmed I/O

Programmed I/O instructions are the result of I/O instructions written in computer program. Each data item transfer is initiated by the instruction in the program.

Usually the program controls data transfer to and from CPU and peripheral. Transferring data under programmed I/O requires constant monitoring of the peripherals by the CPU.

Interrupt Initiated I/O

In the programmed I/O method the CPU stays in the program loop until the I/O unit indicates that it is ready for data transfer. This is time consuming process because it keeps the processor busy needlessly.

This problem can be overcome by using interrupt initiated I/O. In this when the interface determines that the peripheral is ready for data transfer, it generates an interrupt. After receiving the interrupt signal, the CPU stops the task which it is processing and service the I/O transfer and then returns back to its previous processing task.

Direct Memory Access

Removing the CPU from the path and letting the peripheral device manage the memory buses directly would improve the speed of transfer. This technique is known as DMA.

In this, the interface transfer data to and from the memory through memory bus. A DMA controller manages to transfer data between peripherals and memory unit. Many hardware systems use DMA such as disk drive controllers, graphic cards, network cards and sound cards etc. It is also used for intra chip data transfer in multi-core processors. In DMA, CPU would initiate the transfer, do other operations while the transfer is in progress and receive an interrupt from the DMA controller when the transfer has been completed.

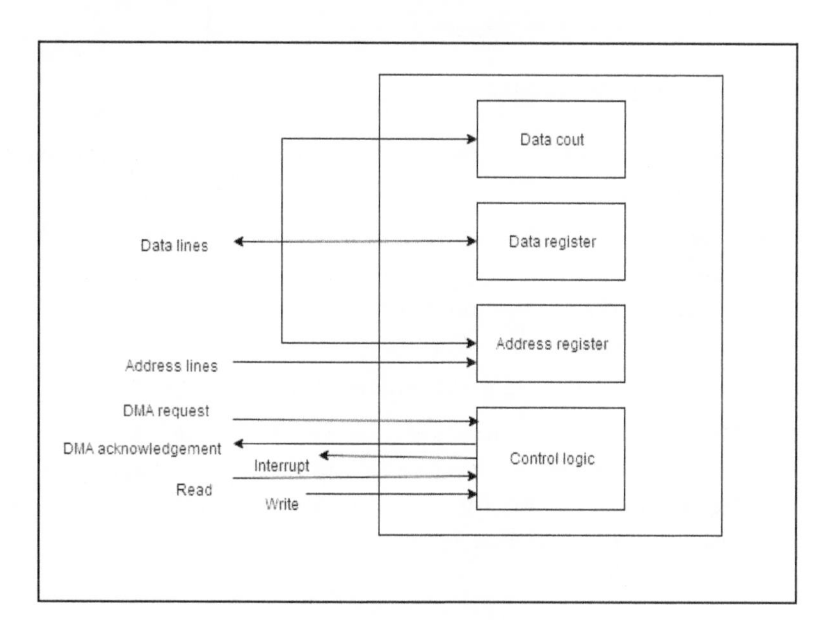

The data transfer between a fast storage media such as magnetic disk and memory unit is limited by the speed of the CPU. Thus we can allow the peripherals directly communicate with each other using the memory buses, removing the intervention of the CPU. This type of data transfer technique is known as DMA or direct memory access. During DMA the CPU is idle and it has no control over the memory buses. The DMA controller takes over the buses to manage the transfer directly between the I/O devices and the memory unit.

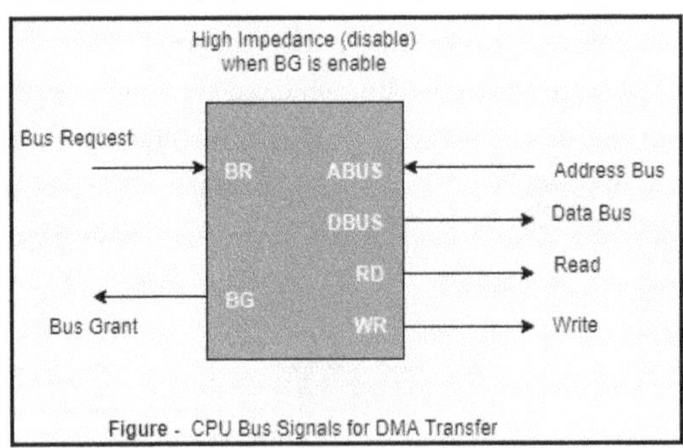

Figure - CPU Bus Signals for DMA Transfer

Bus Request : It is used by the DMA controller to request the CPU to relinquish the control of the buses.

Bus Grant : It is activated by the CPU to Inform the external DMA controller that the buses are in high impedance state and the requesting DMA can take control of the buses. Once the DMA has taken the control of the buses it transfers the data. This transfer can take place in many ways.

Types of DMA transfer using DMA controller:

Burst Transfer :DMA returns the bus after complete data transfer. A register is used as a byte count, being decremented for each byte transfer, and upon the byte count reaching zero, the DMAC will release the bus. When the DMAC operates in burst mode, the CPU is halted for the duration of the data transfer.

Steps involved are:

- Bus grant request time.
- Transfer the entire block of data at transfer rate of device because the device is usually slow than the speed at which the data can be transferred to CPU.
- Release the control of the bus back to CPU

So, total time taken to transfer the N bytes= Bus grant request time + (N) * (memory transfer rate) + Bus release control time.

Where,

X μsec =data transfer time or preparation time (words/block)

Y μsec =memory cycle time or cycle time or transfer time (words/block)

% CPU idle (Blocked)=(Y/X+Y)*100

% CPU Busy=(X/X+Y)*100

Cyclic Stealing :An alternative method in which DMA controller transfers one word at a time after which it must return the control of the buses to the CPU. The CPU delays its operation only for one memory cycle to allow the direct memory I/O transfer to "steal" one memory cycle.

Steps Involved are:

- Buffer the byte into the buffer
- Inform the CPU that the device has 1 byte to transfer (i.e. bus grant request)
- Transfer the byte (at system bus speed)
- Release the control of the bus back to CPU.

Before moving on transfer next byte of data, device performs step 1 again so that bus isn't tied up and the transfer won't depend upon the transfer rate of device.

So, for 1 byte of transfer of data,

time taken by using cycle stealing mode (T).= time required for bus grant + 1 bus cycle to transfer data + time required to release the bus, it will be N x T

In cycle stealing mode we always follow pipelining concept that when one byte is getting transferred then Device is parallel preparing the next byte. "The fraction of CPU time to the data transfer time" if asked then cycle stealing mode is used.

Where,

X μsec =data transfer time or preparation time (words/block)

Y μsec =memory cycle time or cycle time or transfer time (words/block)

% CPU idle (Blocked) =(Y/X)*100

% CPU busy=(X/Y)*100

Interleaved mode: In this technique , the DMA controller takes over the system bus when the microprocessor is not using it. An alternate half cycle i.e. half cycle DMA + half cycle processor.

Figure in the next page shows the block diagram of a typical DMA controller. The unit communicates with the CPU via the data bus and control lines. The registers in the DMA are selected by the CPU through the address bus by enabling the DS (DMA select) and RS (register select) inputs. The RD (read) and WR (write) inputs are bidirectional. When the BG (bus grant) input is 0, the CPU can communicate with the DMA registers through the data bus to read from or write to the DMA registers. When BG = 1, the CPU has relinquished the buses and the DMA can communicate directly with the memory by specifying an address in the address bus and activating the RD or WR control. ; The DMA communicates with the external peripheral through the request and acknowledge lines by using a prescribed handshaking procedure.

The DMA controller has three registers: an address register, a word count register, and a control register. The address register contains an address to specify the desired location in memory. The address bits go through bus buffers into the address bus. The address register is incremented after each word that is transferred to memory. The word count register is incremented after each word that is transferred to memory .

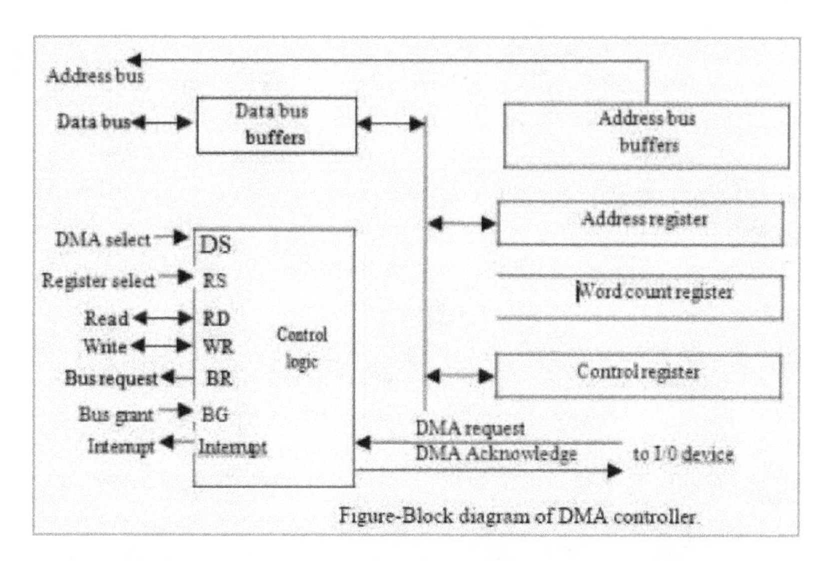

Figure-Block diagram of DMA controller

The DMA is first initialized by the CPU. After that, the DMA starts and continues to transfer data between memory and peripheral unit until an entire block is transferred. The initialization process is essentially a program consisting of I/O instructions that include the address for selecting particular DMA registers. The CPU initializes the DMA by sending the following information through the data bus:

1. The starting address of the memory block where data are available (for read) or where data are to be stored (for write)
2. The word count, which is the number of words in the memory block
3. Control to specify the mode of transfer such as read or write
4. A control to start the DMA transfer

The starting address is stored in the address register. The word count is stored in the word count register, and the control information in the control register. Once the DMA is initialized, the CPU stops communicating with the DMA unless it receives an interrupt signal or if it wants to check how many words have been transferred.

DMA TRANSFER

The position of the DMA controller among the other components in a computer system is illustrated in below Fig. The CPU communicates with the DMA through the address and data buses as with any interface unit. The DMA has its own address, which activates the DS and RS lines. The CPU initializes the DMA through the data bus. Once the DMA receives the start control command, it can start the transfer between the peripheral device and the memory.

When the peripheral device sends a DMA request, the DMA controller activates the BR line, informing the CPU to relinquish the buses. The CPU responds with its BG line, informing the DMA that its buses are disabled. The DMA then puts the current value of its address register into the address bus, initiates the RD or WR signal, and sends a DMA acknowledge to the peripheral device. Note that the RD and WR lines in the DMA controller are bidirectional. The direction of transfer depends on the status of the BG line. When BG line. When BG = 0, the RD and WR are input lines allowing the CPU to communicate with the internal DMA registers. When BG = 1, the RD and WR and output lines from the DMA controller to the random- access memory to specify the read or write operation for the data.

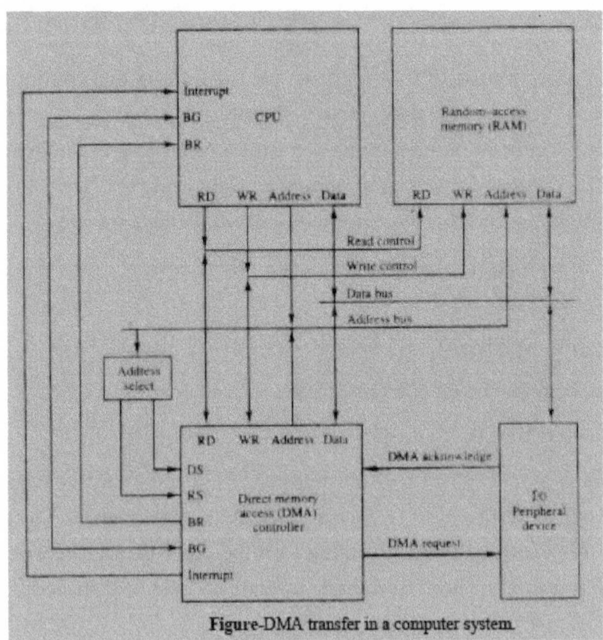

Figure-DMA transfer in a computer system.

In cycle stealing mode we always follow pipelining concept that when one byte is getting transferred then Device is parallel preparing the next byte. "The fraction of CPU time to the data transfer time" if asked then cycle stealing mode is used.

Where,

X μsec =data transfer time or preparation time (words/block)

Y μsec =memory cycle time or cycle time or transfer time (words/block)

% CPU idle (Blocked) =(Y/X)*100

% CPU busy=(X/Y)*100

Interleaved mode: In this technique , the DMA controller takes over the system bus when the microprocessor is not using it. An alternate half cycle i.e. half cycle DMA + half cycle processor.

COA-Asynchronous Data Transfer

We know that, the internal operations in individual unit of digital system are synchronized by means of clock pulse, means clock pulse is given to all registers within a unit, and all data transfer among internal registers occur simultaneously during occurrence of clock pulse. Now, suppose any two units of digital system are designed independently such as CPU and I/O interface.

And if the registers in the interface (I/O interface) share a common clock with CPU registers, then transfer between the two units is said to be synchronous. But in most cases, the internal timing in each unit is independent from each other in such a way that each uses its own private clock for its internal registers. In that case, the two units are said to be asynchronous to each other, and if data transfer occur between them this data transfer is said to be Asynchronous Data Transfer.

But, the Asynchronous Data Transfer between two independent units requires that control signals be transmitted between the communicating units so that the time can be indicated at which they send data.

This asynchronous way of data transfer can be achieved by two methods:

- One way is by means of strobe pulse which is supplied by one of the units to other unit. When transfer has to occur. This method is known as "**Strobe Control**".
- Another method commonly used is to accompany each data item being transferred with a control signal that indicates the presence of data in the bus. The unit receiving the data item responds with another signal to acknowledge receipt of the data. This method of data transfer between two independent units is said to be **"Handshaking".**

The strobe pulse and handshaking method of asynchronous data transfer are not restricted to I/O transfer. In fact, they are used extensively on numerous occasion requiring transfer of data between two independent units. So, here we consider the transmitting unit as source and receiving unit as destination.

As an example: The CPU, is the source during an output or write transfer and is the destination unit during input or read transfer. And thus, the sequence of control during an asynchronous transfer depends on whether the transfer is initiated by the source or by the destination. So, while discussing each way of data transfer asynchronously we see the sequence of control in both terms when it is initiated by source or when it is initiated by destination. In this way, each way of data transfer, can be further divided into parts, source initiated and destination initiated. We can also specify, asynchronous transfer between two independent units by means of a timing diagram that shows the timing relationship that exists between the control and the data buses.

Now, we will discuss each method of asynchronous data transfer in detail one by one.

1. Strobe Control:

The Strobe Control method of asynchronous data transfer employs a single control line to time each transfer .This control line is also known as strobe and it may be achieved either by source or destination, depending on which initiate transfer.

Source initiated strobe for data transfer:

The block diagram and timing diagram of strobe initiated by source unit is shown in figure below:

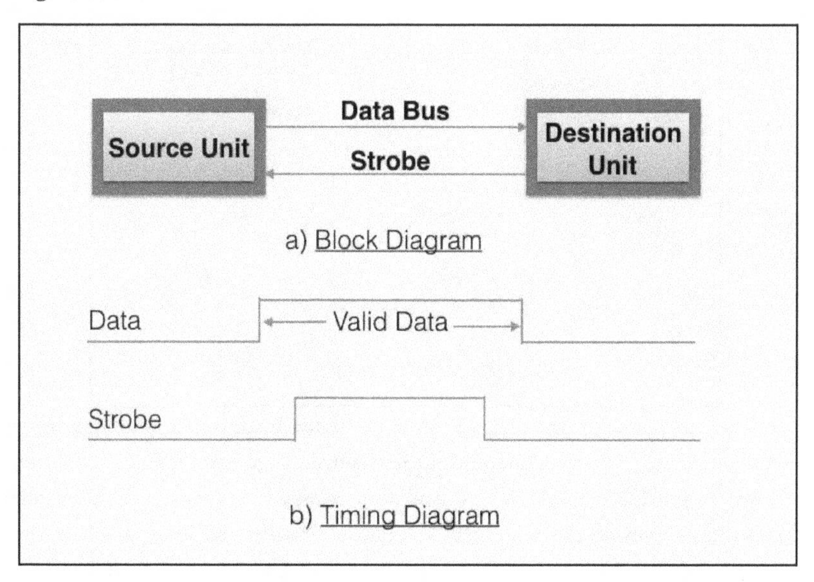

a) Block Diagram

b) Timing Diagram

In block diagram we see that strobe is initiated by source, and as shown in timing diagram, the source unit first places the data on the data bus. After a brief delay to ensure that the data settle to a steady value, the source activates a strobe pulse. The information on data bus and strobe control signal remain in the active state for a sufficient period of time to allow the destination unit to receive the data. Actually, the destination unit, uses a falling edge of strobe control to transfer the contents of data bus to one of its internal registers. The source removes the data from the data bus after it disables its strobe pulse. New valid data will be available only after the strobe is enabled again.

Destination-initiated strobe for data transfer:

The block diagram and timing diagram of strobe initiated by destination is shown in figure below:

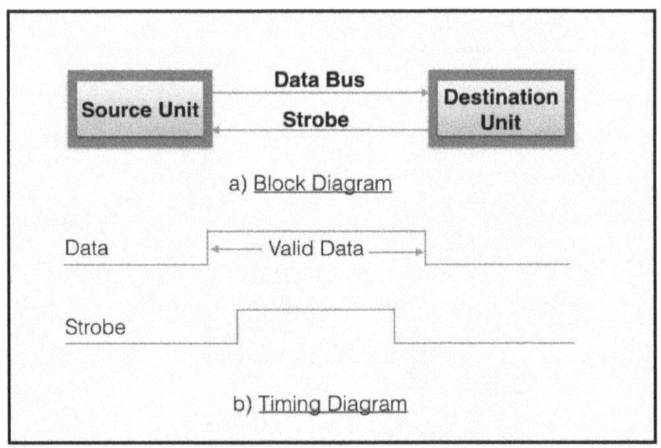

a) Block Diagram

b) Timing Diagram

In block diagram, we see that, the strobe initiated by destination, and as shown in timing diagram, the destination unit first activates the strobe pulse, informing the source to provide the data. The source unit responds by placing the requested binary information on the data bus. The data must be valid and remain in the bus long enough for the destination unit to accept it. The falling edge of strobe pulse can be used again to trigger a destination register. The destination unit then disables the strobe. And source removes the data from data bus after a per determine time interval.

Now, actually in computer, in the first case means in strobe initiated by source - the strobe may be a memory-write control signal from the CPU to a memory unit. The source, CPU, places the word on the data bus and informs the memory unit, which is the destination, that this is a write operation. And in the second case i.e., in the strobe initiated by destination - the strobe may be a memory read control from the CPU to a memory unit. The destination, the CPU, initiates the read operation to inform the memory, which is a source unit, to place selected word into the data bus.

2. Handshaking:

The disadvantage of strobe method is that source unit that initiates the transfer has no way of knowing whether the destination has actually received the data that was placed in the bus. Similarly, a destination unit that initiates the transfer has no way of knowing whether the source unit, has actually placed data on the bus. This problem can be solved by handshaking method. Hand shaking method introduce a second control signal line that provides a replay to the unit that initiates the transfer. In it, one control line is in the same direction as the data flow in the bus from the source to destination. It is used by source unit to inform the destination unit whether there are valid data in the bus. The other control line is in the other direction from destination to the source. It is used by the destination unit to inform the source whether it can accept data. And in it also, sequence of control depends on unit that initiate transfer. Means sequence of control depends whether transfer is initiated by source and destination. Sequence of control in both of them are described below:

Source initiated Handshaking:

The source initiated transfer using handshaking lines is shown in figure below:

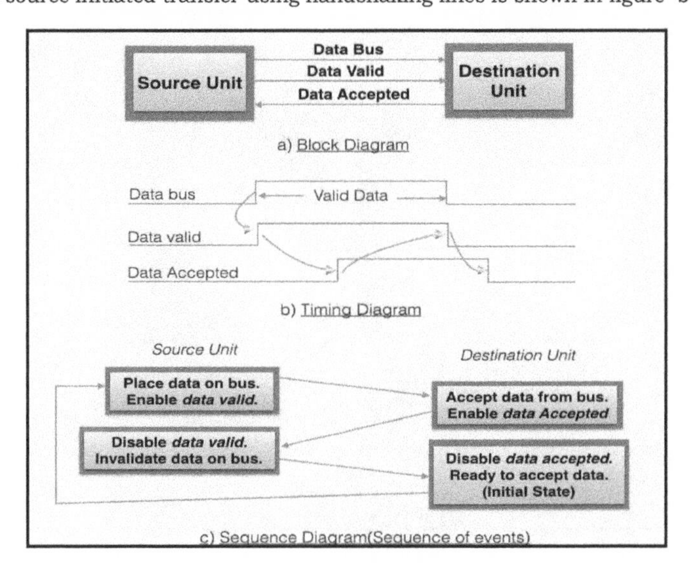

In its block diagram, we se that two handshaking lines are "data valid", which is generated by the source unit, and "data accepted", generated by the destination unit. The timing diagram shows the timing relationship of exchange of signals between the two units. Means as shown in its timing diagram, the source initiates a transfer by placing data on the bus and enabling its data valid signal. The data accepted signal is then activated by destination unit after it accepts the data from the bus. The source unit then disable its data valid signal which invalidates the data on the bus. After this, the destination unit disables its data accepted signal and the system goes into initial state. The source unit does not send the next data item until after the destination unit shows its readiness to accept new data by disabling the data accepted signal. This sequence of events described in its sequence diagram, which shows the above sequence in which the system is present, at any given time.

Destination initiated handshaking:

The destination initiated transfer using handshaking lines is shown in figure below:

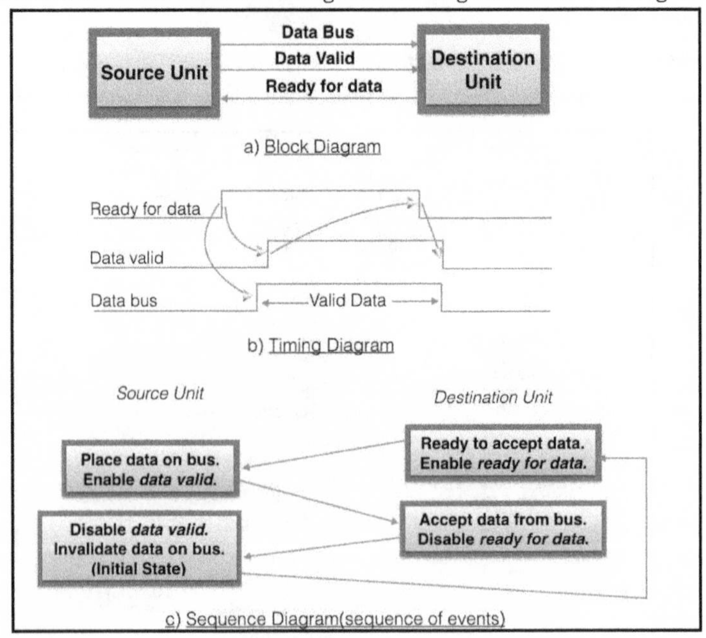

a) Block Diagram

b) Timing Diagram

c) Sequence Diagram(sequence of events)

In its block diagram, we see that the two handshaking lines are "data valid", generated by the source unit, and "ready for data" generated by destination unit. Note that the name of signal data accepted generated by destination unit has been changed to ready for data to reflect its new meaning. In it, transfer is initiated by destination, so source unit does not place data on data bus until it receives ready for data signal from destination unit. After that, hand shaking process is some as that of source initiated. The sequence of event in it are shown in its sequence diagram and timing relationship between signals is shown in its timing diagram.

Thus, here we can say that, sequence of events in both cases would be identical. If we consider ready for data signal as the complement of data accept. Means, the only difference between source and destination initiated transfer is in their choice of initial state.

COA-Priority Interrupt

In a typical application, a number of I/O devices are attached to computer, with each device being able to originate an interrupt request, so to provide services to device which initiate interrupt request, the task of interrupt system is to identify the of interrupt and then provide services to them. But, in most cases there is a possibility that several sources will request service simultaneously. So, in this case, the interrupt system must also need to decide which device to service first. But, these simple interrupt system are not able for that, so, another system known as Priority interrupt system is provided. Priority Interrupt are systems, that establishes a Priority over the various sources (interrupt devices) to determine which condition is to be serviced first when two or more requests arrive simultaneously. This system may also determine which condition are permitted to interrupt to the computer while another interrupt is being serviced.

Usually, in Priority Systems, higher-priority interrupt levels are served first, as if they delayed or interrupted, could have serious consequences. And the devices with high-speed transfer such as magnetic disks are given high-priority, and slow devices such as keyboards receives low-priority.

Establishing Priority of Simultaneous Interrupt:

The priority of simultaneous interrupts can be established either by software method or hardware.

The software method which gives priority to simultaneous interrupt is:

- Polling

And the hardware method which gives priority to simultaneous interrupt is:

- Daisy-Chaining Priority

Now, we will explore to each one of them one by one.

1. Polling:

Polling is the software method of establishing priority of simultaneous interrupt. In this method, when the processor detects an interrupt, it branches to an interrupt service routine whose job is to pull each I/O module to determine which module caused the interrupt.

The poll could be in the form of separate command line(e.g., Test I/O). In this case, the processor raises the Test I/O and places the address of particular I/O module on the address line. If it has interrupt that is, if interrupt is identified in it. And, it is the order in which they are tested i.e., the order in which they appear on address line (Service Routine) determine the priority of each interrupt. As while testing, highest priority source (devices) are tested first then lower-priority devices. This is very simple method of establishing priority on simultaneous interrupt. But the disadvantage of polling is that it is very time consuming.

2. Daisy-Chaining Priority:

The Daisy–Chaining method of establishing priority on interrupt sources uses the hardware i.e., it is the hardware means of establishing priority. In this method, all the device, whether they are interrupt sources or not, connected in a serial manner. Means the device with highest priority is placed in the first position, which is followed by lowest priority device. And all device share a common interrupt request line, and the interrupt acknowledge line is daisy chained through the modules.

The figure shown below, this method of connection with three devices and the CPU.

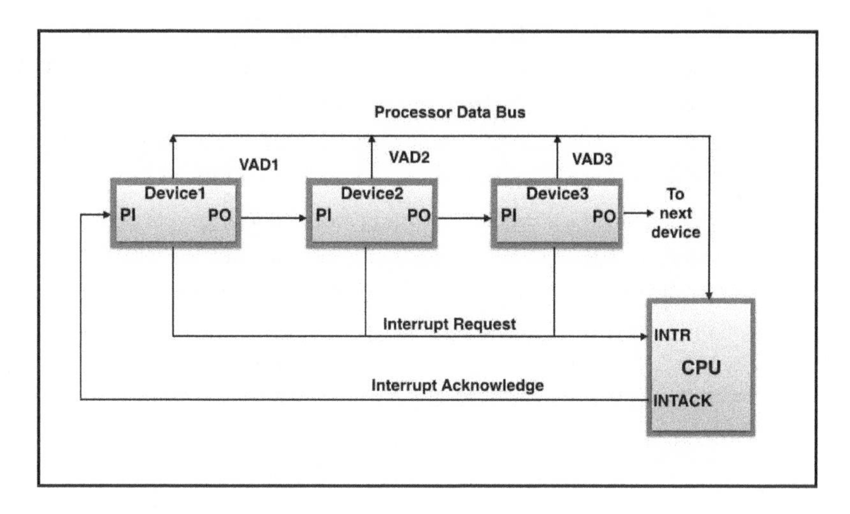

It works as follows:

When any device raise an interrupt, the interrupt request line goes activated, the processor when sense it, it sends out an interrupt acknowledge which is first received by device1.If device1 does not need service, i.e., processor checks, whether the device has pending interrupt or initiate interrupt request, if the result is no, then the signal is passed to device2 by placing 1 in the PO(Priority Out) of device1.

And if device need service then service is given to them by placing first 0 in the PO of device1, which indicate the next-lower-priority device that acknowledge signal has been blocked. And device that have processor responds by inserting its own interrupt vector address (VAD) into the data bus for the CPU to use during interrupt cycle. In this way, it gave services to interrupt source according to their priority. And thus, we can say that, it is the order of device in chain that determine the priority of interrupt sources.

Input-output Processor (IOP)

The IOP is similar to a CPU except that it is designed to handle the details of I/O processing. Unlike the DMA controller that must be set up entirely by the CPU, the IOP can fetch and execute its own instructions. IOP instructions are specially designed to facilitate I/O transfers. In addition, the IOP can perform other processing tasks, such as arithmetic, logic, branching, and code translation.

The block diagram of a computer with two processors is shown in below Figure. The memory unit occupies a central position and can communicate with each processor by means of direct memory access. The CPU is responsible for processing data needed in the solution of computational tasks. The IOP provides a path for transfer of data between various peripheral devices and the memory unit.

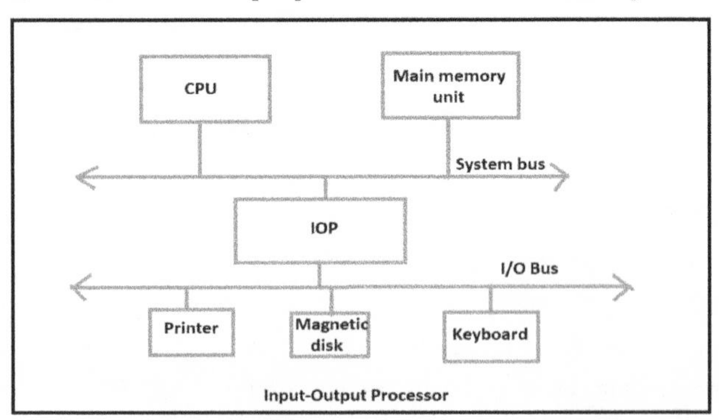

Input-Output Processor

The data formats of peripheral devices differ from memory and CPU data formats. The IOP must structure data words from many different sources. For example, it may be necessary to take four bytes from an input device and pack them into one 32 -bit word before the transfer to memory. Data are gathered in the IOP at the device rate and bit capacity while the CPU is executing its own program. After the input data are assembled into a memory word, they are transferred from IOP directly into memory by "stealing" one memory cycle from the CPU. Similarly, an output word transferred from memory to the IOP is directed from the IOP to the output device at the device rate and bit capacity.

The communication between the IOP and the devices attached to it is similar to the program control method of transfer. The way by which the CPU and IOP communicate depends on the level of sophistication included in the system. In most computer systems, the CPU is the master while the IOP is a slave processor. The CPU is assigned the task of initiating all operations, but I/O instructions are execute in the IOP. CPU instructions provide operations to start an I/O transfer and also to test I/O status conditions needed for making decisions on various I/O activities. The IOP, in turn, typically asks for CPU attention by means of an interrupt. It also responds to CPU requests by placing a status word in a prescribed location in memory to be examined later by a CPU program. When an I/O operation is desired, the CPU informs the IOP where to find the I/O program and then leaves the transfer details to the IOP.

CPU-IOP Communication

The communication between CPU and IOP. These are depending on the particular computer considered. In most cases the memory unit acts as a message center where each processor leaves information for the other. To appreciate the operation of a typical IOP, we will illustrate by a specific example the method by which the CPU and IOP communicate. This is a simplified example that omits many operating details in order to provide an overview of basic concepts.

The sequence of operations may be carried out as shown in the flowchart of below Fig. The CPU sends an instruction to test the IOP path. The IOP responds by inserting a status word in memory for the CPU to check. The bits of the status word indicate the condition of the IOP and I/O device, such as IOP overload condition, device busy with another transfer, or device ready for I/O transfer. The CPU refers to the status word in memory to decide what to do next. If all is in order, the CPU sends the instruction to start I/O transfer. The memory address received with this instruction tells the IOP where to find its program.

The CPU can now continue with another program while the IOP is busy with the I/O program. Both programs refer to memory by means of DMA transfer. When the IOP terminates the execution of its program, it sends an interrupt request to the CPU.

The CPU responds to the interrupt by issuing an instruction to read the status from the IOP. The IOP responds by placing the contents of its status report into a specified memory location.

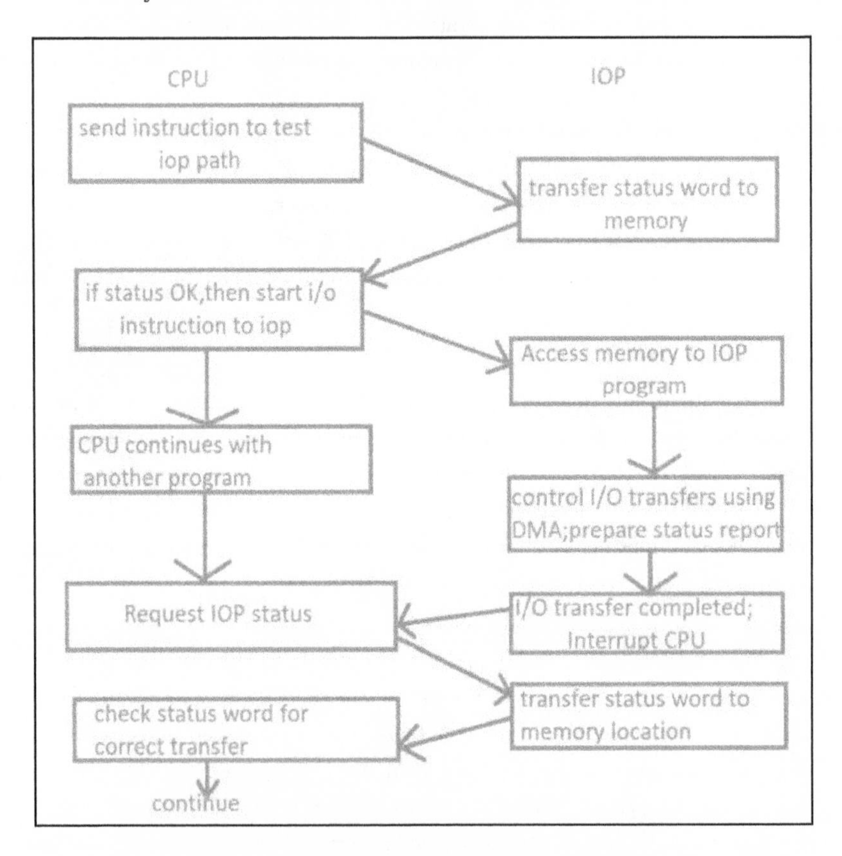

The IOP takes care of all data transfers between several I/O units and the memory while the CPU is processing another program. The IOP and CPU are competing for the use of memory, so the number of devices that can be in operation is limited by the access time of the memory.

Serial Communication

Introduction

Serial communication is the most widely used approach to transfer information between data processing equipment and peripherals. In general, communication means interchange of information between individuals through written documents, verbal words, audio and video lessons.

Every device might it be your Personal computer or mobile runs on serial protocol. The protocol is the secure and reliable form of communication having a set of rules addressed by the source host (sender) and destination host (receiver). To have a better insight, I have explained the concept of serial communication.

In embedded system, Serial communication is the way of exchanging data using different methods in the form of serial digital binary. Some of the well-known interfaces used for the data exchange are RS-232, RS-485, I2C, SPI etc.

What is Serial communication?

In serial communication, data is in the form of binary pulses. In other words, we can say Binary One represents a logic HIGH or 5 Volts, and zero represents a logic LOW or 0 Volts. Serial communication can take many forms depending on the type of transmission mode and data transfer. The **transmission modes** are classified as Simplex, Half Duplex, and Full Duplex. There will be a source (also known as a sender) and destination (also called a receiver) for each transmission mode.

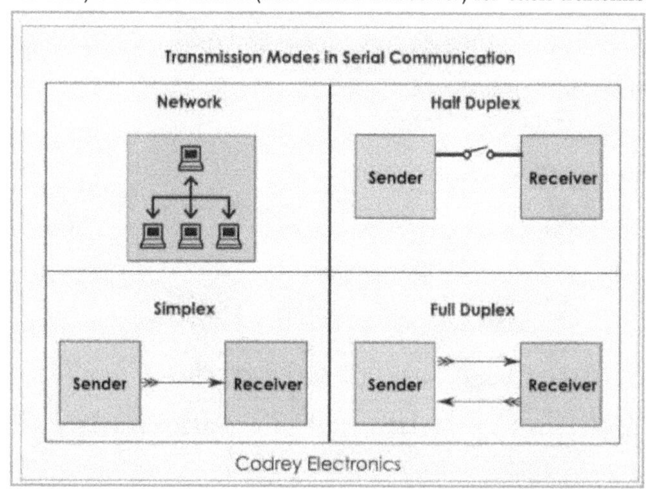

The Simplex method is a one-way communication technique. Only one client (either the sender or receiver is active at a time). If a sender transmits, the receiver can only accept. Radio and Television transmission are the examples of simplex mode.

In Half Duplex mode, both sender and receiver are active but not at a time, i.e. if a sender transmits, the receiver can accept but cannot send and vice versa. A good example is an internet. If a client (laptop) sends a request for a web page, the web server processes the application and sends back the information.

The Full Duplex mode is widely used communication in the world. Here both sender and receiver can transmit and receive at the same time. An example is your Smartphone.

Beyond the transmission modes, we have to consider the endianness and protocol design of the host computer (sender or receiver). **Endianness** is the way of storing the data at a particular memory address. Depending on the data alignment endian is classified as

- Little Endian and
- Big Endian.

Take this example to understand the concept of endianness. Suppose, we have a 32-bit hexadecimal data ABCD87E2. How is this data stored in memory? To have a clear idea, I have explained the difference between Little Endian and Big Endian.

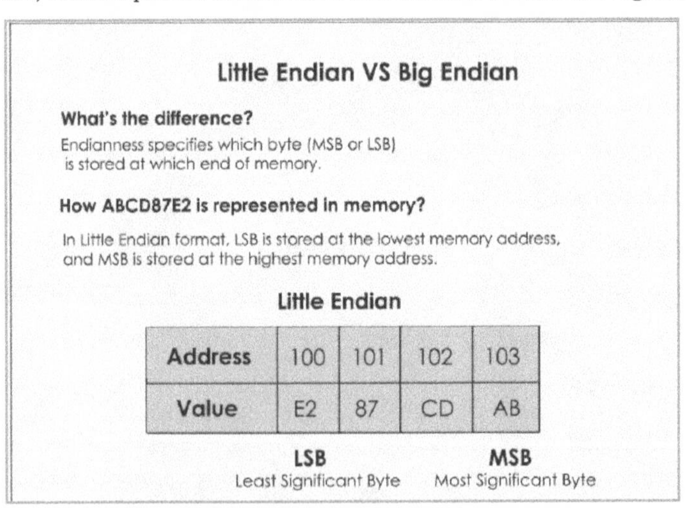

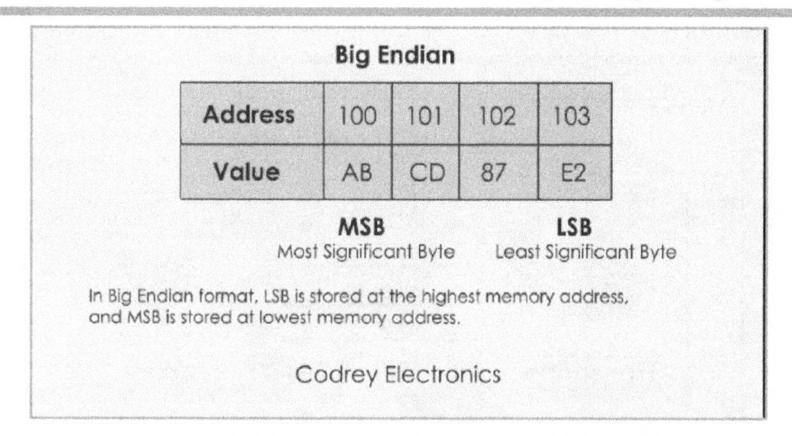

Data transfer can happen in two ways. They are serial communication and parallel communication. Serial communication is a technique used to send data bit by bit using a two-wires i.e. transmitter (sender) and receiver.

For example, I want to send an 8-bit binary data 11001110 from the transmitter to the receiver. But, which bit goes out first? Most Significant Bit – MSB (7th bit) or Least Significant Bit- LSB (0th Bit). We cannot say. Here I am considering LSB is moving first (for little Endian).

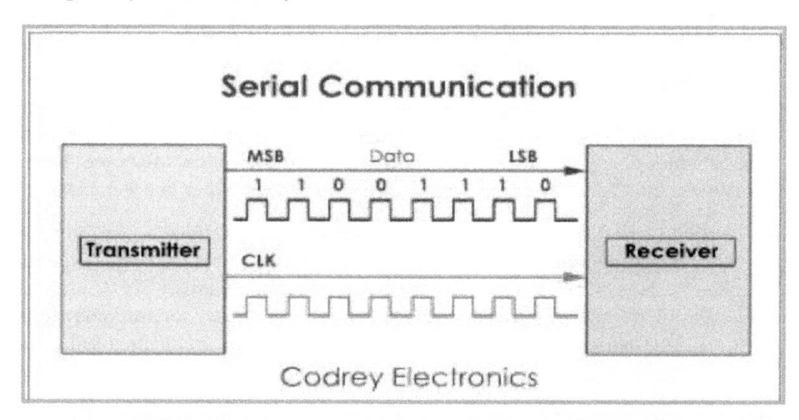

From the above diagram, for every clock pulse; the transmitter sends a single bit of data to the receiver.

Parallel communication moves 8,16, or 32 bits of data at a time. Printers and Xerox machines use parallel communication for faster data transfer.

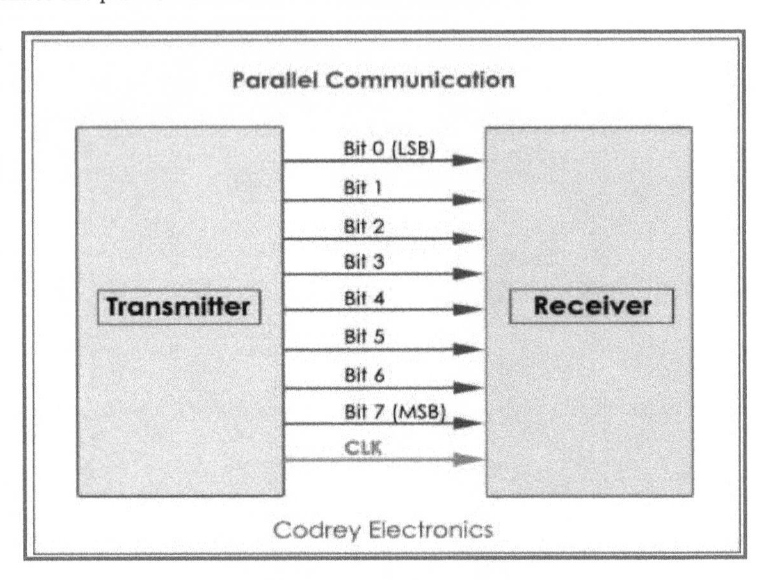

Difference between Serial and Parallel communication

Serial communication sends only one bit at a time. so, these require fewer I/O (input-output) lines. Hence, occupying less space and more resistant to cross-talk. The main advantage of serial communication is, the cost of the entire embedded system becomes cheap and transmits the information over a long distance. Serial transfer is used in DCE (Data communication Equipment) devices like a modem.

In parallel communication, a chunk of data (8,16 or 32 bit) is sent at a time. So, each bit of data requires a separate physical I/O line. The advantage of parallel communication is it is fast but its drawback is it use more number of I/O (input-output) lines. Parallel transfer is used in PC (personal computer) for interconnecting CPU (central processing unit), RAM (random access memory), modems, audio, video and network hardware.

Note: If your Integrated Circuit or processor supports less amount of Input/output pins it is better to opt serial communication .

Serial Communication	Parallel Communication
Sends data bit by bit at one clock pulse	Transfers a chunk of data at a time
Requires one wire to transmit the data	Requires 'n' number of lines for transmitting 'n' bits
Communication speed is slow	Communication speed is fast
Installation cost is low	Installation cost is high
Preferred for long distance communication	Used for short distance communication
Example: Computer to Computer	Computer to multi function printer.

RS-232 protocol

RS232 is the first serial protocol used for connecting modems for telephony. RS stands for Recommended Standard, and now it has changed to EIA (Electronic Industries Alliance) / TIA (Telecommunication Industry Association). It is also used in modem, mouse, and CNC (computed numerical computing) machines. You can connect only a single transmitter to a single receiver.

It supports full duplex communication and allows baud rate up to 1Mbps. Cable length is limited to 50 feet. As you know, the data stored in the memory are in the form of bytes. You may have a doubt How is the byte-wise data converted to binary bits? The answer is a Serial port. The serial port has an internal chip called **UART**. UART is an acronym for Universal Asynchronous Receiver Transmitter which converts the parallel data (byte) into the bitwise serial form.

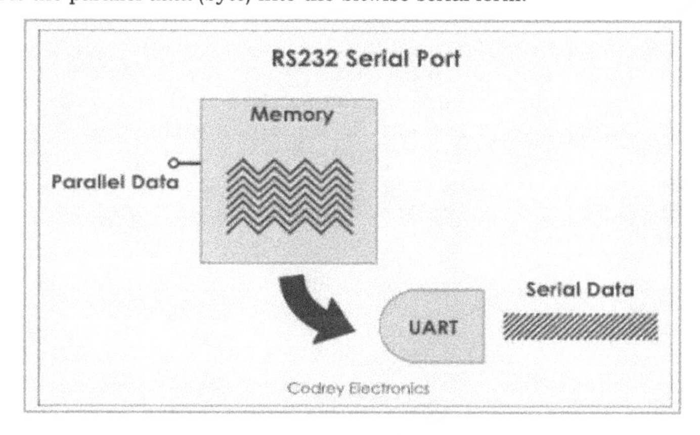

RS-232 Wiring Connection

The RS232 serial port has nine pins, male or female type models. RS 232C serial communication interface is the later version of RS232. All the features present in RS232 is present in the RS232C model except it has 25 pins. Out of 25 or 9 pins, we use only three pins for the connection of terminal devices.

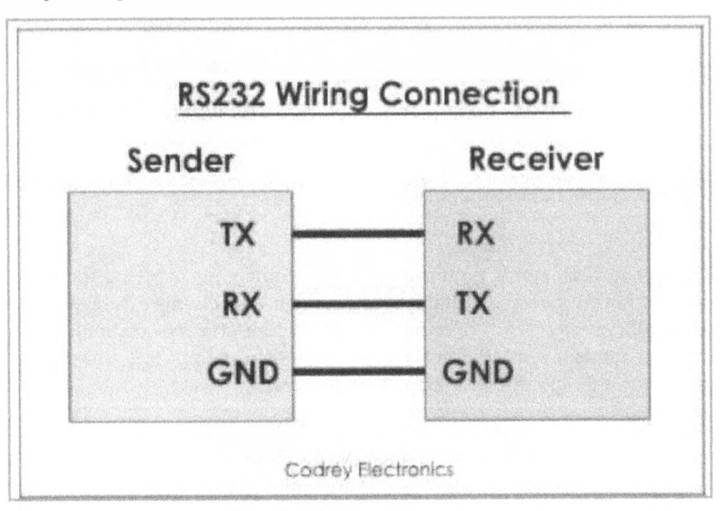

IEEE 1394

IEEE 1394, High Performance Serial Bus, is an electronics standard for connecting devices to your personal computer. IEEE 1394 provides a single plug-and-socket connection on which up to 63 devices can be attached with data transfer speeds up to 400 Mbps (megabit s per second). The standard describes a serial bus or pathway between one or more peripheral devices and your computer's microprocessor . Many peripheral devices now come equipped to meet IEEE 1394. Two popular implementations of IEEE 1394 are Apple's **FireWire** and Sony's **i.LINK** . IEEE 1394 implementations provide:

- A simple common plug-in serial connector on the back of your computer and on many different types of peripheral devices
- A thin serial cable rather than the thicker parallel cable you now use to your printer, for example

- A very high-speed rate of data transfer that will accommodate multimedia applications (100 and 200 megabits per second today; with much higher rates later)
- Hot-plug and plug and play capability without disrupting your computer
- The ability to chain devices together in a number of different ways without terminators or complicated set-up requirements

In time, IEEE 1394 implementations are expected to replace and consolidate today's serial and parallel interfaces, including Centronics parallel , RS-232C , and Small Computer System Interface (SCSI). The first products to be introduced with FireWire include digital camera s, digital video disks (DVD s), digital video tapes, digital camcorders, and music systems. Because IEEE 1394 is a peer-to-peer interface, one camcorder can dub to another without being plugged into a computer. With a computer equipped with the socket and bus capability, any device (for example, a video camera) can be plugged in while the computer is running.

Briefly How It Works

There are two levels of interface in IEEE 1394, one for the backplane bus within the computer and another for the point-to-point interface between device and computer on the serial cable. A simple bridge connects the two environments. The backplane bus supports 12.5, 25, or 50 megabits per second data transfer. The cable interface supports 100, 200, or 400 megabits per second. Each of these interfaces can handle any of the possible data rates and change from one to another as needed.

The serial bus functions as though devices were in slots within the computer sharing a common memory space. A 64-bit device address allows a great deal of flexibility in configuring devices in chains and trees from a single socket.

IEEE 1394 provides two types of data transfer: asynchronous and isochronous . Asynchronous is for traditional load-and-store applications where data transfer can be initiated and an application interrupted as a given length of data arrives in a buffer . Isochronous data transfer ensures that data flows at a pre-set rate so that an application can handle it in a timed way. For multimedia applications, this kind of data transfer reduces the need for buffering and helps ensure a continuous presentation for the viewer.

The 1394 standard requires that a device be within 4.5 meters of the bus socket. Up to 16 devices can be connected in a single chain, each with the 4.5 meter maximum (before signal attenuation begins to occur) so theoretically you could have a device as far away as 72 meters from the computer.

Another new approach to connecting devices, the Universal Serial Bus (USB), provides the same "hot plug" capability as the 1394 standard. It's a less expensive technology but data transfer is limited to 12 Mbps (million bits per second). Small Computer System Interface offers a high data transfer rate (up to 40 megabytes per second) but requires address preassignment and a device terminator on the last device in a chain. FireWire can work with the latest internal computer bus standard, Peripheral Component Interconnect (PCI), but higher data transfer rates may require special design considerations to minimize undesired buffering for transfer rate mismatches.

Peripheral Component Interconnect (PCI)

PCI stands for Peripheral Component Interconnect. It could be a standard information transport that was common in computers from 1993 to 2007 or so. It was for a long time the standard transport for extension cards in computers, like sound cards, network cards, etc. It was a parallel transport, that, in its most common shape, had a clock speed of 66 MHz, and can either be 32 or 64 bits wide. It has since been replaced by PCI Express, which could be a serial transport as contradicted to PCI. A PCI port, or, more precisely, PCI opening, is essentially the connector that's utilized to put through the card to the transport. When purge, it basically sits there and does nothing.

Types of PCI : These are various types of PCI:

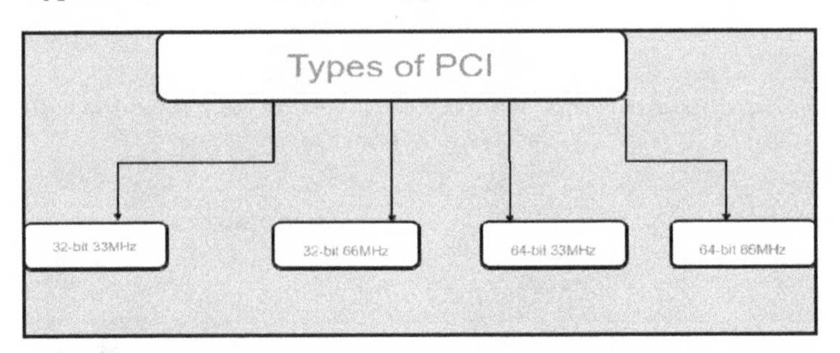

- PCI 32 bits have a transport speed of 33 MHz and work at 132 MBps.
- PCI 64 bits have a transport speed of 33 MHz and work at 264 MBps.
- PCI 64 bits have a transport speed of 66 MHz and work at 512 MBps.
- PCI 64 bits have a transport speed of 66 MHz and work at 1 GBps.

Function of PCI :

PCI slots are utilized to install sound cards, Ethernet and remote cards and presently strong state drives utilizing NVMe innovation to supply SSD drive speeds that are numerous times speedier than SATA SSD speeds. PCI openings too permit discrete design cards to be included to a computer as well.

PCI openings (and their variations) permit you to include expansion cards to a motherboard. The extension cards increment the machines capabilities past what the motherboard may create alone, such as: upgraded illustrations, extended sound, expanded USB and difficult drive controller, and extra arrange interface options, to title a couple of.

Advantage of PCI :

- You'll interface a greatest of five components to the PCI and you'll be able moreover supplant each of them by settled gadgets on the motherboard.
- You have different PCI buses on the same computer.
- The PCI transport will improve the speed of the exchanges from 33MHz to 133 MHz with a transfer rate of 1 gigabyte per second.
- The PCI can handle gadgets employing a greatest of 5 volts and the pins utilized can exchange more that one flag through one stick.

Disadvantage of PCI :

- PCI Graphics Card cannot get to system memory.
- PCI does not support pipeline.

USB

What is the full form of USB?

The full form of USB is Universal Serial Bus it is a common platform that allows communication between devices and a host controller such as a PC (computer). Such buses are handy when we are concerned about how to link the computer to the electronic system we have. They are used for networking, contact, or power supply purposes.

Universal Serial Bus is productive and reduces the workload to serve the function of transferring data and electrical power supply between different peripherals gadgets such as mice, printers, digital cameras, keyboards, scanners, flash drives and external hard drives etc.. It also reduces power consumption, which is best used for storing data.

History of USB

Seven companies in a group developed USB in 1994, namely Microsoft, Compaq, Intel, Nortel, DEC, IBM and NEC. USB was designed to simplify the work and make the user comfortable connecting external devices to a computer. Windows, Mac etc. using a USB device and consider it a very useful tool.

Connection of USB with Computer

Insert the USB device into the USB port of the pc to make the connection between the USB and computers. It will automatically detect the device after you insert it and work on it further. Rebooting of the computer after the USB device has been inserted into the computer is not required. There are different size of Universal Serial Bus (USB) devices are available.

Micro size USB

Mini size USB

Standard size USB

Advantages

1. LOw power consumption.
2. USB is less expensive
3. Each device containing the USB port fits in with USB.
4. The USB can be of various sizes and its connections also come in several ways.

Disadvantages

1. Compared with other systems, data transmission is not much quicker.
2. Single messages can only be exchanged between the peripheral and host, and the Universal Serial Bus does not include the broadcast functionality.
3. Performance and functionality of USB are within limits.

Chapter-4

Operating Systems Overview

Memory Management

Principles of Deadlock

Overview of Computer Operating Systems Functions

An operating system (OS) is a collection of software that manages computer hardware resources and provides common services for computer programs. The operating system is a vital component of the system software in a computer system. This tutorial will take you through step by step approach while learning Operating System concepts.

Why to Learn Operating System?

An Operating System (OS) is an interface between a computer user and computer hardware. An operating system is a software which performs all the basic tasks like file management, memory management, process management, handling input and output, and controlling peripheral devices such as disk drives and printers.

Some popular Operating Systems include Linux Operating System, Windows Operating System, VMS, OS/400, AIX, z/OS, etc.

Following are some of important functions of an operating System.

- Memory Management
- Processor Management
- Device Management
- File Management
- Security
- Control over system performance
- Job accounting
- Error detecting aids
- Coordination between other software and users

Applications of Operating System

Following are some of the important activities that an Operating System performs –

Security – By means of password and similar other techniques, it prevents unauthorized access to programs and data.

Control over system performance – Recording delays between request for a service and response from the system.

Job accounting – Keeping track of time and resources used by various jobs and users.

Error detecting aids – Production of dumps, traces, error messages, and other debugging and error detecting aids.

Coordination between other softwares and users – Coordination and assignment of compilers, interpreters, assemblers and other software to the various users of the computer systems.

Overview

An Operating System (OS) is an interface between a computer user and computer hardware. An operating system is a software which performs all the basic tasks like file management, memory management, process management, handling input and output, and controlling peripheral devices such as disk drives and printers.

Some popular Operating Systems include Linux Operating System, Windows Operating System, VMS, OS/400, AIX, z/OS, etc.

Definition

An operating system is a program that acts as an interface between the user and the computer hardware and controls the execution of all kinds of programs.

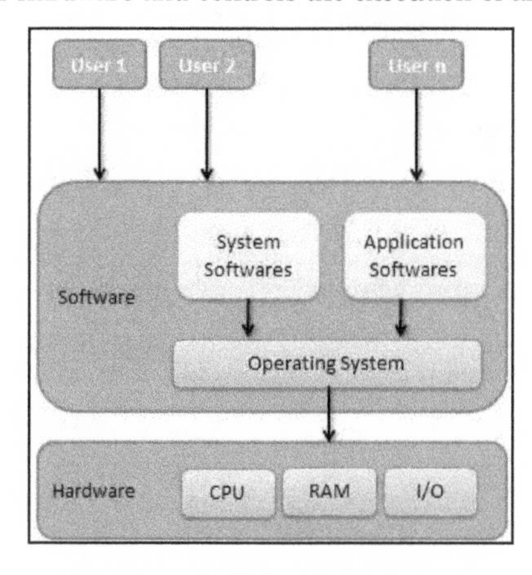

Following are some of important functions of an operating System.

- Memory Management
- Processor Management
- Device Management
- File Management
- Security
- Control over system performance
- Job accounting
- Error detecting aids
- Coordination between other software and users

Memory Management

Memory management refers to management of Primary Memory or Main Memory. Main memory is a large array of words or bytes where each word or byte has its own address.

Main memory provides a fast storage that can be accessed directly by the CPU. For a program to be executed, it must in the main memory. An Operating System does the following activities for memory management –

1. Keeps tracks of primary memory, i.e., what part of it are in use by whom, what part are not in use.
2. In multiprogramming, the OS decides which process will get memory when and how much.
3. Allocates the memory when a process requests it to do so.
4. De-allocates the memory when a process no longer needs it or has been terminated.

Processor Management

In multiprogramming environment, the OS decides which process gets the processor when and for how much time. This function is called process scheduling. An Operating System does the following activities for processor management –

1. Keeps tracks of processor and status of process. The program responsible for this task is known as traffic controller.
2. Allocates the processor (CPU) to a process.
3. De-allocates processor when a process is no longer required.

Device Management

An Operating System manages device communication via their respective drivers. It does the following activities for device management –

1. Keeps tracks of all devices. Program responsible for this task is known as the I/O controller.
2. Decides which process gets the device when and for how much time.
3. Allocates the device in the efficient way.
4. De-allocates devices.

File Management

A file system is normally organized into directories for easy navigation and usage. These directories may contain files and other directions.

An Operating System does the following activities for file management –

1. Keeps track of information, location, uses, status etc. The collective facilities are often known as file system.
2. Decides who gets the resources.
3. Allocates the resources.
4. De-allocates the resources.

Types of Operating System

Operating systems are there from the very first computer generation and they keep evolving with time. In this chapter, we will discuss some of the important types of operating systems which are most commonly used.

Batch operating system

The users of a batch operating system do not interact with the computer directly. Each user prepares his job on an off-line device like punch cards and submits it to the computer operator. To speed up processing, jobs with similar needs are batched together and run as a group. The programmers leave their programs with the operator and the operator then sorts the programs with similar requirements into batches.

The problems with Batch Systems are as follows –

- Lack of interaction between the user and the job.
- CPU is often idle, because the speed of the mechanical I/O devices is slower than the CPU.
- Difficult to provide the desired priority.

Time-sharing operating systems

Time-sharing is a technique which enables many people, located at various terminals, to use a particular computer system at the same time. Time-sharing or multitasking is a logical extension of multiprogramming. Processor's time which is shared among multiple users simultaneously is termed as time-sharing.

The main difference between Multiprogrammed Batch Systems and Time-Sharing Systems is that in case of Multiprogrammed batch systems, the objective is to maximize processor use, whereas in Time-Sharing Systems, the objective is to minimize response time.

Multiple jobs are executed by the CPU by switching between them, but the switches occur so frequently. Thus, the user can receive an immediate response. For example, in a transaction processing, the processor executes each user program in a short burst or quantum of computation.

That is, if n users are present, then each user can get a time quantum. When the user submits the command, the response time is in few seconds at most.

The operating system uses CPU scheduling and multiprogramming to provide each user with a small portion of a time. Computer systems that were designed primarily as batch systems have been modified to time-sharing systems.

Advantages of Timesharing operating systems are as follows –

- Provides the advantage of quick response.
- Avoids duplication of software.
- Reduces CPU idle time.

Disadvantages of Time-sharing operating systems are as follows –

- Problem of reliability.
- Question of security and integrity of user programs and data.
- Problem of data communication.

Distributed operating System

Distributed systems use multiple central processors to serve multiple real-time applications and multiple users. Data processing jobs are distributed among the processors accordingly.

The processors communicate with one another through various communication lines (such as high-speed buses or telephone lines). These are referred as loosely coupled systems or distributed systems. Processors in a distributed system may vary in size and function. These processors are referred as sites, nodes, computers, and so on.

The advantages of distributed systems are as follows –

- With resource sharing facility, a user at one site may be able to use the resources available at another.
- Speedup the exchange of data with one another via electronic mail.
- If one site fails in a distributed system, the remaining sites can potentially continue operating.

- Better service to the customers.
- Reduction of the load on the host computer.
- Reduction of delays in data processing.

Network operating System

A Network Operating System runs on a server and provides the server the capability to manage data, users, groups, security, applications, and other networking functions. The primary purpose of the network operating system is to allow shared file and printer access among multiple computers in a network, typically a local area network (LAN), a private network or to other networks.

Examples of network operating systems include Microsoft Windows Server 2003, Microsoft Windows Server 2008, UNIX, Linux, Mac OS X, Novell NetWare, and BSD.

The advantages of network operating systems are as follows –

- Centralized servers are highly stable.
- Security is server managed.
- Upgrades to new technologies and hardware can be easily integrated into the system.
- Remote access to servers is possible from different locations and types of systems.

The disadvantages of network operating systems are as follows –

- High cost of buying and running a server.
- Dependency on a central location for most operations.
- Regular maintenance and updates are required.

Real Time operating System

A real-time system is defined as a data processing system in which the time interval required to process and respond to inputs is so small that it controls the environment. The time taken by the system to respond to an input and display of required updated information is termed as the response time. So in this method, the response time is very less as compared to online processing.

Real-time systems are used when there are rigid time requirements on the operation of a processor or the flow of data and real-time systems can be used as a control device in a dedicated application. A real-time operating system must have well-defined, fixed time constraints, otherwise the system will fail. For example, Scientific experiments, medical imaging systems, industrial control systems, weapon systems, robots, air traffic control systems, etc. There are two types of real-time operating systems.

Hard real-time systems

Hard real-time systems guarantee that critical tasks complete on time. In hard real-time systems, secondary storage is limited or missing and the data is stored in ROM. In these systems, virtual memory is almost never found.

Soft real-time systems

Soft real-time systems are less restrictive. A critical real-time task gets priority over other tasks and retains the priority until it completes. Soft real-time systems have limited utility than hard real-time systems. For example, multimedia, virtual reality, Advanced Scientific Projects like undersea exploration and planetary rovers, etc.

Operating System - Services

An Operating System provides services to both the users and to the programs.

It provides programs an environment to execute.

It provides users the services to execute the programs in a convenient manner.

Following are a few common services provided by an operating system –

- Program execution
- I/O operations
- File System manipulation
- Communication
- Error Detection
- Resource Allocation
- Protection

- **User Interfaces** - Means by which users can issue commands to the system. Depending on the system these may be a command-line interface (e.g. sh, csh, ksh, tcsh, etc.), a GUI interface (e.g. Windows, X-Windows, KDE, Gnome, etc.), or a batch command systems.

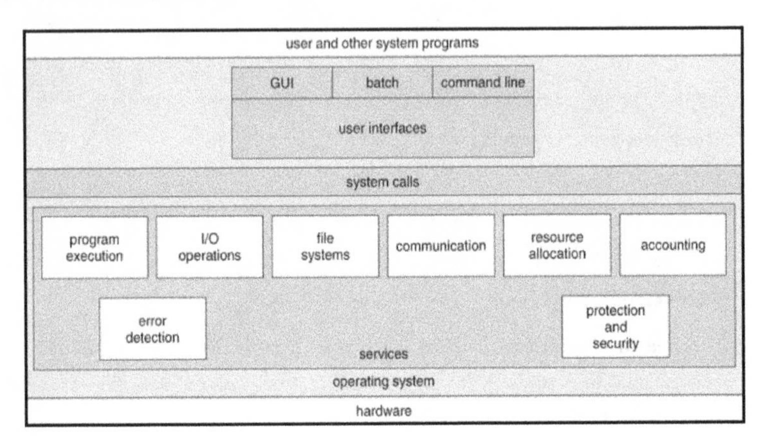

User Operating-System Interface

Command Interpreter

- Gets and processes the next user request, and launches the requested programs.
- In some systems the CI may be incorporated directly into the kernel.
- More commonly the CI is a separate program that launches once the user logs in or otherwise accesses the system.
- UNIX, for example, provides the user with a choice of different shells, which may either be configured to launch automatically at login, or which may be changed on the fly. (Each of these shells uses a different configuration file of initial settings and commands that are executed upon startup.)
- Different shells provide different functionality, in terms of certain commands that are implemented directly by the shell without launching any external programs.

Most provide at least a rudimentary command interpretation structure for use in shell script programming (loops, decision constructs, variables, etc.)

- An interesting distinction is the processing of wild card file naming and I/O re-direction. On UNIX systems those details are handled by the shell, and the program which is launched sees only a list of filenames generated by the shell from the wild cards. On a DOS system, the wild cards are passed along to the programs, which can interpret the wild cards as the program sees fit.

Graphical User Interface, GUI

Generally implemented as a desktop metaphor, with file folders, trash cans, and resource icons. Icons represent some item on the system, and respond accordingly when the icon is activated. First developed in the early 1970's at Xerox PARC research facility. In some systems the GUI is just a front end for activating a traditional command line interpreter running in the background. In others the GUI is a true graphical shell in its own right. Mac has traditionally provided ONLY the GUI interface. With the advent of OSX (based partially on UNIX), a command line interface has also become available.

Because mice and keyboards are impractical for small mobile devices, these normally use a touch-screen interface today, that responds to various patterns of swipes or "gestures". When these first came out they often had a physical keyboard and/or a trackball of some kind built in, but today a virtual keyboard is more commonly implemented on the touch screen.

Choice of interface

Most modern systems allow individual users to select their desired interface, and to customize its operation, as well as the ability to switch between different interfaces as needed. System administrators generally determine which interface a user starts with when they first log in.

GUI interfaces usually provide an option for a terminal emulator window for entering command-line commands.

Command-line commands can also be entered into shell scripts, which can then be run like any other programs.

Program execution

Operating systems handle many kinds of activities from user programs to system programs like printer spooler, name servers, file server, etc. Each of these activities is encapsulated as a process.

A process includes the complete execution context (code to execute, data to manipulate, registers, OS resources in use). Following are the major activities of an operating system with respect to program management –

- Loads a program into memory.
- Executes the program.
- Handles program's execution.
- Provides a mechanism for process synchronization.
- Provides a mechanism for process communication.
- Provides a mechanism for deadlock handling.

I/O Operation

An I/O subsystem comprises of I/O devices and their corresponding driver software. Drivers hide the peculiarities of specific hardware devices from the users.

An Operating System manages the communication between user and device drivers.

- I/O operation means read or write operation with any file or any specific I/O device.
- Operating system provides the access to the required I/O device when required.

File system manipulation

A file represents a collection of related information. Computers can store files on the disk (secondary storage), for long-term storage purpose. Examples of storage media include magnetic tape, magnetic disk and optical disk drives like CD, DVD. Each of these media has its own properties like speed, capacity, data transfer rate and data access methods.

A file system is normally organized into directories for easy navigation and usage. These directories may contain files and other directions. Following are the major activities of an operating system with respect to file management –

- Program needs to read a file or write a file.
- The operating system gives the permission to the program for operation on file.
- Permission varies from read-only, read-write, denied and so on.
- Operating System provides an interface to the user to create/delete files.
- Operating System provides an interface to the user to create/delete directories.
- Operating System provides an interface to create the backup of file system.

Communication

In case of distributed systems which are a collection of processors that do not share memory, peripheral devices, or a clock, the operating system manages communications between all the processes. Multiple processes communicate with one another through communication lines in the network.

The OS handles routing and connection strategies, and the problems of contention and security. Following are the major activities of an operating system with respect to communication –

- Two processes often require data to be transferred between them
- Both the processes can be on one computer or on different computers, but are connected through a computer network.

Communication may be implemented by two methods, either by Shared Memory or by Message Passing.

Error handling

Errors can occur anytime and anywhere. An error may occur in CPU, in I/O devices or in the memory hardware. Following are the major activities of an operating system with respect to error handling –

- The OS constantly checks for possible errors.
- The OS takes an appropriate action to ensure correct and consistent computing.

Resource Management

In case of multi-user or multi-tasking environment, resources such as main memory, CPU cycles and files storage are to be allocated to each user or job. Following are the major activities of an operating system with respect to resource management –

- The OS manages all kinds of resources using schedulers.
- CPU scheduling algorithms are used for better utilization of CPU.

Protection

Considering a computer system having multiple users and concurrent execution of multiple processes, the various processes must be protected from each other's activities.

Protection refers to a mechanism or a way to control the access of programs, processes, or users to the resources defined by a computer system. Following are the major activities of an operating system with respect to protection –

- The OS ensures that all access to system resources is controlled.
- The OS ensures that external I/O devices are protected from invalid access attempts.
- The OS provides authentication features for each user by means of passwords.

Operating-System Structures

Operating system can be implemented with the help of various structures. The structure of the OS depends mainly on how the various common components of the operating system are interconnected and melded into the kernel. Depending on this we have following structures of the operating system:

Simple structure:

Such operating systems do not have well defined structure and are small, simple and limited systems. The interfaces and levels of functionality are not well separated. MS-DOS is an example of such operating system. In MS-DOS application programs are able to access the basic I/O routines. These types of operating system cause the entire system to crash if one of the user programs fails. Diagram of the structure of MS-DOS is shown below.

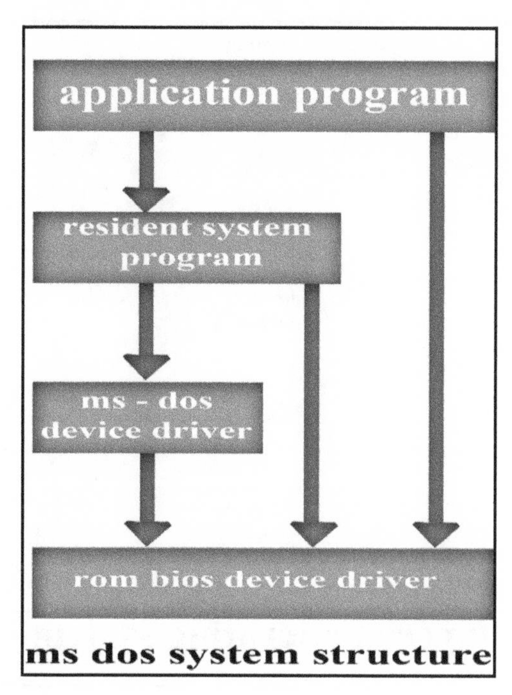

ms dos system structure

Layered structure:

An OS can be broken into pieces and retain much more control on system. In this structure the OS is broken into number of layers (levels). The bottom layer (layer 0) is the hardware and the topmost layer (layer N) is the user interface. These layers are so designed that each layer uses the functions of the lower level layers only. This simplifies the debugging process as if lower level layers are debugged and an error occurs during debugging then the error must be on that layer only as the lower level layers have already been debugged.

The main disadvantage of this structure is that at each layer, the data needs to be modified and passed on which adds overhead to the system. Moreover careful planning of the layers is necessary as a layer can use only lower level layers. UNIX is an example of this structure.

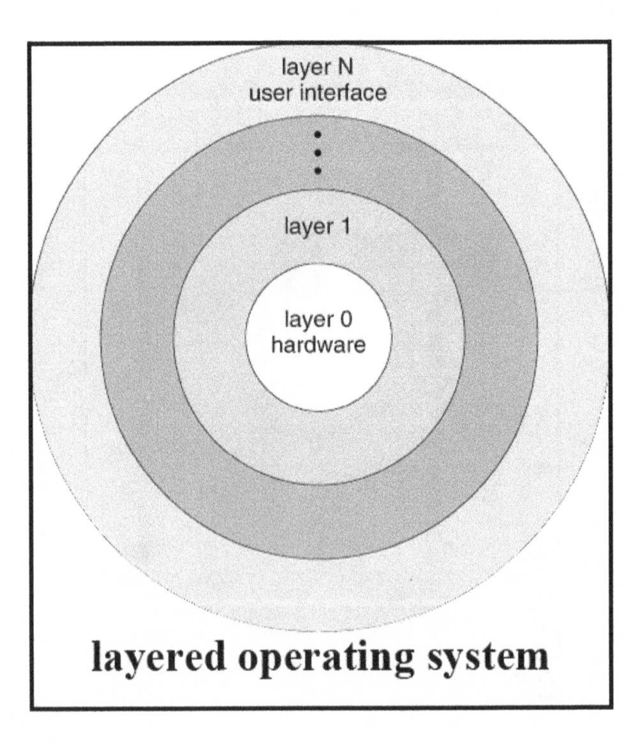

Micro-kernel:

This structure designs the operating system by removing all non-essential components from the kernel and implementing them as system and user programs. This result in a smaller kernel called the micro-kernel. Advantages of this structure are that all new services need to be added to user space and does not require the kernel to be modified. Thus it is more secure and reliable as if a service fails then rest of the operating system remains untouched. Mac OS is an example of this type of OS.

Modular structure or approach:

It is considered as the best approach for an OS. It involves designing of a modular kernel. The kernel has only set of core components and other services are added as dynamically loadable modules to the kernel either during run time or boot time. It resembles layered structure due to the fact that each kernel has defined and protected interfaces but it is more flexible than the layered structure as a module can call any other module.

For example Solaris OS is organized as shown in the figure.

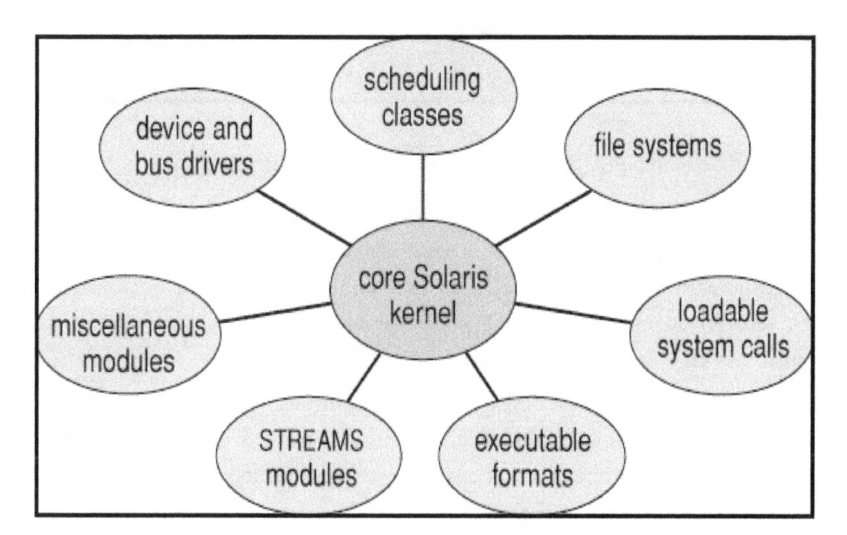

System Calls

System calls provide a means for user or application programs to call upon the services of the operating system. Generally written in C or C++, although some are written in assembly for optimal performance. Figure illustrates the sequence of system calls required to copy a file:

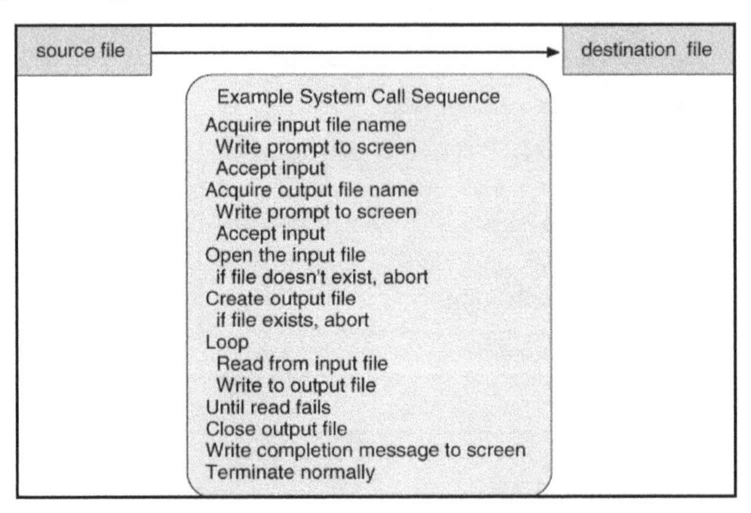

Figure - Example of how system calls are used.

You can use "***strace***" to see more examples of the large number of system calls invoked by a single simple command. Read the man page for strace, and try some simple examples. (strace ***mkdir*** temp, strace ***cd*** temp, strace date > ***t.t***, strace cp t.t t.2, etc.)Most programmers do not use the low-level system calls directly, but instead use an "Application Programming Interface", API.

The use of APIs instead of direct system calls provides for greater program portability between different systems. The API then makes the appropriate system calls through the system call interface, using a table lookup to access specific numbered system calls, as shown in Figure

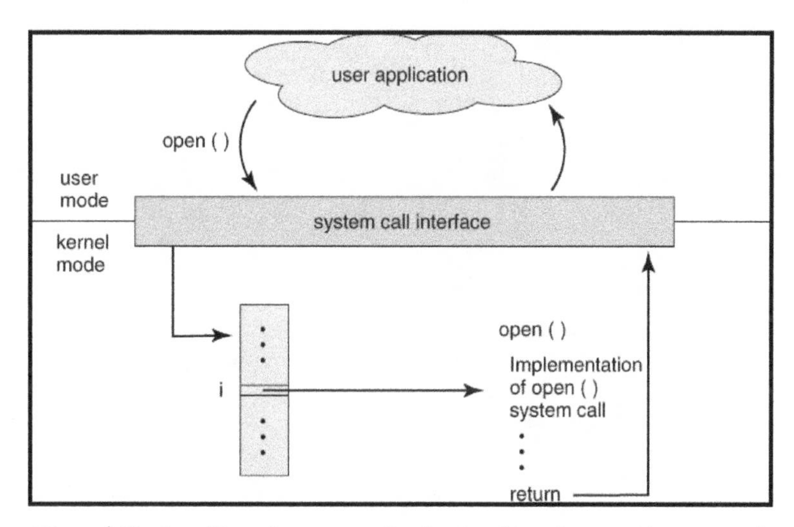

Figure - The handling of a user application invoking the open( ) system call

Parameters are generally passed to system calls via registers, or less commonly, by values pushed onto the stack. Large blocks of data are generally accessed indirectly, through a memory address passed in a register or on the stack, as shown in Figure .

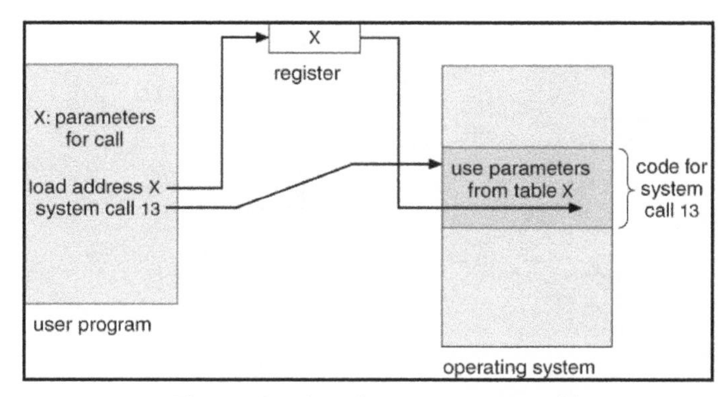

Figure - Passing of parameters as a table

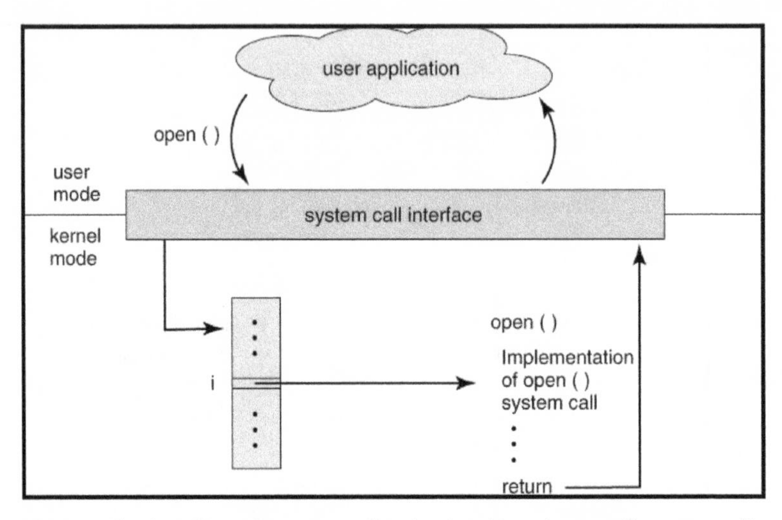

Figure - The handling of a user application invoking the open( ) system call .

Parameters are generally passed to system calls via registers, or less commonly, by values pushed onto the stack. Large blocks of data are generally accessed indirectly, through a memory address passed in a register or on the stack, as shown in Figure .

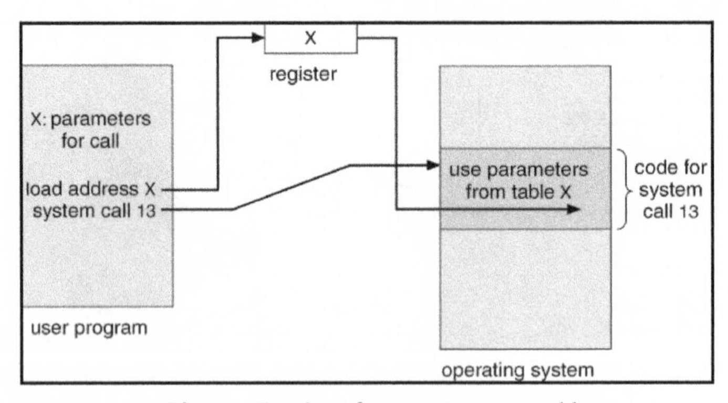

Figure - Passing of parameters as a table

Types of System Calls

- Process control
- File management
- Device management
- Information maintenance
- Communications
- Protection

Process Control

A running program needs to be able to halt its execution either normally (end) or abnormally (abort). If a system call is made to terminate the currently running program abnormally, or if the program runs into a problem and causes an error trap, a dump of memory is sometimes taken and an error message generated. The dump is written to disk and may be examined by a debugger—a system program designed to aid the programmer in finding and correcting bugs—to determine the cause of the problem. Under either normal or abnormal circumstances, the operating system must transfer control to the invoking command interpreter. The command interpreter then reads the next command. In an interactive system, the command interpreter simply continues with the next command; it is assumed that the user will issue an appropriate command to respond to any error.

File Management

We first need to be able to create and delete files. Either system call requires the name of the file and perhaps some of the file's attributes. Once the file is created, we need to open it and to use it. We may also read, write, or reposition (rewinding or skipping to the end of the file, for example). Finally, we need to close the file, indicating that we are no longer using it. We may need these same sets of operations for directories if we have a directory structure for organizing files in the file system. In addition, for either files or directories, we need to be able to determine the values of various attributes and perhaps to reset them if necessary. File attributes include the file name, a file type, protection codes, accounting information, and so on .

At least two system calls, get file attribute and set file attribute, are required for this function. Some operating systems provide many more calls, such as calls for file move and copy.

Device Management

A process may need several resources to execute—main memory, disk drives, access to files, and so on. If the resources are available, they can be granted, and control can be returned to the user process. Otherwise, the process will have to wait until sufficient resources are available. The various resources controlled by the operating system can be thought of as devices. Some of these devices are physical devices (for example, tapes), while others can be thought of as abstract or virtual devices (for example, files). If there are multiple users of the system, the system may require us to first request the device, to ensure exclusive use of it. After we are finished with the device, we release it. These functions are similar to the open and close system calls for files.

Information Maintenance

Many system calls exist simply for the purpose of transferring information between the user program and the operating system. For example, most systems have a system call to return the current t I m e and date . Other system calls may return information about the system, such as the number of current users, the version number of the operating system, the amount of free memory or disk space, and so on. In addition, the operating system keeps information about all its processes, and system calls are used to access this information. Generally, calls are also used to reset the process information (get process attributes and set process attributes) .

Communication

There are two common models of inter process communication: the message passing model and the shared-memory model. In the message-passing model, the communicating processes exchange messages with one another to transfer information. Messages can be exchanged between the processes either directly or indirectly through a common mailbox.

Before communication can take place, a connection must be opened. The name of the other communicator must be known, be it another process on the same system or a process on another computer connected by a communications network. Each computer in a network has a host name by which it is commonly known. A host also has a network identifier, such as an IP address. Similarly, each process has a process name, and this name is translated into an identifier by which the operating system can refer to the process. The get host id and get processed system calls do this translation. The identifiers are then passed to the general purpose open and close calls provided by the file system or to specific open connection and close connection system calls, depending on the system's model of communication.

In the shared-memory model, processes use shared memory creates and shared memory attaches system calls to create and gain access to regions of memory owned by other processes. Recall that, normally, the operating system tries to prevent one process from accessing another process's memory. Shared memory requires that two or more processes agree to remove this restriction. They can then exchange information by reading and writing data in the shared areas. The form of the data and the location are determined by the processes and are not under the operating system's control. The processes are also responsible for ensuring that they are not writing to the same location simultaneously.

System Programs

At the lowest level is hardware. Next are the operating system, then the system programs, and finally the application programs. System programs provide a convenient environment for program development and execution. Some of them are simply user interfaces to system calls; others are considerably more complex. They can be divided into these categories:

File management. These programs create, delete, copy, rename, print, dump, list, and generally manipulate files and directories.

Status information. Some programs simply ask the system for the date, time, amount of available memory or disk space, number of users, or similar status information. Others are more complex, providing detailed -

-performance, logging, and debugging information. Typically, these programs format and print the output to the terminal or other output devices or files or display it in a window of the GUI. Some systems also support a registry, which is used to store and retrieve configuration information .

File modification. Several text editors may be available to create and modify the content of files stored on disk or other storage devices. There may also be special commands to search contents of files or perform transformations of the text.

Programming-language support. Compilers, assemblers, debuggers and interpreters for common programming languages (such as C, C++, Java, Visual Basic, and PERL) are often provided to the user with the operating system.

Program loading and execution. Once a program is assembled or compiled, it must be loaded into memory to be executed. The system may provide absolute loaders, relocatable loaders, linkage editors, and overlay loaders. Debugging systems for either higher-level languages or machine language are needed as well.

Communications. These programs provide the mechanism for creating virtual connections among processes, users, and computer systems. They allow users to send messages to one another's screens, to browse web pages, to send electronic-mail messages, to log in remotely, or to transfer files from one machine to another.

In addition to systems programs, most In addition to systems programs, most operating systems are supplied with programs that are useful in solving common problems or performing common operations. Such programs include web browsers, word processors and text formatters, spreadsheets, database systems, compilers, plotting and statistical-analysis packages, and games. These programs are known as system utilities or application programs.

Protection

Protection provides mechanisms for controlling which users / processes have access to which system resources.

- System calls allow the access mechanisms to be adjusted as needed, and for non-privileged users to be granted elevated access permissions under carefully controlled temporary circumstances.
- Once only of concern on multi-user systems, protection is now important on all systems, in the age of ubiquitous network connectivity.

Operating-System Generation

OSes may be designed and built for a specific HW configuration at a specific site, but more commonly they are designed with a number of variable parameters and components, which are then configured for a particular operating environment.

Systems sometimes need to be re-configured after the initial installation, to add additional resources, capabilities, or to tune performance, logging, or security.

Information that is needed to configure an OS include:

- What CPU(s) are installed on the system, and what optional characteristics does each have?
- How much RAM is installed? (This may be determined automatically, either at install or boot time.)
- What devices are present? The OS needs to determine which device drivers to include, as well as some device-specific characteristics and parameters.
- What OS options are desired, and what values to set for particular OS parameters. The latter may include the size of the open file table, the number of buffers to use, process scheduling (priority) parameters, disk scheduling algorithms, number of slots in the process table, etc.

At one extreme the OS source code can be edited, re-compiled, and linked into a new kernel. More commonly configuration tables determine which modules to link into the new kernel, and what values to set for some key important parameters. This approach may require the configuration of complicated make files, which can be done either automatically or through interactive configuration programs; Then make is used to actually generate the new kernel specified by the new parameters.

At the other extreme a system configuration may be entirely defined by table data, in which case the "rebuilding" of the system merely requires editing data tables. Once a system has been regenerated, it is usually required to reboot the system to activate the new kernel. Because there are possibilities for errors, most systems provide some mechanism for booting to older or alternate kernels.

Protection and Security

Protection is any mechanism for controlling the access of processes or users to the resources defined by a computer system. This mechanism must provide means for specification of the controls to be imposed and means for enforcement. Protection can improve reliability by detecting latent errors at the interfaces between component subsystems. Early detection of interface errors can often prevent contamination of a healthy subsystem by another subsystem that is malfunctioning. An unprotected resource cannot defend against use (or misuse) by an unauthorized or incompetent user. A protection-oriented system provides a means to distinguish between authorized and unauthorized usage, A system can have adequate protection but still be prone to failure and allow inappropriate access.

It is the job of s**ecurity** to defend a system from external and internal attacks. Such attacks spread across a huge range and include viruses and worms, denial-of service attacks Protection and security require the system to be able to distinguish among all its users. Most operating systems maintain a list of user names and associated user identifiers (user IDs).

- User ID then associated with all files, processes of that user to determine access control
- Group identifier (group ID) allows set of users to be defined and controls managed, then also associated with each process, file Privilege escalation allows user to change to effective ID with more rights

Operating System - Security

Security refers to providing a protection system to computer system resources such as CPU, memory, disk, software programs and most importantly data/information stored in the computer system. If a computer program is run by an unauthorized user, then he/she may cause severe damage to computer or data stored in it. So a computer system must be protected against unauthorized access, malicious access to system memory, viruses, worms etc. We're going to discuss following :

- Authentication
- One Time passwords
- Program Threats
- System Threats
- Computer Security Classifications

Authentication

Authentication refers to identifying each user of the system and associating the executing programs with those users. It is the responsibility of the Operating System to create a protection system which ensures that a user who is running a particular program is authentic. Operating Systems generally identifies/authenticates users using following three ways –

Username / Password – User need to enter a registered username and password with Operating system to login into the system.

User card/key – User need to punch card in card slot, or enter key generated by key generator in option provided by operating system to login into the system.

User attribute - fingerprint/ eye retina pattern/ signature – User need to pass his/her attribute via designated input device used by operating system to login into the system.

One Time passwords

One-time passwords provide additional security along with normal authentication. In One-Time Password system, a unique password is required every time user tries to login into the system. Once a one-time password is used, then it cannot be used again. One-time password are implemented in various ways.

Random numbers – Users are provided cards having numbers printed along with corresponding alphabets. System asks for numbers corresponding to few alphabets randomly chosen.

Secret key – User are provided a hardware device which can create a secret id mapped with user id. System asks for such secret id which is to be generated every time prior to login.

Network password – Some commercial applications send one-time passwords to user on registered mobile/ email which is required to be entered prior to login.

Program Threats

Operating system's processes and kernel do the designated task as instructed. If a user program made these process do malicious tasks, then it is known as Program Threats. One of the common example of program threat is a program installed in a computer which can store and send user credentials via network to some hacker. Following is the list of some well-known program threats.

Trojan Horse – Such program traps user login credentials and stores them to send to malicious user who can later on login to computer and can access system resources.

Trap Door – If a program which is designed to work as required, have a security hole in its code and perform illegal action without knowledge of user then it is called to have a trap door.

Logic Bomb – Logic bomb is a situation when a program misbehaves only when certain conditions met otherwise it works as a genuine program. It is harder to detect.

Virus – Virus as name suggest can replicate themselves on computer system. They are highly dangerous and can modify/delete user files, crash systems. A virus is generally a small code embedded in a program. As user accesses the program, the virus starts getting embedded in other files/ programs and can make system unusable for user

System Threats

System threats refers to misuse of system services and network connections to put user in trouble. System threats can be used to launch program threats on a complete network called as program attack. System threats creates such an environment that operating system resources/ user files are misused. Following is the list of some well-known system threats.

Worm – Worm is a process which can choked down a system performance by using system resources to extreme levels. A Worm process generates its multiple copies where each copy uses system resources, prevents all other processes to get required resources. Worms processes can even shut down an entire network.

Port Scanning – Port scanning is a mechanism or means by which a hacker can detects system vulnerabilities to make an attack on the system.

Denial of Service – Denial of service attacks normally prevents user to make legitimate use of the system. For example, a user may not be able to use internet if denial of service attacks browser's content settings.

Computer Security Classifications

As per the U.S. Department of Defense Trusted Computer System's Evaluation Criteria there are four security classifications in computer systems: A, B, C, and D. This is widely used specifications to determine and model the security of systems and of security solutions. Following is the brief description of each classification.

Classification Type & Description

- **Type A**

  Highest Level. Uses formal design specifications and verification techniques. Grants a high degree of assurance of process security.

- **Type B**

  Provides mandatory protection system. Have all the properties of a class C2 system. Attaches a sensitivity label to each object. It is of three types.

  1. **B1** – Maintains the security label of each object in the system. Label is used for making decisions to access control.
  2. **B2** – Extends the sensitivity labels to each system resource, such as storage objects, supports covert channels and auditing of events.
  3. **B3** – Allows creating lists or user groups for access-control to grant access or revoke access to a given named object.

- **Type C**

  Provides protection and user accountability using audit capabilities. It is of two types.

  1. **C1** – Incorporates controls so that users can protect their private information and keep other users from accidentally reading / deleting their data. UNIX versions are mostly Cl class.
  2. **C2** – Adds an individual-level access control to the capabilities of a Cl level system.

- **Type D**

  Lowest level. Minimum protection. MS-DOS, Window 3.1 fall in this category.

Memory Management:

Background

Obviously memory accesses and memory management are a very important part of modern computer operation. Every instruction has to be fetched from memory before it can be executed, and most instructions involve retrieving data from memory or storing data in memory or both.

The advent of multi-tasking OSes compounds the complexity of memory management, because because as processes are swapped in and out of the CPU, so must their code and data be swapped in and out of memory, all at high speeds and without interfering with any other processes.

Shared memory, virtual memory, the classification of memory as read-only versus read-write, and concepts like copy-on-write forking all further complicate the issue.

Basic Hardware

It should be noted that from the memory chips point of view, all memory accesses are equivalent. The memory hardware doesn't know what a particular part of memory is being used for, nor does it care. This is almost true of the OS as well, although not entirely.

The CPU can only access its registers and main memory. It cannot, for example, make direct access to the hard drive, so any data stored there must first be transferred into the main memory chips before the CPU can work with it. (Device drivers communicate with their hardware via interrupts and "memory" accesses, sending short instructions for example to transfer data from the hard drive to a specified location in main memory. The disk controller monitors the bus for such instructions, transfers the data, and then notifies the CPU that the data is there with another interrupt, but the CPU never gets direct access to the disk.).

Memory accesses to registers are very fast, generally one clock tick, and a CPU may be able to execute more than one machine instruction per clock tick. Memory accesses to main memory are comparatively slow, and may take a number of clock ticks to complete. This would require intolerable waiting by the CPU if it were not for an intermediary fast memory cache built into most modern CPUs.

The basic idea of the cache is to transfer chunks of memory at a time from the main memory to the cache, and then to access individual memory locations one at a time from the cache.

User processes must be restricted so that they only access memory locations that "belong" to that particular process. This is usually implemented using a base register and a limit register for each process, as shown in Figures and below. Every memory access made by a user process is checked against these two registers, and if a memory access is attempted outside the valid range, then a fatal error is generated. The OS obviously has access to all existing memory locations, as this is necessary to swap users' code and data in and out of memory. It should also be obvious that changing the contents of the base and limit registers is a privileged activity, allowed only to the OS kernel.

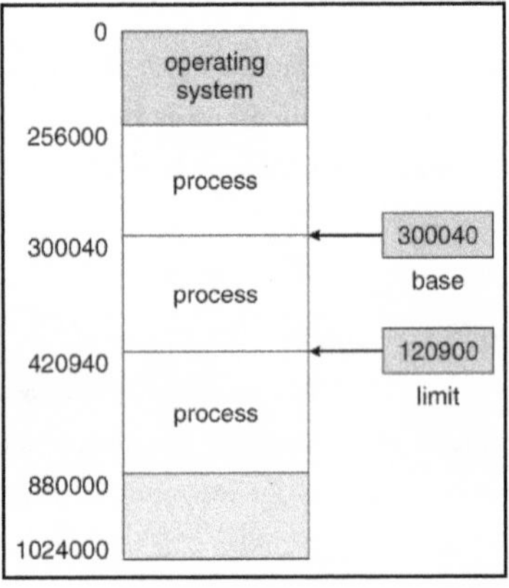

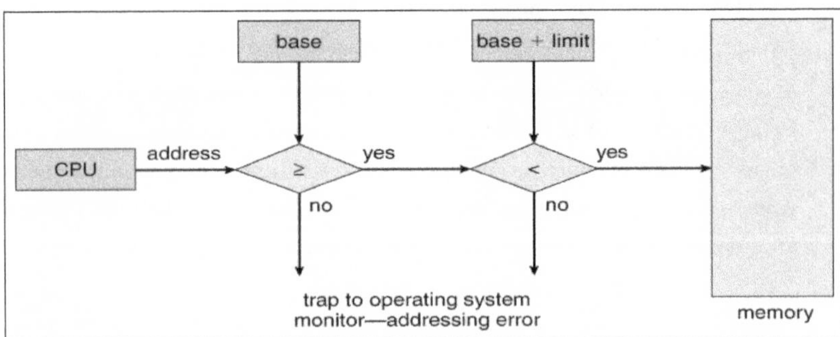

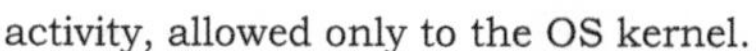

The basic idea of the cache is to transfer chunks of memory at a time from the main memory to the cache, and then to access individual memory locations one at a time from the cache.

User processes must be restricted so that they only access memory locations that "belong" to that particular process. This is usually implemented using a base register and a limit register for each process, as shown in Figures and below. Every memory access made by a user process is checked against these two registers, and if a memory access is attempted outside the valid range, then a fatal error is generated. The OS obviously has access to all existing memory locations, as this is necessary to swap users' code and data in and out of memory. It should also be obvious that changing the contents of the base and limit registers is a privileged activity, allowed only to the OS kernel.

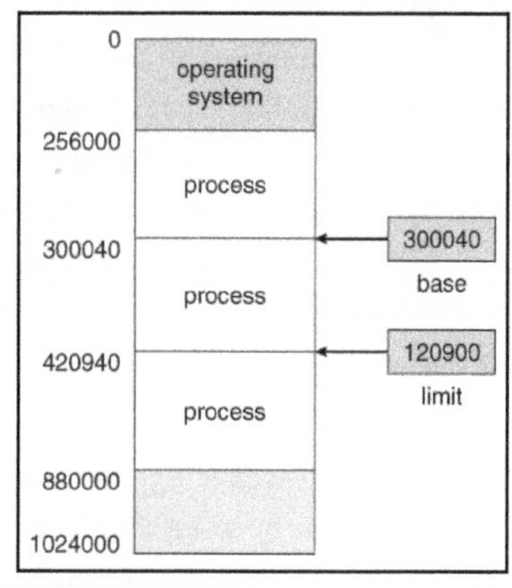

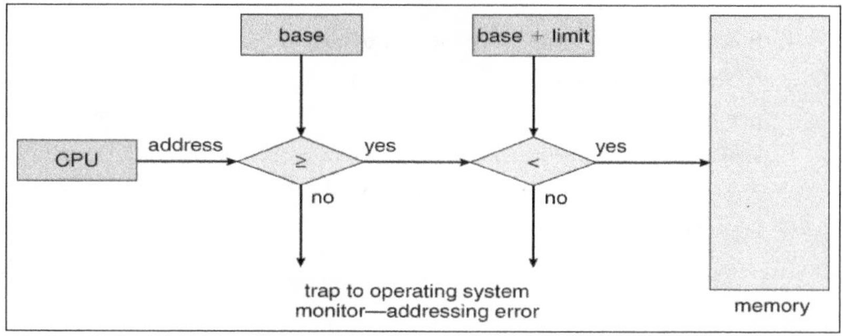

Swapping

A process must be loaded into memory in order to execute. If there is not enough memory available to keep all running processes in memory at the same time, then some processes who are not currently using the CPU may have their memory swapped out to a fast local disk called the backing store.

Standard Swapping

- If compile-time or load-time address binding is used, then processes must be swapped back into the same memory location from which they were swapped out. If execution time binding is used, then the processes can be swapped back into any available location.
- Swapping is a very slow process compared to other operations. For example, if a user process occupied 10 MB and the transfer rate for the backing store were 40 MB per second, then it would take 1/4 second (250 milliseconds) just to do the data transfer. Adding in a latency lag of 8 milliseconds and ignoring head seek time for the moment, and further recognizing that swapping involves moving old data out as well as new data in, the overall transfer time required for this swap is 512 milliseconds, or over half a second. For efficient processor scheduling the CPU time slice should be significantly longer than this lost transfer time.
- To reduce swapping transfer overhead, it is desired to transfer as little information as possible, which requires that the system know how much memory a process is using, as opposed to how much it might use. Programmers can help with this by freeing up dynamic memory that they are no longer using.
- It is important to swap processes out of memory only when they are idle, or more to the point, only when there are no pending I/O operations. (Otherwise the pending I/O operation could write into the wrong process's memory space.) The solution is to either swap only totally idle processes, or do I/O operations only into and out of OS buffers, which are then transferred to or from process's main memory as a second step.

- Most modern OSes no longer use swapping, because it is too slow and there are faster alternatives available. (e.g. Paging.) However some UNIX systems will still invoke swapping if the system gets extremely full, and then discontinue swapping when the load reduces again. Windows 3.1 would use a modified version of swapping that was somewhat controlled by the user, swapping process's out if necessary and then only swapping them back in when the user focused on that particular window.

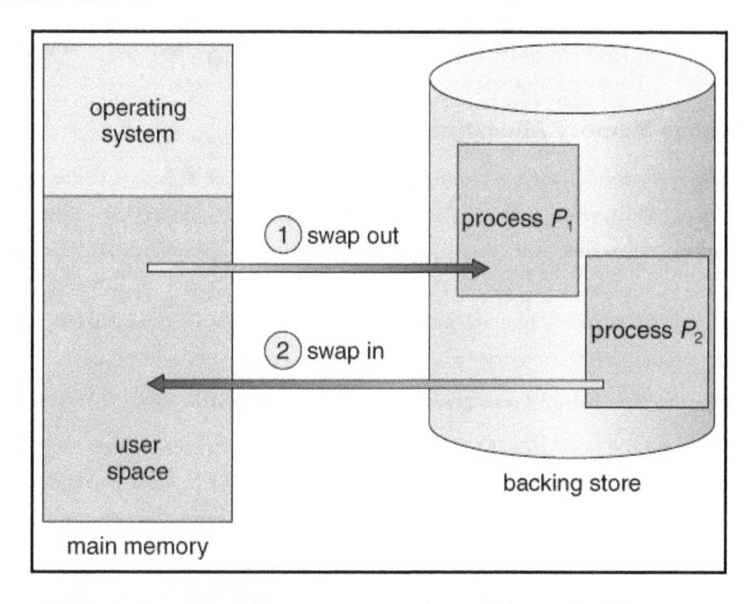

Figure - Swapping of two processes using a disk as a backing store.

Swapping on Mobile Systems

Swapping is typically not supported on mobile platforms, for several reasons:

- Mobile devices typically use flash memory in place of more spacious hard drives for persistent storage, so there is not as much space available.
- Flash memory can only be written to a limited number of times before it becomes unreliable.

- The bandwidth to flash memory is also lower.

Apple's IOS asks applications to voluntarily free up memory

- Read-only data, e.g. code, is simply removed, and reloaded later if needed.
- Modified data, e.g. the stack, is never removed, but . . .
- Apps that fail to free up sufficient memory can be removed by the OS

Android follows a similar strategy.

- Prior to terminating a process, Android writes its application state to flash memory for quick restarting.

Contiguous Memory Allocation

One approach to memory management is to load each process into a contiguous space. The operating system is allocated space first, usually at either low or high memory locations, and then the remaining available memory is allocated to processes as needed. (The OS is usually loaded low, because that is where the interrupt vectors are located, but on older systems part of the OS was loaded high to make more room in low memory (within the 640K barrier) for user processes.)

Memory Protection (was Memory Mapping and Protection)

The system shown in Figure below allows protection against user programs accessing areas that they should not, allows programs to be relocated to different memory starting addresses as needed, and allows the memory space devoted to the OS to grow or shrink dynamically as needs change.

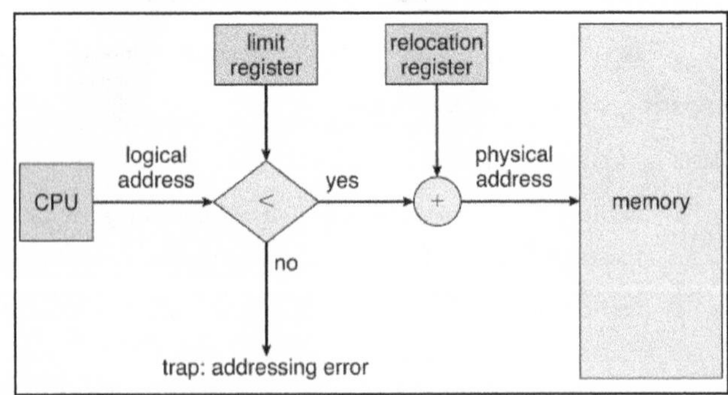

Memory Allocation

One method of allocating contiguous memory is to divide all available memory into equal sized partitions, and to assign each process to their own partition. This restricts both the number of simultaneous processes and the maximum size of each process, and is no longer used.

An alternate approach is to keep a list of unused (free) memory blocks (holes), and to find a hole of a suitable size whenever a process needs to be loaded into memory. There are many different strategies for finding the "best" allocation of memory to processes, including the three most commonly discussed:

1. **First fit** - Search the list of holes until one is found that is big enough to satisfy the request, and assign a portion of that hole to that process. Whatever fraction of the hole not needed by the request is left on the free list as a smaller hole. Subsequent requests may start looking either from the beginning of the list or from the point at which this search ended.
2. **Best fit** - Allocate the smallest hole that is big enough to satisfy the request. This saves large holes for other process requests that may need them later, but the resulting unused portions of holes may be too small to be of any use, and will therefore be wasted. Keeping the free list sorted can speed up the process of finding the right hole.
3. **Worst fit** - Allocate the largest hole available, thereby increasing the likelihood that the remaining portion will be usable for satisfying future requests.

Simulations show that either first or best fit are better than worst fit in terms of both time and storage utilization. First and best fits are about equal in terms of storage utilization, but first fit is faster.

Fragmentation

All the memory allocation strategies suffer from **external fragmentation**, though first and best fits experience the problems more so than worst fit.

External fragmentation means that the available memory is broken up into lots of little pieces, none of which is big enough to satisfy the next memory requirement, although the sum total could.

The amount of memory lost to fragmentation may vary with algorithm, usage patterns, and some design decisions such as which end of a hole to allocate and which end to save on the free list.

Statistical analysis of first fit, for example, shows that for N blocks of allocated memory, another 0.5 N will be lost to fragmentation.

Internal fragmentation also occurs, with all memory allocation strategies. This is caused by the fact that memory is allocated in blocks of a fixed size, whereas the actual memory needed will rarely be that exact size. For a random distribution of memory requests, on the average 1/2 block will be wasted per memory request, because on the average the last allocated block will be only half full.

- Note that the same effect happens with hard drives, and that modern hardware gives us increasingly larger drives and memory at the expense of ever larger block sizes, which translates to more memory lost to internal fragmentation.
- Some systems use variable size blocks to minimize losses due to internal fragmentation.

If the programs in memory are relocatable, (using execution-time address binding), then the external fragmentation problem can be reduced via compaction, i.e. moving all processes down to one end of physical memory. This only involves updating the relocation register for each process, as all internal work is done using logical addresses.

Another solution as we will see in upcoming sections is to allow processes to use non-contiguous blocks of physical memory, with a separate relocation register for each block.

Segmentation

Basic Method

Most users (programmers) do not think of their programs as existing in one continuous linear address space. Rather they tend to think of their memory in multiple segments, each dedicated to a particular use, such as code, data, the stack, the heap, etc.

Memory segmentation supports this view by providing addresses with a segment number (mapped to a segment base address) and an offset from the beginning of that segment. For example, a C compiler might generate 5 segments for the user code, library code, global (static) variables, the stack, and the heap, as shown in Figure :

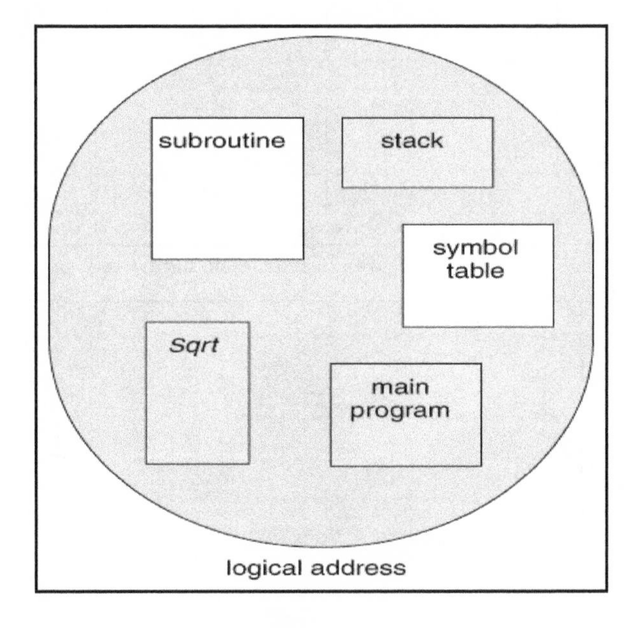

Figure: Programmer's view of a program.

Segmentation Hardware

A segment table maps segment-offset addresses to physical addresses, and simultaneously checks for invalid addresses, using a system similar to the page tables and relocation base registers discussed previously. (Note that at this point in the discussion of segmentation, each segment is kept in contiguous memory and may be of different sizes, but that segmentation can also be combined with paging as we shall see shortly.).

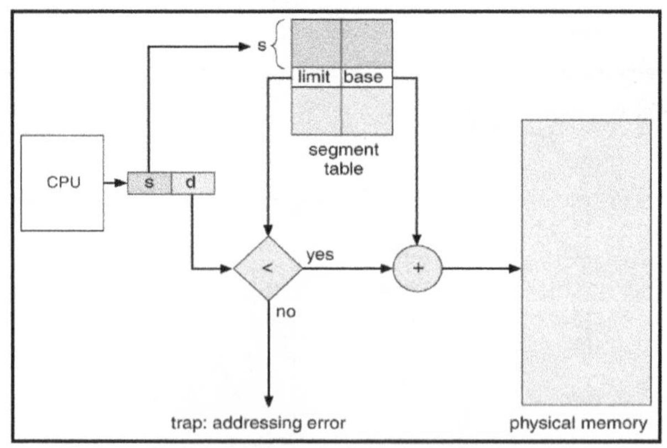

Figure : Segmentation hardware

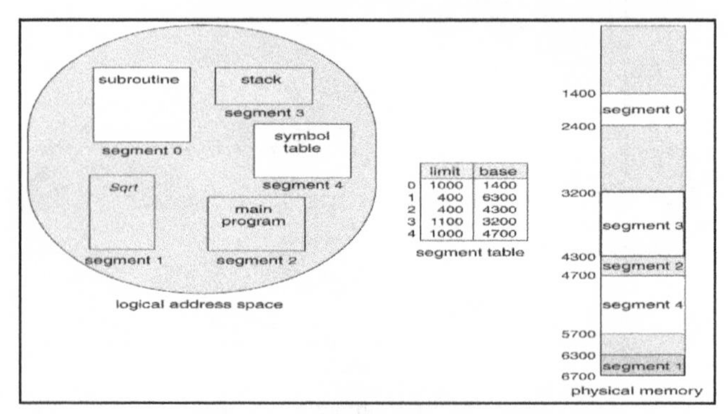

Figure - Example of segmentation

Paging

Paging is a memory management scheme that allows processes physical memory to be discontinuous, and which eliminates problems with fragmentation by allocating memory in equal sized blocks known as pages. Paging eliminates most of the problems of the other methods discussed previously, and is the predominant memory management technique used today.

Basic Method

The basic idea behind paging is to divide physical memory into a number of equal sized blocks called frames, and to divide a programs logical memory space into blocks of the same size called pages. Any page (from any process) can be placed into any available frame. The page table is used to look up what frame a particular page is stored in at the moment. In the following example, for instance, page 2 of the program's logical memory is currently stored in frame 3 of physical memory:

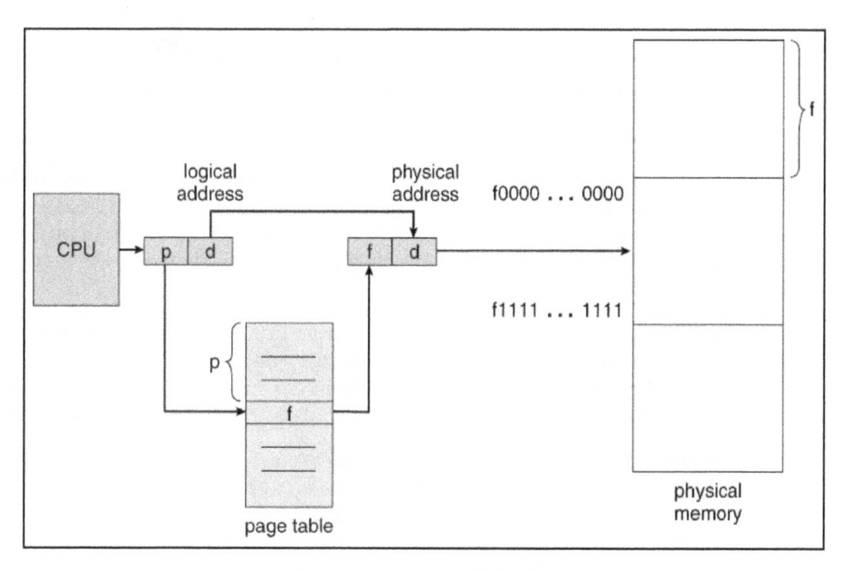

Figure - Paging hardware

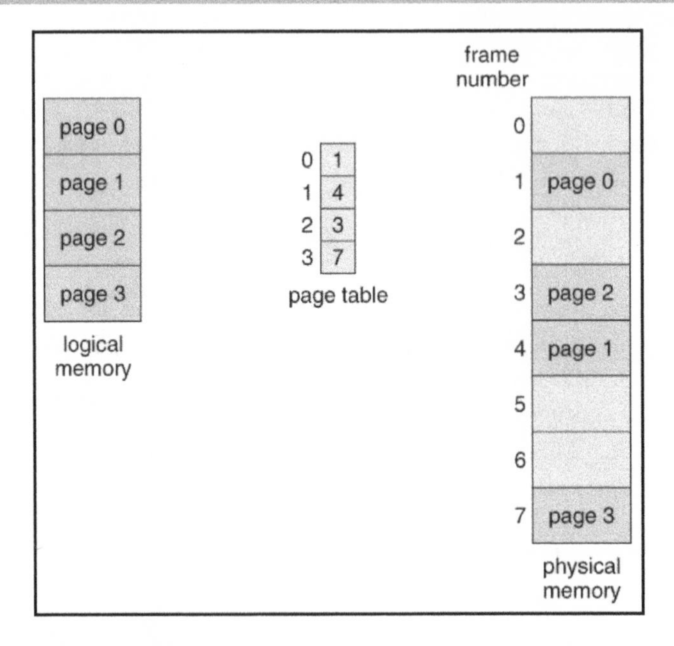

Figure - Paging model of logical and physical memory.

A logical address consists of two parts: A page number in which the address resides, and an offset from the beginning of that page. (The number of bits in the page number limits how many pages a single process can address. The number of bits in the offset determines the maximum size of each page, and should correspond to the system frame size.)

The page table maps the page number to a frame number, to yield a physical address which also has two parts: The frame number and the offset within that frame. The number of bits in the frame number determines how many frames the system can address, and the number of bits in the offset determines the size of each frame.

Page numbers, frame numbers, and frame sizes are determined by the architecture, but are typically powers of two, allowing addresses to be split at a certain number of bits. For example, if the logical address size is 2^m and the page size is 2^n, then the high-order m-n bits of a logical address designate the page number and the remaining n bits represent the offset.

Note also that the number of bits in the page number and the number of bits in the frame number do not have to be identical. The former determines the address range of the logical address space, and the latter relates to the physical address space.

page number	page offset
p	d
$m - n$	n

(DOS used to use an addressing scheme with 16 bit frame numbers and 16-bit offsets, on hardware that only supported 24-bit hardware addresses. The result was a resolution of starting frame addresses finer than the size of a single frame, and multiple frame-offset combinations that mapped to the same physical hardware address.). Consider the following micro example, in which a process has 16 bytes of logical memory, mapped in 4 byte pages into 32 bytes of physical memory. (Presumably some other processes would be consuming the remaining 16 bytes of physical memory.)

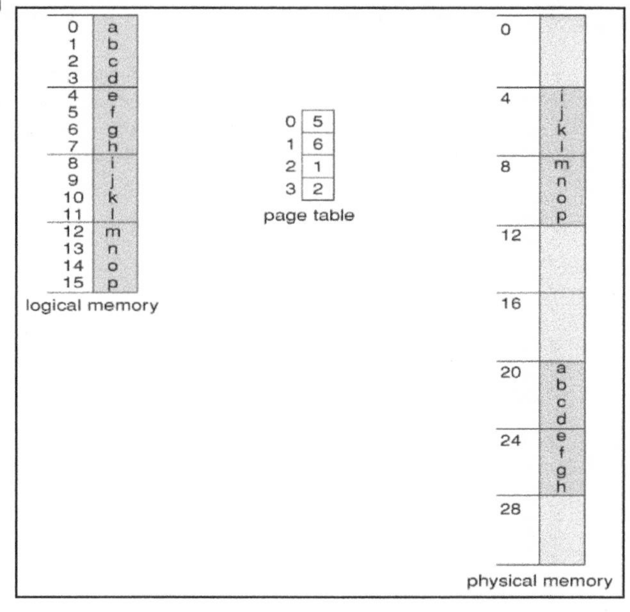

Figure - Paging example for a 32-byte memory with 4-byte pages

Note that paging is like having a table of relocation registers, one for each page of the logical memory. There is no external fragmentation with paging. All blocks of physical memory are used, and there are no gaps in between and no problems with finding the right sized hole for a particular chunk of memory. There is, however, internal fragmentation. Memory is allocated in chunks the size of a page, and on the average, the last page will only be half full, wasting on the average half a page of memory per process. (Possibly more, if processes keep their code and data in separate pages.) Larger page sizes waste more memory, but are more efficient in terms of overhead. Modern trends have been to increase page sizes, and some systems even have multiple size pages to try and make the best of both worlds. Page table entries (frame numbers) are typically 32 bit numbers, allowing access to 2^32 physical page frames. If those frames are 4 KB in size each, that translates to 16 TB of addressable physical memory. (32 + 12 = 44 bits of physical address space.)

When a process requests memory (e.g. when its code is loaded in from disk), free frames are allocated from a free-frame list, and inserted into that process's page table. Processes are blocked from accessing anyone else's memory because all of their memory requests are mapped through their page table. There is no way for them to generate an address that maps into any other process's memory space. The operating system must keep track of each individual process's page table, updating it whenever the process's pages get moved in and out of memory, and applying the correct page table when processing system calls for a particular process. This all increases the overhead involved when swapping processes in and out of the CPU. (The currently active page table must be updated to reflect the process that is currently running.).

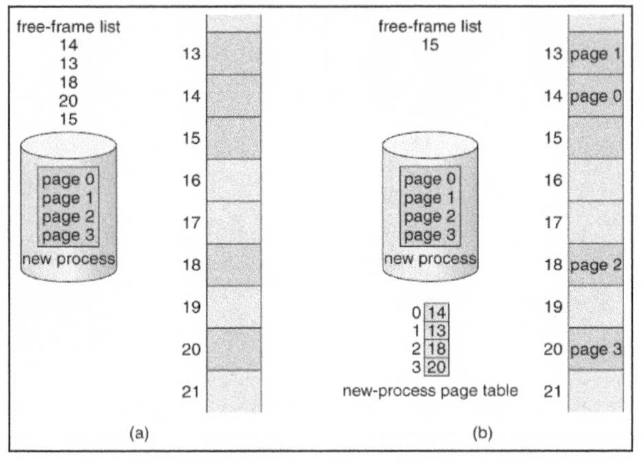

Figure - Free frames (a) before allocation and (b) after allocation .

Hardware Support

Page lookups must be done for every memory reference, and whenever a process gets swapped in or out of the CPU, its page table must be swapped in and out too, along with the instruction registers, etc. It is therefore appropriate to provide hardware support for this operation, in order to make it as fast as possible and to make process switches as fast as possible also. One option is to use a set of registers for the page table. For example, the DEC PDP-11 uses 16-bit addressing and 8 KB pages, resulting in only 8 pages per process. (It takes 13 bits to address 8 KB of offset, leaving only 3 bits to define a page number.) An alternate option is to store the page table in main memory, and to use a single register (called the page-table base register, PTBR) to record where in memory the page table is located. Process switching is fast, because only the single register needs to be changed.

However memory access just got half as fast, because every memory access now requires two memory accesses - One to fetch the frame number from memory and then another one to access the desired memory location. The solution to this problem is to use a very special high-speed memory device called the translation look-aside buffer, TLB. The benefit of the TLB is that it can search an entire table for a key value in parallel, and if it is found anywhere in the table, then the corresponding lookup value is returned.

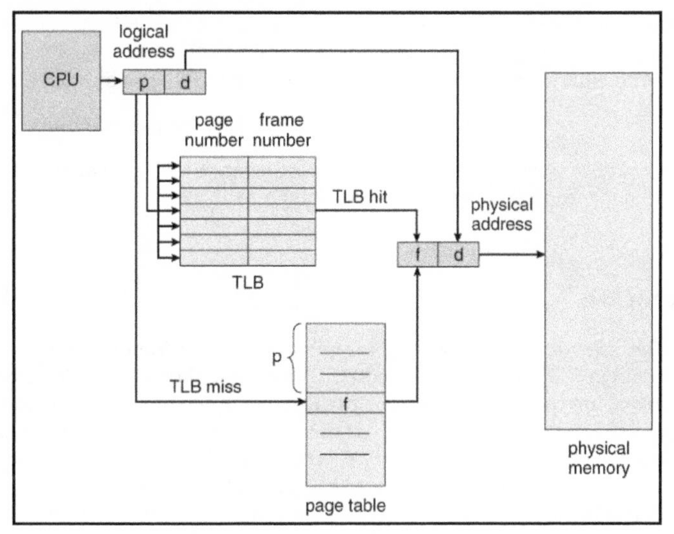

Figure - Paging hardware with TLB

The TLB is very expensive, however, and therefore very small. (Not large enough to hold the entire page table.) It is therefore used as a cache device. Addresses are first checked against the TLB, and if the info is not there (a TLB miss), then the frame is looked up from main memory and the TLB is updated. If the TLB is full, then replacement strategies range from least-recently used, LRU to random. Some TLBs allow some entries to be wired down, which means that they cannot be removed from the TLB. Typically these would be kernel frames.

Some TLBs store address-space identifiers, ASIDs, to keep track of which process "owns" a particular entry in the TLB. This allows entries from multiple processes to be stored simultaneously in the TLB without granting one process access to some other process's memory location. Without this feature the TLB has to be flushed clean with every process switch. The percentage of time that the desired information is found in the TLB is termed the hit ratio. For example, suppose that it takes 100 nanoseconds to access main memory, and only 20 nanoseconds to search the TLB. So a TLB hit takes 120 nanoseconds total (20 to find the frame number and then another 100 to go get the data), and a TLB miss takes 220 (20 to search the TLB, 100 to go get the frame number, and then another 100 to go get the data.) So with an 80% TLB hit ratio, the average memory access time would be:

$$0.80 * 120 + 0.20 * 220 = 140 \text{ nanoseconds}$$

for a 40% slowdown to get the frame number. A 98% hit rate would yield 122 nanoseconds average access time (you should verify this), for a 22% slowdown. The ninth edition ignores the 20 nanoseconds required to search the TLB, yielding

$$0.80 * 100 + 0.20 * 200 = 120 \text{ nanoseconds}$$

for a 20% slowdown to get the frame number. A 99% hit rate would yield 101 nanoseconds average access time (you should verify this), for a 1% slowdown.

Protection

The page table can also help to protect processes from accessing memory that they shouldn't, or their own memory in ways that they shouldn't. A bit or bits can be added to the page table to classify a page as read-write, read-only, read-write-execute, or some combination of these sorts of things. Then each memory reference can be checked to ensure it is accessing the memory in the appropriate mode. Valid / invalid bits can be added to "mask off" entries in the page table that are not in use by the current process, as shown by example in Figure below.

Note that the valid / invalid bits described above cannot block all illegal memory accesses, due to the internal fragmentation. (Areas of memory in the last page that are not entirely filled by the process, and may contain data left over by whoever used that frame last.)

Many processes do not use all of the page table available to them, particularly in modern systems with very large potential page tables. Rather than waste memory by creating a full-size page table for every process, some systems use a page-table length register, PTLR, to specify the length of the page table.

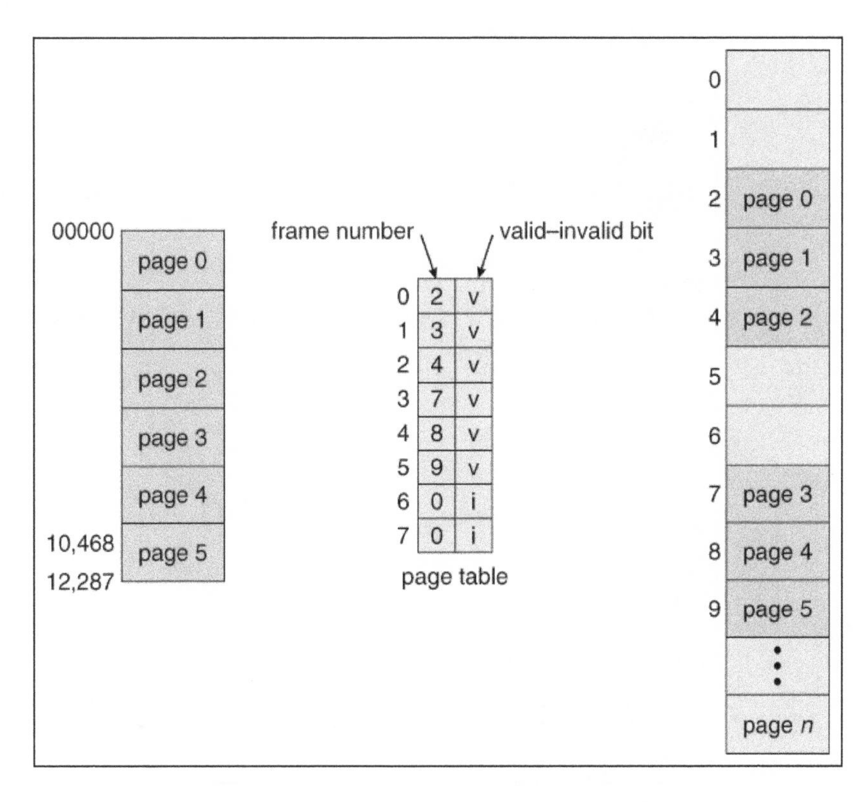

Figure - Valid (v) or invalid (i) bit in page table

Shared Pages

Paging systems can make it very easy to share blocks of memory, by simply duplicating page numbers in multiple page frames. This may be done with either code or data. If code is reentrant, that means that it does not write to or change the code in any way (it is non self-modifying), and it is therefore safe to re-enter it. More importantly, it means the code can be shared by multiple processes, so long as each has their own copy of the data and registers, including the instruction register. In the example given below, three different users are running the editor simultaneously, but the code is only loaded into memory (in the page frames) one time. Some systems also implement shared memory in this fashion.

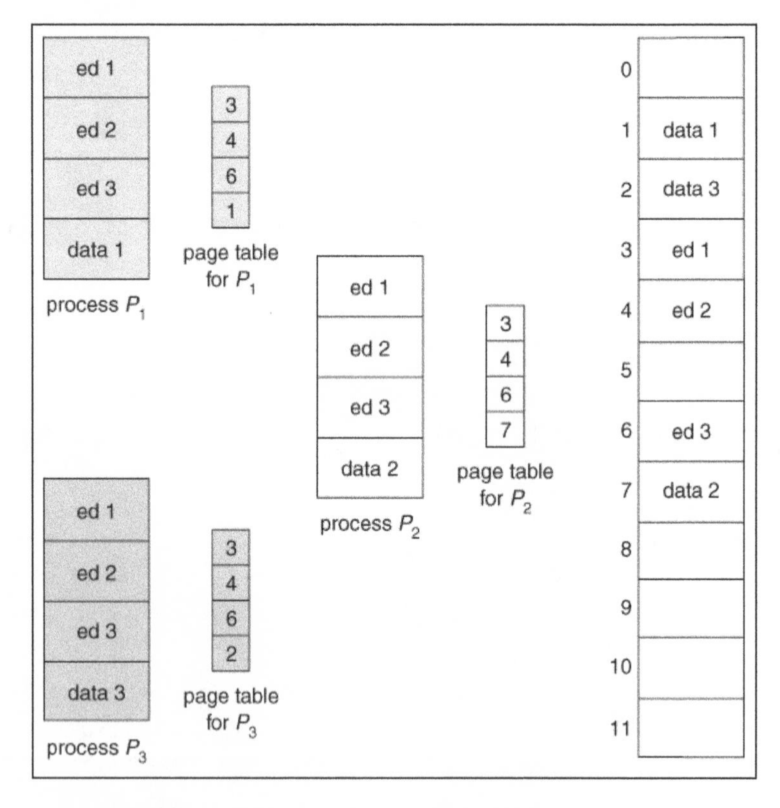

Figure - Sharing of code in a paging environment

Structure of the Page Table

Hierarchical Paging

Most modern computer systems support logical address spaces of 2^32 to 2^64. With a 2^32 address space and 4K (2^12) page sizes, this leave 2^20 entries in the page table. At 4 bytes per entry, this amounts to a 4 MB page table, which is too large to reasonably keep in contiguous memory. (And to swap in and out of memory with each process switch.) Note that with 4K pages, this would take 1024 pages just to hold the page table! One option is to use a two-tier paging system, i.e. to page the page table.

For example, the 20 bits described above could be broken down into two 10-bit page numbers. The first identifies an entry in the outer page table, which identifies where in memory to find one page of an inner page table. The second 10 bits finds a specific entry in that inner page table, which in turn identifies a particular frame in physical memory. (The remaining 12 bits of the 32 bit logical address are the offset within the 4K frame.).

page number		page offset
p_1	p_2	d
10	10	12

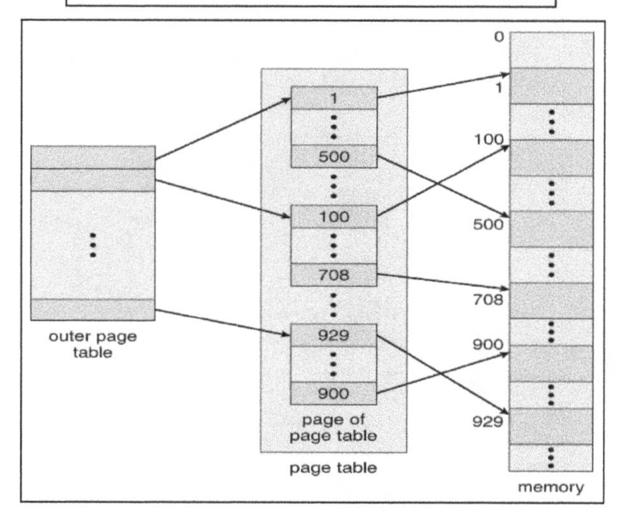

Figure : A two-level page-table scheme

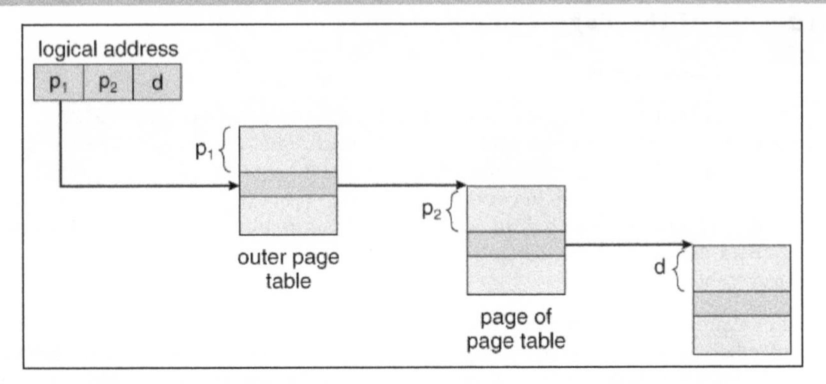

Figure - Address translation for a two-level 32-bit paging architecture .

VAX Architecture divides 32-bit addresses into 4 equal sized sections, and each page is 512 bytes, yielding an address form of:

section	page	offset
s	*p*	*d*
2	21	9

With a 64-bit logical address space and 4K pages, there are 52 bits worth of page numbers, which is still too many even for two-level paging. One could increase the paging level, but with 10-bit page tables it would take 7 levels of indirection, which would be prohibitively slow memory access. So some other approach must be used.

outer page	inner page	offset
p_1	p_2	*d*
42	10	12

64-bits Two-tiered leaves 42 bits in outer table

2nd outer page	outer page	inner page	offset
p_1	p_2	p_3	*d*
32	10	10	12

Going to a fourth level still leaves 32 bits in the outer table.

Virtual Memory

A computer can address more memory than the amount physically installed on the system. This extra memory is actually called virtual memory and it is a section of a hard disk that's set up to emulate the computer's RAM. The main visible advantage of this scheme is that programs can be larger than physical memory. Virtual memory serves two purposes. First, it allows us to extend the use of physical memory by using disk. Second, it allows us to have memory protection, because each virtual address is translated to a physical address.

Following are the situations, when entire program is not required to be loaded fully in main memory.

1. User written error handling routines are used only when an error occurred in the data or computation.
2. Certain options and features of a program may be used rarely.
3. Many tables are assigned a fixed amount of address space even though only a small amount of the table is actually used.
4. The ability to execute a program that is only partially in memory would counter many benefits.
5. Less number of I/O would be needed to load or swap each user program into memory.
6. A program would no longer be constrained by the amount of physical memory that is available.
7. Each user program could take less physical memory, more programs could be run the same time, with a corresponding increase in CPU utilization and throughput.

Modern microprocessors intended for general-purpose use, a memory management unit, or MMU, is built into the hardware. The MMU's job is to translate virtual addresses into physical addresses.

Virtual memory is commonly implemented by demand paging. It can also be implemented in a segmentation system. Demand segmentation can also be used to provide virtual memory.

A basic example is given below –

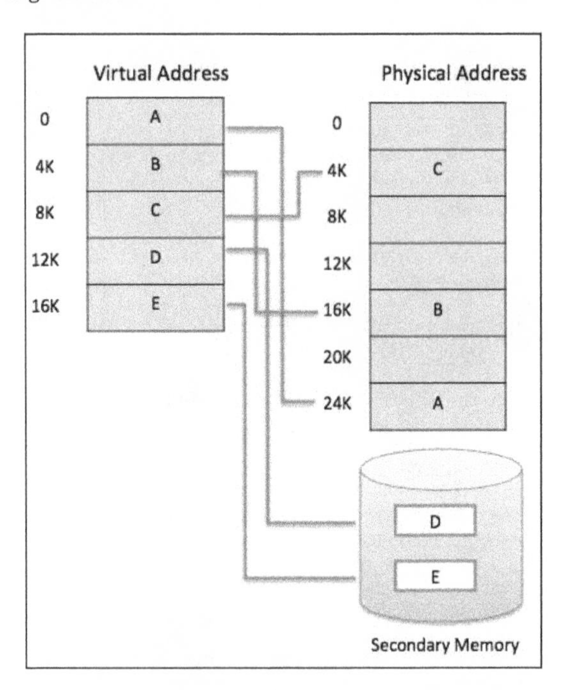

Demand Paging

A demand paging system is quite similar to a paging system with swapping where processes reside in secondary memory and pages are loaded only on demand, not in advance. When a context switch occurs, the operating system does not copy any of the old program's pages out to the disk or any of the new program's pages into the main memory Instead, it just begins executing the new program after loading the first page and fetches that program's pages as they are referenced.

While executing a program, if the program references a page which is not available in the main memory because it was swapped out a little ago, the processor treats this invalid memory reference as a page fault and transfers control from the program to the operating system to demand the page back into the memory.

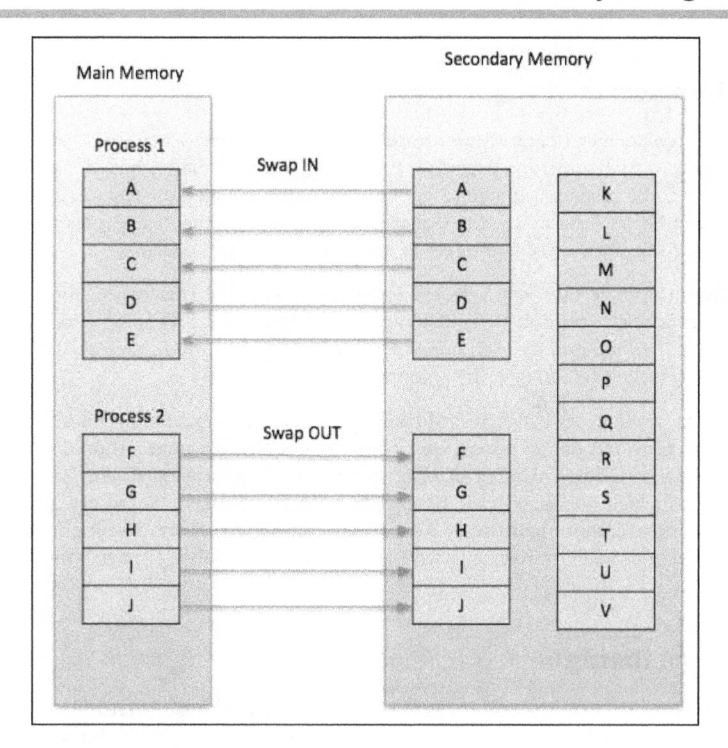

Advantages

- Following are the advantages of Demand Paging –
- Large virtual memory.
- More efficient use of memory.
- There is no limit on degree of multiprogramming.

Disadvantages

- Number of tables and the amount of processor overhead for handling page interrupts are greater than in the case of the simple paged management techniques.

Page Replacement Algorithm

Page replacement algorithms are the techniques using which an Operating System decides which memory pages to swap out, write to disk when a page of memory needs to be allocated. Paging happens whenever a page fault occurs and a free page cannot be used for allocation purpose accounting to reason that pages are not available or the number of free pages is lower than required pages.

When the page that was selected for replacement and was paged out, is referenced again, it has to read in from disk, and this requires for I/O completion. This process determines the quality of the page replacement algorithm: the lesser the time waiting for page-ins, the better is the algorithm.

A page replacement algorithm looks at the limited information about accessing the pages provided by hardware, and tries to select which pages should be replaced to minimize the total number of page misses, while balancing it with the costs of primary storage and processor time of the algorithm itself. There are many different page replacement algorithms. We evaluate an algorithm by running it on a particular string of memory reference and computing the number of page faults.

Reference String

The string of memory references is called reference string. Reference strings are generated artificially or by tracing a given system and recording the address of each memory reference. The latter choice produces a large number of data, where we note two things.

- For a given page size, we need to consider only the page number, not the entire address.
- If we have a reference to a page p, then any immediately following references to page p will never cause a page fault. Page p will be in memory after the first reference; the immediately following references will not fault.
- For example, consider the following sequence of addresses – 123,215,600,1234,76,96
- If page size is 100, then the reference string is 1,2,6,12,0,0

First In First Out (FIFO) algorithm

Oldest page in main memory is the one which will be selected for replacement. Easy to implement, keep a list, replace pages from the tail and add new pages at the head. A simple and obvious page replacement strategy is FIFO, i.e. first-in-first-out.

As new pages are brought in, they are added to the tail of a queue, and the page at the head of the queue is the next victim. In the following example, 20 page requests result in 15 page faults:

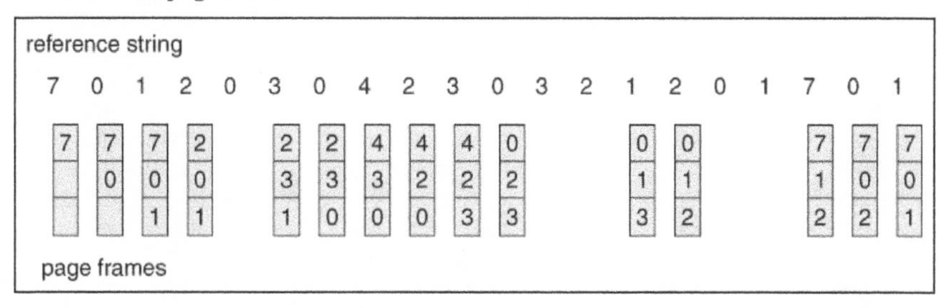

Although FIFO is simple and easy, it is not always optimal, or even efficient. An interesting effect that can occur with FIFO is Belady's anomaly, in which increasing the number of frames available can actually increase the number of page faults that occur! Consider, for example, the following chart based on the page sequence (1, 2, 3, 4, 1, 2, 5, 1, 2, 3, 4, 5) and a varying number of available frames. Obviously the maximum number of faults is 12 (every request generates a fault), and the minimum number is 5 (each page loaded only once), but in between there are some interesting results:

Optimal Page Replacement

The discovery of Belady's anomaly lead to the search for an optimal page-replacement algorithm, which is simply that which yields the lowest of all possible page-faults, and which does not suffer from Belady's anomaly. Such an algorithm does exist, and is called OPT or MIN. This algorithm is simply "Replace the page that will not be used for the longest time in the future."

For example, Figure 9.14 shows that by applying OPT to the same reference string used for the FIFO example, the minimum number of possible page faults is 9. Since 6 of the page-faults are unavoidable (the first reference to each new page), FIFO can be shown to require 3 times as many (extra) page faults as the optimal algorithm. (Note: The book claims that only the first three page faults are required by all algorithms, indicating that FIFO is only twice as bad as OPT.). Unfortunately OPT cannot be implemented in practice, because it requires foretelling the future, but it makes a nice benchmark for the comparison and evaluation of real proposed new algorithms.

In practice most page-replacement algorithms try to approximate OPT by predicting (estimating) in one fashion or another what page will not be used for the longest period of time. The basis of FIFO is the prediction that the page that was brought in the longest time ago is the one that will not be needed again for the longest future time, but as we shall see, there are many other prediction methods, all striving to match the performance of OPT.

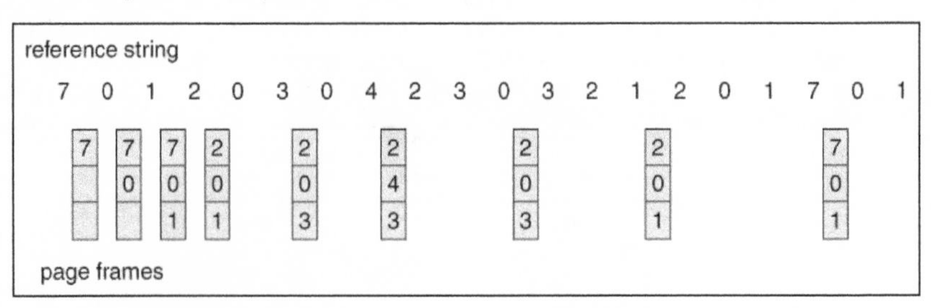

LRU Page Replacement

The prediction behind LRU, the Least Recently Used, algorithm is that the page that has not been used in the longest time is the one that will not be used again in the near future. (Note the distinction between FIFO and LRU: The former looks at the oldest load time, and the latter looks at the oldest use time.)

Some view LRU as analogous to OPT, except looking backwards in time instead of forwards. (OPT has the interesting property that for any reference string S and its reverse R, OPT will generate the same number of page faults for S and for R. It turns out that LRU has this same property.)

Figure illustrates LRU for our sample string, yielding 12 page faults, (as compared to 15 for FIFO and 9 for OPT.).

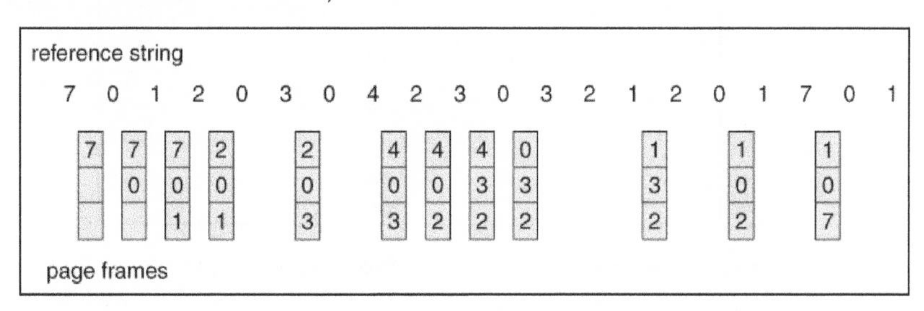

LRU is considered a good replacement policy, and is often used. The problem is how exactly to implement it. There are two simple approaches commonly used:

- **Counters.** Every memory access increments a counter, and the current value of this counter is stored in the page table entry for that page. Then finding the LRU page involves simple searching the table for the page with the smallest counter value. Note that overflowing of the counter must be considered.

- **Stack.** Another approach is to use a stack, and whenever a page is accessed, pull that page from the middle of the stack and place it on the top. The LRU page will always be at the bottom of the stack. Because this requires removing objects from the middle of the stack, a doubly linked list is the recommended data structure.

Note that both implementations of LRU require hardware support, either for incrementing the counter or for managing the stack, as these operations must be performed for every memory access.

Neither LRU or OPT exhibit Belady's anomaly. Both belong to a class of page-replacement algorithms called stack algorithms, which can never exhibit Belady's anomaly. A stack algorithm is one in which the pages kept in memory for a frame set of size N will always be a subset of the pages kept for a frame size of N + 1. In the case of LRU, (and particularly the stack implementation thereof), the top N pages of the stack will be the same for all frame set sizes of N or anything larger.

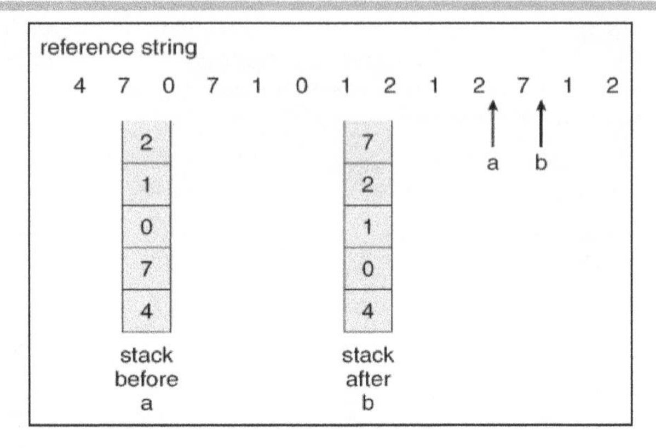

Figure - Use of a stack to record the most recent page references.

Allocation of Frames

We said earlier that there were two important tasks in virtual memory management: a page-replacement strategy and a frame-allocation strategy. This section covers the second part of that pair.

Minimum Number of Frames

The absolute minimum number of frames that a process must be allocated is dependent on system architecture, and corresponds to the worst-case scenario of the number of pages that could be touched by a single (machine) instruction. If an instruction (and its operands) spans a page boundary, then multiple pages could be needed just for the instruction fetch.

Memory references in an instruction touch more pages, and if those memory locations can span page boundaries, then multiple pages could be needed for operand access also.

The worst case involves indirect addressing, particularly where multiple levels of indirect addressing are allowed. Left unchecked, a pointer to a pointer to a pointer to a pointer to a . . . could theoretically touch every page in the virtual address space in a single machine instruction, requiring every virtual page be loaded into physical memory simultaneously. For this reason architectures place a limit (say 16) on the number of levels of indirection allowed in an instruction, which is enforced with a counter initialized to the limit and decremented with every level of indirection in an instruction - If the counter reaches zero, then an "excessive indirection" trap occurs. This example would still require a minimum frame allocation of 17 per process.

Allocation Algorithms

Equal Allocation - If there are m frames available and n processes to share them, each process gets m / n frames, and the leftovers are kept in a free-frame buffer pool.

Proportional Allocation - Allocate the frames proportionally to the size of the process, relative to the total size of all processes. So if the size of process i is S_i, and S is the sum of all S_i, then the allocation for process P_i is a_i = m * S_i / S. Variations on proportional allocation could consider priority of process rather than just their size. Obviously all allocations fluctuate over time as the number of available free frames, m, fluctuates, and all are also subject to the constraints of minimum allocation. (If the minimum allocations cannot be met, then processes must either be swapped out or not allowed to start until more free frames become available.)

Global versus Local Allocation

One big question is whether frame allocation (page replacement) occurs on a local or global level. With local replacement, the number of pages allocated to a process is fixed, and page replacement occurs only amongst the pages allocated to this process. With global replacement, any page may be a potential victim, whether it currently belongs to the process seeking a free frame or not.

Local page replacement allows processes to better control their own page fault rates, and leads to more consistent performance of a given process over different system load levels. Global page replacement is overall more efficient, and is the more commonly used approach.

Non-Uniform Memory Access

The above arguments all assume that all memory is equivalent, or at least has equivalent access times. This may not be the case in multiple-processor systems, especially where each CPU is physically located on a separate circuit board which also holds some portion of the overall system memory. In these latter systems, CPUs can access memory that is physically located on the same board much faster than the memory on the other boards. The basic solution is akin to processor affinity - At the same time that we try to schedule processes on the same CPU to minimize cache misses, we also try to allocate memory for those processes on the same boards, to minimize access times. The presence of threads complicates the picture, especially when the threads get loaded onto different processors. Solaris uses an *lgroup* as a solution, in a hierarchical fashion based on relative latency. For example, all processors and RAM on a single board would probably be in the same lgroup. Memory assignments are made within the same *lgroup* if possible, or to the next nearest *lgroup* otherwise. (Where "nearest" is defined as having the lowest access time.)

Thrashing

If a process cannot maintain its minimum required number of frames, then it must be swapped out, freeing up frames for other processes. This is an intermediate level of CPU scheduling. But what about a process that can keep its minimum, but cannot keep all of the frames that it is currently using on a regular basis? In this case it is forced to page out pages that it will need again in the very near future, leading to large numbers of page faults. A process that is spending more time paging than executing is said to be thrashing.

Cause of Thrashing

Early process scheduling schemes would control the level of multiprogramming allowed based on CPU utilization, adding in more processes when CPU utilization was low. The problem is that when memory filled up and processes started spending lots of time waiting for their pages to page in, then CPU utilization would lower, causing the schedule to add in even more processes and exacerbating the problem! Eventually the system would essentially grind to a halt. Local page replacement policies can prevent one thrashing process from taking pages away from other processes, but it still tends to clog up the I/O queue, thereby slowing down any other process that needs to do even a little bit of paging (or any other I/O for that matter.).

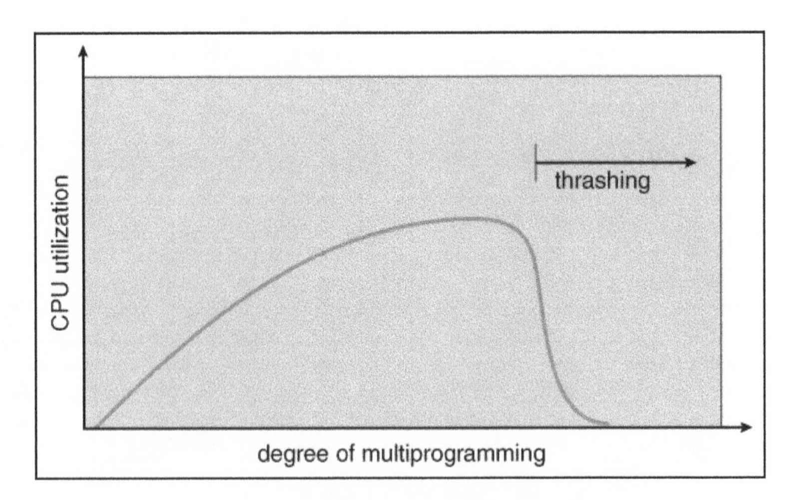

Figure - Thrashing

Working-Set Model

The working set model is based on the concept of locality, and defines a working set window, of length delta. Whatever pages are included in the most recent delta page references are said to be in the processes working set window, and comprise its current working set, as illustrated in Figure :

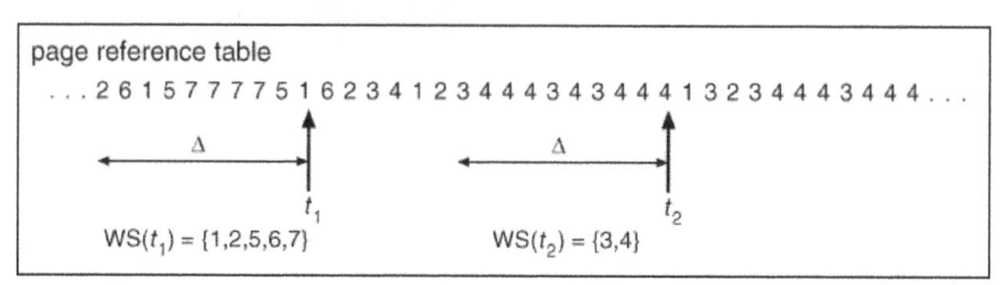

The selection of delta is critical to the success of the working set model - If it is too small then it does not encompass all of the pages of the current locality, and if it is too large, then it encompasses pages that are no longer being frequently accessed.

The total demand, D, is the sum of the sizes of the working sets for all processes. If D exceeds the total number of available frames, then at least one process is thrashing, because there are not enough frames available to satisfy its minimum working set. If D is significantly less than the currently available frames, then additional processes can be launched.

The hard part of the working-set model is keeping track of what pages are in the current working set, since every reference adds one to the set and removes one older page. An approximation can be made using reference bits and a timer that goes off after a set interval of memory references:

For example, suppose that we set the timer to go off after every 5000 references (by any process), and we can store two additional historical reference bits in addition to the current reference bit.

Every time the timer goes off, the current reference bit is copied to one of the two historical bits, and then cleared.

If any of the three bits is set, then that page was referenced within the last 15,000 references, and is considered to be in that processes reference set.

Finer resolution can be achieved with more historical bits and a more frequent timer, at the expense of greater overhead.

Deadlock

System Model

For the purposes of deadlock discussion, a system can be modeled as a collection of limited resources, which can be partitioned into different categories, to be allocated to a number of processes, each having different needs.

Resource categories may include memory, printers, CPUs, open files, tape drives, CD -ROMS, etc.

By definition, all the resources within a category are equivalent, and a request of this category can be equally satisfied by any one of the resources in that category. If this is not the case (i.e. if there is some difference between the resources within a category), then that category needs to be further divided into separate categories. For example, "printers" may need to be separated into "laser printers" and "color inkjet printers".

Some categories may have a single resource.

In normal operation a process must request a resource before using it, and release it when it is done, in the following sequence:

Request - If the request cannot be immediately granted, then the process must wait until the *resource(s)* it needs become available. For example the system calls *open( ), malloc( ), new( ),* and *request( ).*

Use - The process uses the resource, e.g. prints to the printer or reads from the file.

Release - The process relinquishes the resource. so that it becomes available for other processes. For example, *close( ), free( ), delete( ),* and *release( ).*

For all kernel-managed resources, the kernel keeps track of what resources are free and which are allocated, to which process they are allocated, and a queue of processes waiting for this resource to become available. Application-managed resources can be controlled using mutexes or *wait( )* and *signal( )* calls, (i.e. binary or counting semaphores.)

A set of processes is deadlocked when every process in the set is waiting for a resource that is currently allocated to another process in the set (and which can only be released when that other waiting process makes progress.)

Introduction to Deadlock

Every process needs some resources to complete its execution. However, the resource is granted in a sequential order.

1. The process requests for some resource.
2. OS grant the resource if it is available otherwise let the process waits.
3. The process uses it and release on the completion.

A Deadlock is a situation where each of the computer process waits for a resource which is being assigned to some another process. In this situation, none of the process gets executed since the resource it needs, is held by some other process which is also waiting for some other resource to be released.

Let us assume that there are three processes P1, P2 and P3. There are three different resources R1, R2 and R3. R1 is assigned to P1, R2 is assigned to P2 and R3 is assigned to P3. After some time, P1 demands for R1 which is being used by P2. P1 halts its execution since it can't complete without R2.

P2 also demands for R3 which is being used by P3. P2 also stops its execution because it can't continue without R3. P3 also demands for R1 which is being used by P1 therefore P3 also stops its execution. In this scenario, a cycle is being formed among the three processes. None of the process is progressing and they are all waiting. The computer becomes unresponsive since all the processes got blocked.

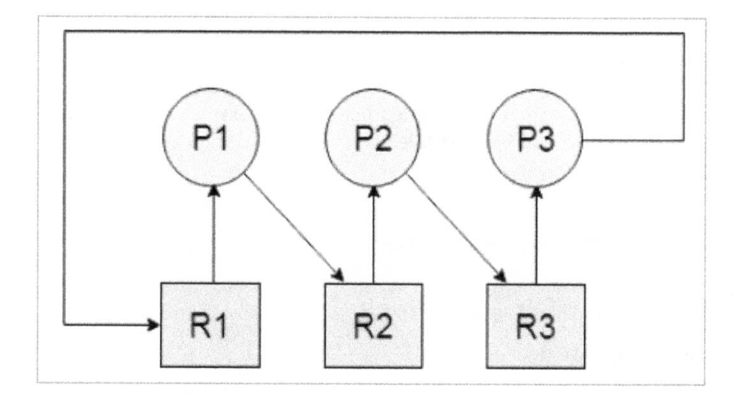

Sr.	Deadlock	Starvation
1	Deadlock is a situation where no process got blocked and no process proceeds	Starvation is a situation where the low priority process got blocked and the high priority processes proceed.
2	Deadlock is an infinite waiting.	Starvation is a long waiting but not infinite.
3	Every Deadlock is always a starvation.	Every starvation need not be deadlock.
4	The requested resource is blocked by the other process.	The requested resource is continuously be used by the higher priority processes.
5	Deadlock happens when Mutual exclusion, hold and wait, No preemption and circular wait occurs simultaneously.	It occurs due to the uncontrolled priority and resource management.

Necessary conditions for Deadlocks

Mutual Exclusion

A resource can only be shared in mutually exclusive manner. It implies, if two process cannot use the same resource at the same time.

Hold and Wait

A process waits for some resources while holding another resource at the same time.

No preemption

The process which once scheduled will be executed till the completion. No other process can be scheduled by the scheduler meanwhile.

Circular Wait

All the processes must be waiting for the resources in a cyclic manner so that the last process is waiting for the resource which is being held by the first process.

Strategies for handling Deadlock

Deadlock Ignorance

Deadlock Ignorance is the most widely used approach among all the mechanism. This is being used by many operating systems mainly for end user uses. In this approach, the Operating system assumes that deadlock never occurs.

It simply ignores deadlock. This approach is best suitable for a single end user system where User uses the system only for browsing and all other normal stuff.

There is always a tradeoff between Correctness and performance. The operating systems like Windows and Linux mainly focus upon performance. However, the performance of the system decreases if it uses deadlock handling mechanism all the time if deadlock happens 1 out of 100 times then it is completely unnecessary to use the deadlock handling mechanism all the time.

In these types of systems, the user has to simply restart the computer in the case of deadlock. Windows and Linux are mainly using this approach.

Deadlock prevention

Deadlock happens only when Mutual Exclusion, hold and wait, No preemption and circular wait holds simultaneously. If it is possible to violate one of the four conditions at any time then the deadlock can never occur in the system.

The idea behind the approach is very simple that we have to fail one of the four conditions but there can be a big argument on its physical implementation in the system.

Deadlock avoidance

In deadlock avoidance, the operating system checks whether the system is in safe state or in unsafe state at every step which the operating system performs. The process continues until the system is in safe state. Once the system moves to unsafe state, the OS has to backtrack one step.

In simple words, The OS reviews each allocation so that the allocation doesn't cause the deadlock in the system.

Deadlock detection and recovery

This approach let the processes fall in deadlock and then periodically check whether deadlock occur in the system or not. If it occurs then it applies some of the recovery methods to the system to get rid of deadlock.

Deadlock Prevention

If we simulate deadlock with a table which is standing on its four legs then we can also simulate four legs with the four conditions which when occurs simultaneously, cause the deadlock.

However, if we break one of the legs of the table then the table will fall definitely. The same happens with deadlock, if we can be able to violate one of the four necessary conditions and don't let them occur together then we can prevent the deadlock.

Deadlock Prevention

If we simulate deadlock with a table which is standing on its four legs then we can also simulate four legs with the four conditions which when occurs simultaneously, cause the deadlock.

However, if we break one of the legs of the table then the table will fall definitely. The same happens with deadlock, if we can be able to violate one of the four necessary conditions and don't let them occur together then we can prevent the deadlock.

Let's see how we can prevent each of the conditions.

1. Mutual Exclusion

Mutual section from the resource point of view is the fact that a resource can never be used by more than one process simultaneously which is fair enough but that is the main reason behind the deadlock. If a resource could have been used by more than one process at the same time then the process would have never been waiting for any resource.

However, if we can be able to violate resources behaving in the mutually exclusive manner then the deadlock can be prevented.

Spooling

For a device like printer, spooling can work. There is a memory associated with the printer which stores jobs from each of the process into it. Later, Printer collects all the jobs and print each one of them according to FCFS. By using this mechanism, the process doesn't have to wait for the printer and it can continue whatever it was doing. Later, it collects the output when it is produced.

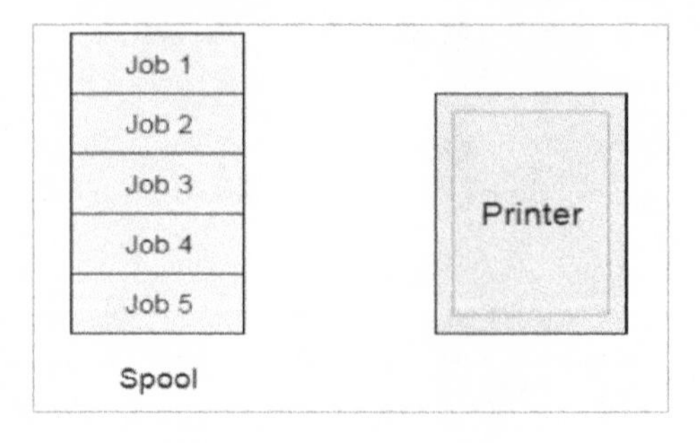

Although, Spooling can be an effective approach to violate mutual exclusion but it suffers from two kinds of problems.

This cannot be applied to every resource. After some point of time, there may arise a race condition between the processes to get space in that spool.

We cannot force a resource to be used by more than one process at the same time since it will not be fair enough and some serious problems may arise in the performance. Therefore, we cannot violate mutual exclusion for a process practically.

2. Hold and Wait

Hold and wait condition lies when a process holds a resource and waiting for some other resource to complete its task. Deadlock occurs because there can be more than one process which are holding one resource and waiting for other in the cyclic order. However, we have to find out some mechanism by which a process either doesn't hold any resource or doesn't wait. That means, a process must be assigned all the necessary resources before the execution starts. A process must not wait for any resource once the execution has been started.

!(Hold and wait) = !hold or !wait (negation of hold and wait is, either you don't hold or you don't wait)

This can be implemented practically if a process declares all the resources initially. However, this sounds very practical but can't be done in the computer system because a process can't determine necessary resources initially.

Process is the set of instructions which are executed by the CPU. Each of the instruction may demand multiple resources at the multiple times. The need cannot be fixed by the OS.

The problem with the approach is:

1. Practically not possible.
2. Possibility of getting starved will be increases due to the fact that some process may hold a resource for a very long time.

3. No Preemption

Deadlock arises due to the fact that a process can't be stopped once it starts. However, if we take the resource away from the process which is causing deadlock then we can prevent deadlock. This is not a good approach at all since if we take a resource away which is being used by the process then all the work which it has done till now can become inconsistent.

Consider a printer is being used by any process. If we take the printer away from that process and assign it to some other process then all the data which has been printed can become inconsistent and ineffective and also the fact that the process can't start printing again from where it has left which causes performance inefficiency.

4. Circular Wait

To violate circular wait, we can assign a priority number to each of the resource. A process can't request for a lesser priority resource. This ensures that not a single process can request a resource which is being utilized by some other process and no cycle will be formed.

Condition	Approach	Is Practically Possible?
Mutual Exclusion	Spooling	✗
Hold and Wait	Request for all the resources initially	✗
No Preemption	Snatch all the resources	✗
Circular Wait	Assign priority to each resources and order resources numerically	✓

Among all the methods, violating Circular wait is the only approach that can be implemented practically.

Deadlock avoidance

In deadlock avoidance, the request for any resource will be granted if the resulting state of the system doesn't cause deadlock in the system. The state of the system will continuously be checked for safe and unsafe states. In order to avoid deadlocks, the process must tell OS, the maximum number of resources a process can request to complete its execution. The simplest and most useful approach states that the process should declare the maximum number of resources of each type it may ever need. The Deadlock avoidance algorithm examines the resource allocations so that there can never be a circular wait condition.

Safe and Unsafe States The resource allocation state of a system can be defined by the instances of available and allocated resources, and the maximum instance of the resources demanded by the processes. A state of a system recorded at some random time is shown below.

Resources Assigned

Process	Type 1	Type 2	Type 3	Type 4
A	3	0	2	2
B	0	0	1	1
C	1	1	1	0
D	2	1	4	0

Resources still needed

Process	Type 1	Type 2	Type 3	Type 4
A	1	1	0	0
B	0	1	1	2
C	1	2	1	0
D	2	1	1	2

E = (7 6 8 4) **P = (6 2 8 3)** **A = (1 4 0 1)**

Above tables and vector E, P and A describes the resource allocation state of a system. There are 4 processes and 4 types of the resources in a system. Table 1 shows the instances of each resource assigned to each process. Table 2 shows the instances of the resources, each process still needs. Vector E is the representation of total instances of each resource in the system. Vector P represents the instances of resources that have been assigned to processes. Vector A represents the number of resources that are not in use. A state of the system is called safe if the system can allocate all the resources requested by all the processes without entering into deadlock. If the system cannot fulfill the request of all processes then the state of the system is called unsafe. The key of Deadlock avoidance approach is when the request is made for resources then the request must only be approved in the case if the resulting state is also a safe state.

Deadlock Detection and Recovery

In this approach, The OS doesn't apply any mechanism to avoid or prevent the deadlocks. Therefore the system considers that the deadlock will definitely occur. In order to get rid of deadlocks, The OS periodically checks the system for any deadlock. In case, it finds any of the deadlock then the OS will recover the system using some recovery techniques. The main task of the OS is detecting the deadlocks. The OS can detect the deadlocks with the help of Resource allocation graph.

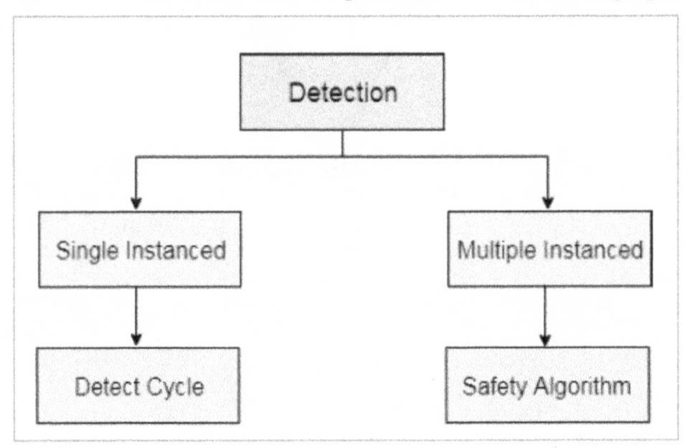

In single instanced resource types, if a cycle is being formed in the system then there will definitely be a deadlock. On the other hand, in multiple instanced resource type graph, detecting a cycle is not just enough. We have to apply the safety algorithm on the system by converting the resource allocation graph into the allocation matrix and request matrix.

In order to recover the system from deadlocks, either OS considers resources or processes.

For Resource

Preempt the resource

We can snatch one of the resources from the owner of the resource (process) and give it to the other process with the expectation that it will complete the execution and will release this resource sooner. Well, choosing a resource which will be snatched is going to be a bit difficult.

Rollback to a safe state

System passes through various states to get into the deadlock state. The operating system can rollback the system to the previous safe state. For this purpose, OS needs to implement check pointing at every state.

The moment, we get into deadlock, we will rollback all the allocations to get into the previous safe state.

For Process

Kill a process

Killing a process can solve our problem but the bigger concern is to decide which process to kill. Generally, Operating system kills a process which has done least amount of work until now.

Kill all process

This is not a suggestible approach but can be implemented if the problem becomes very serious. Killing all process will lead to inefficiency in the system because all the processes will execute again from starting.

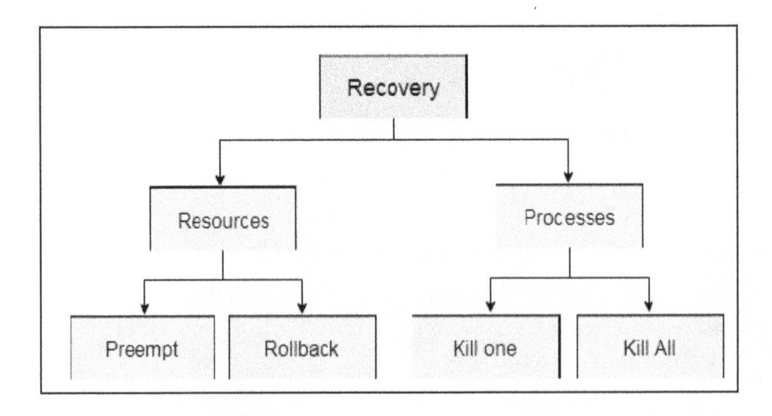

Chapter-5

File System Interface

File System Implementation

File-System Interface

File Concept

File Attributes

Different OSes keep track of different file attributes, including:

1. **Name** - Some systems give special significance to names, and particularly extensions (.exe, .txt, etc.), and some do not. Some extensions may be of significance to the OS (.exe), and others only to certain applications (.jpg)
2. **Identifier** (e.g. inode number)
3. **Type** - Text, executable, other binary, etc.
4. **Location** - on the hard drive.
5. **Size.**
6. **Protection**
7. **Time & Date**
8. **User ID**

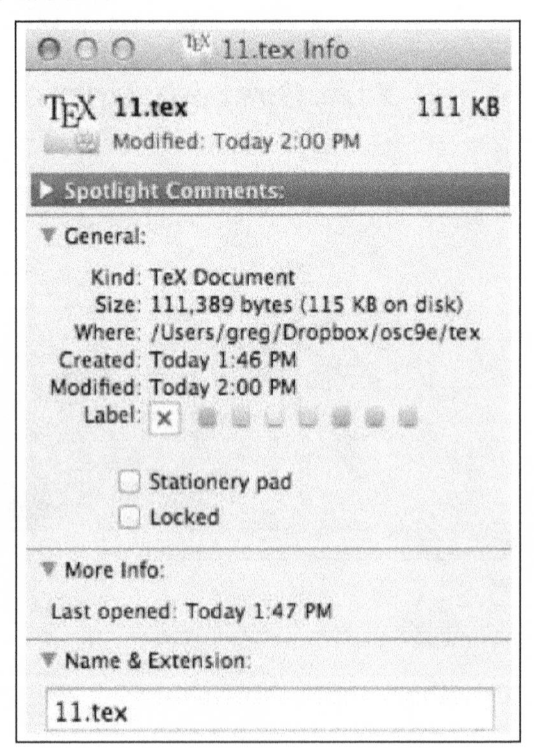

File Operations

The file ADT supports many common operations:

1. Creating a file
2. Writing a file
3. Reading a file
4. Repositioning within a file
5. Deleting a file
6. Truncating a file.

Most OSes require that files be ***opened*** before access and ***closed*** after all access is complete. Normally the programmer must open and close files explicitly, but some rare systems open the file automatically at first access. Information about currently open files is stored in an ***open file table***, containing for example:

1. **File pointer** - records the current position in the file, for the next read or write access.
2. **File-open count** - How many times has the current file been opened (simultaneously by different processes) and not yet closed? When this counter reaches zero the file can be removed from the table.
3. **Disk location of the file.**
4. **Access rights**

Some systems provide support for file locking.

1. A **shared lock** is for reading only.
2. A **exclusive lock** is for writing as well as reading.
3. An **advisory lock** is informational only, and not enforced. (A "Keep Out" sign, which may be ignored.)
4. A **mandatory lock** is enforced. (A truly locked door.)
5. UNIX used **advisory locks**, and Windows uses mandatory locks.

File Types

Windows (and some other systems) use special file extensions to indicate the type of each file:

file type	usual extension	function
executable	exe, com, bin or none	ready-to-run machine-language program
object	obj, o	compiled, machine language, not linked
source code	c, cc, java, perl, asm	source code in various languages
batch	bat, sh	commands to the command interpreter
markup	xml, html, tex	textual data, documents
word processor	xml, rtf, docx	various word-processor formats
library	lib, a, so, dll	libraries of routines for programmers
print or view	gif, pdf, jpg	ASCII or binary file in a format for printing or viewing
archive	rar, zip, tar	related files grouped into one file, sometimes compressed, for archiving or storage
multimedia	mpeg, mov, mp3, mp4, avi	binary file containing audio or A/V information

Figure - Common file types.

Macintosh stores a creator attribute for each file, according to the program that first created it with the create( ) system call.

UNIX stores magic numbers at the beginning of certain files. (Experiment with the "file" command, especially in directories such as /bin and /dev)

File Structure

Some files contain an internal structure, which may or may not be known to the OS.

For the OS to support particular file formats increases the size and complexity of the OS.UNIX treats all files as sequences of bytes, with no further consideration of the internal structure. (With the exception of executable binary programs, which it must know how to load and find the first executable statement, etc.)

Macintosh files have two forks - a **resource fork**, and a **data fork**. The resource fork contains information relating to the UI, such as icons and button images, and can be modified independently of the data fork, which contains the code or data as appropriate.

Internal File Structure

Disk files are accessed in units of physical blocks, typically 512 bytes or some power -of-two multiple thereof. (Larger physical disks use larger block sizes, to keep the range of block numbers within the range of a 32-bit integer.) . Internally files are organized in units of logical units, which may be as small as a single byte, or may be a larger size corresponding to some data record or structure size.

The number of logical units which fit into one physical block determines its packing, and has an impact on the amount of internal fragmentation (wasted space) that occurs. As a general rule, half a physical block is wasted for each file, and the larger the block sizes the more space is lost to internal fragmentation.

Access Methods

Sequential Access

A sequential access file emulates magnetic tape operation, and generally supports a few operations:

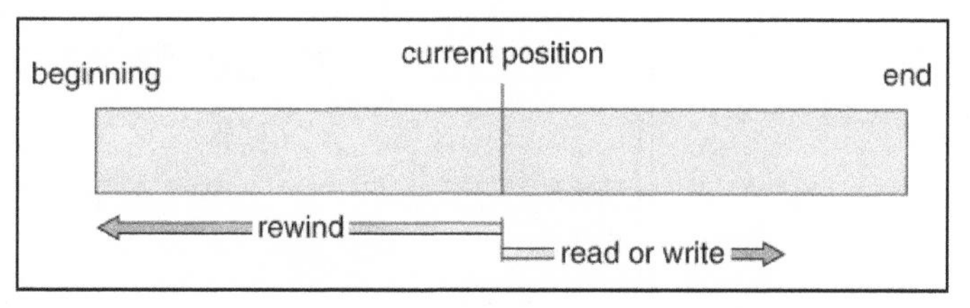

- ***read next*** - read a record and advance the tape to the next position.
- ***write next*** - write a record and advance the tape to the next position.
- ***rewind***
- ***skip n records*** - May or may not be supported. N may be limited to positive numbers, or may be limited to +/- 1.

Direct Access

Jump to any record and read that record. Operations supported include:
read n - read record number n. (Note an argument is now required.)
write n - write record number n. (Note an argument is now required.)

jump to record n - could be 0 or the end of file.

Query current record - used to return back to this record later.

Sequential access can be easily emulated using direct access. The inverse is complicated and inefficient.

sequential access	implementation for direct access
reset	cp = 0;
read_next	read cp ; cp = cp + 1;
write_next	write cp; cp = cp + 1;

Figure - Simulation of sequential access on a direct-access file.

Other Access Methods

An indexed access scheme can be easily built on top of a direct access system. Very large files may require a multi-tiered indexing scheme, i.e. indexes of indexes.

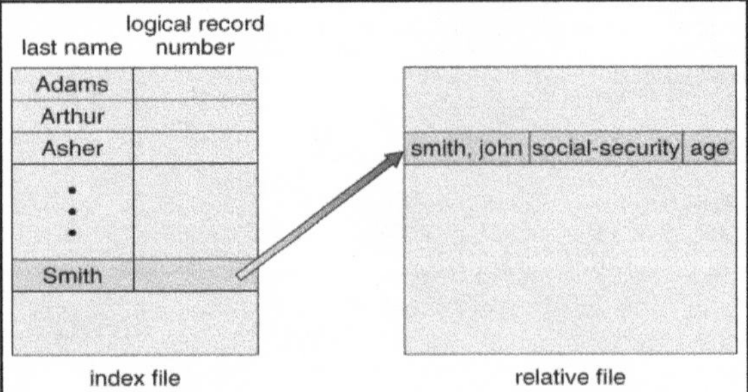

Directory Structure

Storage Structure

A disk can be used in its entirety for a file system. Alternatively a physical disk can be broken up into multiple partitions, slices, or mini-disks, each of which becomes a virtual disk and can have its own file system. (or be used for raw storage, swap space, etc.). Or, multiple physical disks can be combined into one volume, i.e. a larger virtual disk, with its own file system spanning the physical disks.

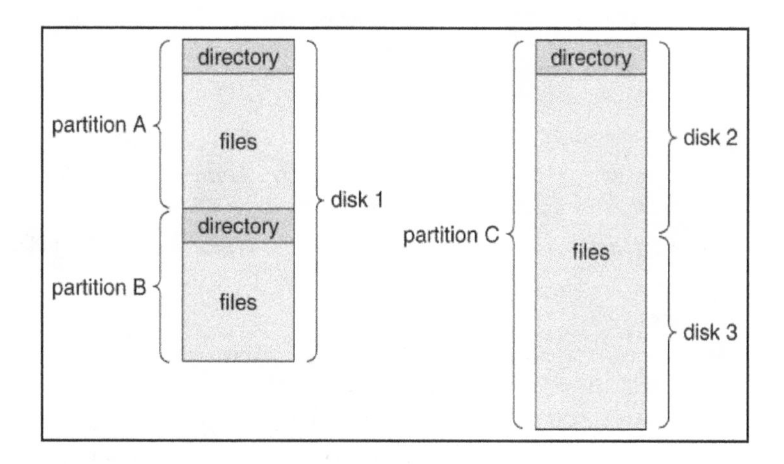

Figure - A typical file-system organization.

Directory Overview

Directory operations to be supported include:

- Search for a file
- Create a file - add to the directory
- Delete a file - erase from the directory
- List a directory - possibly ordered in different ways.
- Rename a file - may change sorting order
- Traverse the file system.

Single-Level Directory

Simple to implement, but each file must have a unique name.

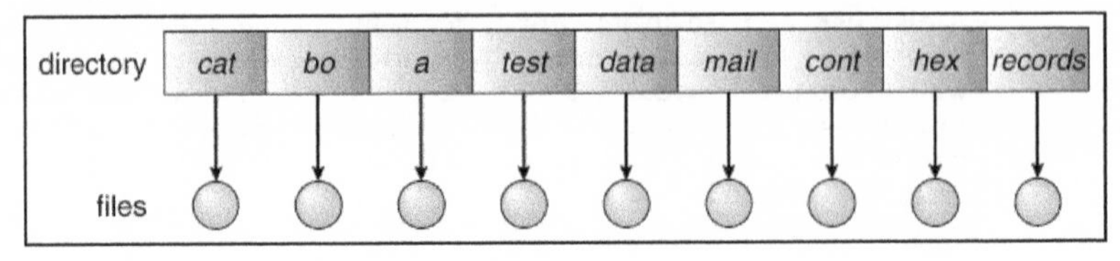

Figure - Single-level directory.

Two-Level Directory

- Each user gets their own directory space.
- File names only need to be unique within a given user's directory.
- A master file directory is used to keep track of each users directory, and must be maintained when users are added to or removed from the system.
- A separate directory is generally needed for system (executable) files.
- Systems may or may not allow users to access other directories besides their own
- If access to other directories is allowed, then provision must be made to specify the directory being accessed.
- If access is denied, then special consideration must be made for users to run programs located in system directories. A search path is the list of directories in which to search for executable programs, and can be set uniquely for each user.

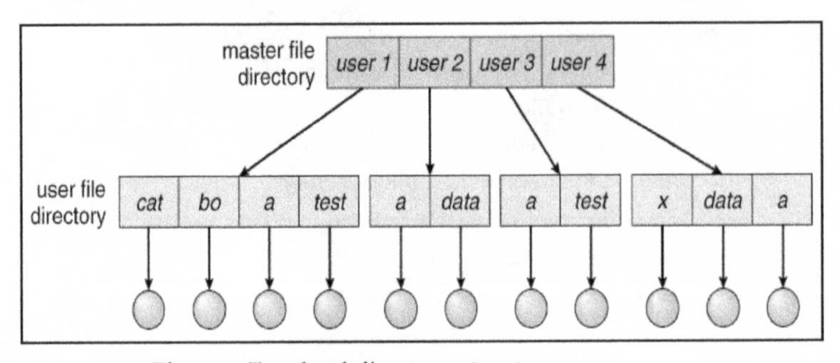

Figure - Two-level directory structure.

Tree-Structured Directories

An obvious extension to the two-tiered directory structure, and the one with which we are all most familiar. Each user / process has the concept of a current directory from which all (relative) searches take place. Files may be accessed using either absolute pathnames (relative to the root of the tree) or relative pathnames (relative to the current directory.)

Directories are stored the same as any other file in the system, except there is a bit that identifies them as directories, and they have some special structure that the OS understands. One question for consideration is whether or not to allow the removal of directories that are not empty - Windows requires that directories be emptied first, and UNIX provides an option for deleting entire sub-trees.

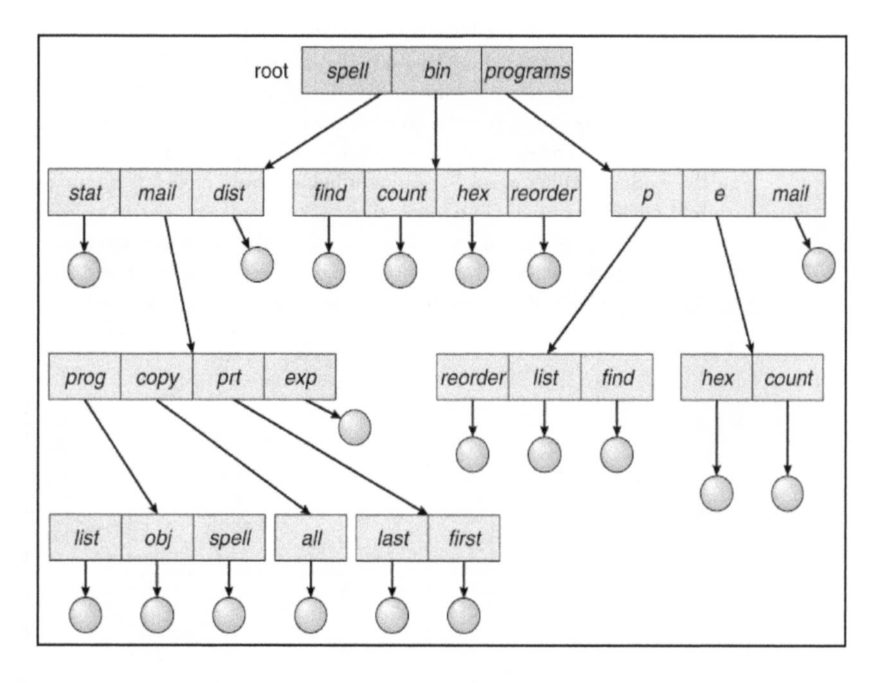

Figure - Tree-structured directory structure.

Acyclic-Graph Directories

When the same files need to be accessed in more than one place in the directory structure (e.g. because they are being shared by more than one user / process), it can be useful to provide an acyclic-graph structure. (Note the directed arcs from parent to child.) UNIX provides two types of links for implementing the acyclic-graph structure. (See "man ln" for more details.)

A hard link (usually just called a link) involves multiple directory entries that both refer to the same file. Hard links are only valid for ordinary files in the same file system. A symbolic link, that involves a special file, containing information about where to find the linked file. Symbolic links may be used to link directories and/or files in other file systems, as well as ordinary files in the current file system.

Windows only supports symbolic links, termed shortcuts. Hard links require a reference count, or link count for each file, keeping track of how many directory entries are currently referring to this file. Whenever one of the references is removed the link count is reduced, and when it reaches zero, the disk space can be reclaimed. For symbolic links there is some question as to what to do with the symbolic links when the original file is moved or deleted: One option is to find all the symbolic links and adjust them also. Another is to leave the symbolic links dangling, and discover that they are no longer valid the next time they are used. What if the original file is removed, and replaced with another file having the same name before the symbolic link is next used?

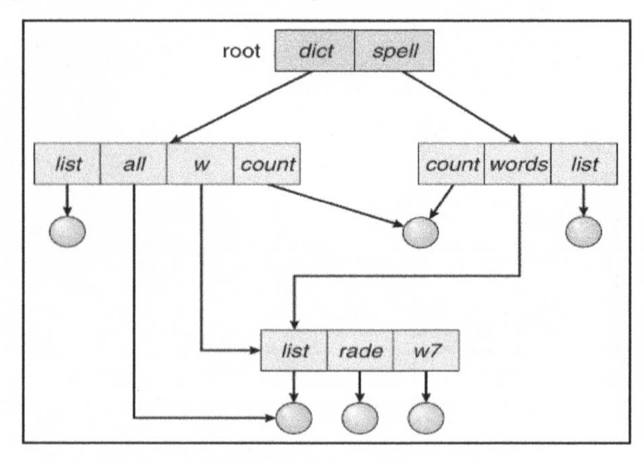

Figure - Acyclic-graph directory structure.

General Graph Directory

If cycles are allowed in the graphs, then several problems can arise:

Search algorithms can go into infinite loops. One solution is to not follow links in search algorithms. (Or not to follow symbolic links, and to only allow symbolic links to refer to directories.)

Sub-trees can become disconnected from the rest of the tree and still not have their reference counts reduced to zero. Periodic garbage collection is required to detect and resolve this problem. (chkdsk in DOS and fsck in UNIX search for these problems, among others, even though cycles are not supposed to be allowed in either system. Disconnected disk blocks that are not marked as free are added back to the file systems with made-up file names, and can usually be safely deleted.).

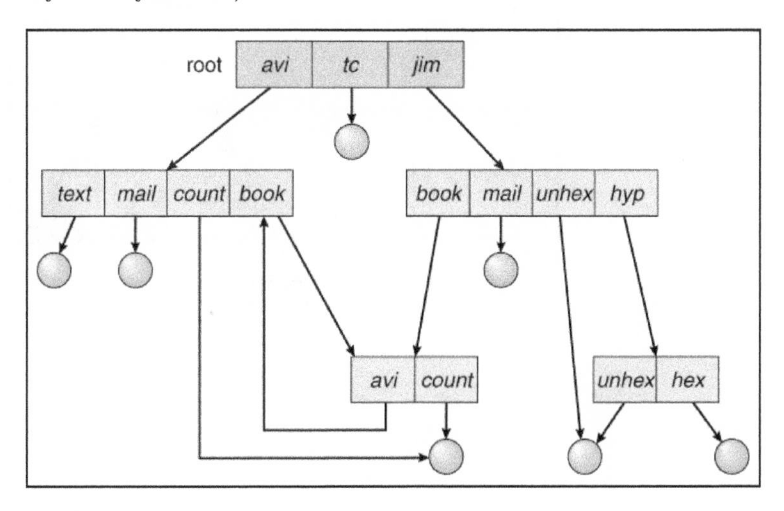

File-System Mounting

The basic idea behind mounting file systems is to combine multiple file systems into one large tree structure. The mount command is given a file system to mount and a mount point (directory) on which to attach it. Once a file system is mounted onto a mount point, any further references to that directory actually refer to the root of the mounted file system.

Any files (or sub-directories) that had been stored in the mount point directory prior to mounting the new file system are now hidden by the mounted file system, and are no longer available. For this reason some systems only allow mounting onto empty directories.

File systems can only be mounted by root, unless root has previously configured certain file systems to be mountable onto certain pre-determined mount points. (E.g. root may allow users to mount floppy file systems to /mnt or something like it.) Anyone can run the mount command to see what file systems are currently mounted.

File systems may be mounted read-only, or have other restrictions imposed

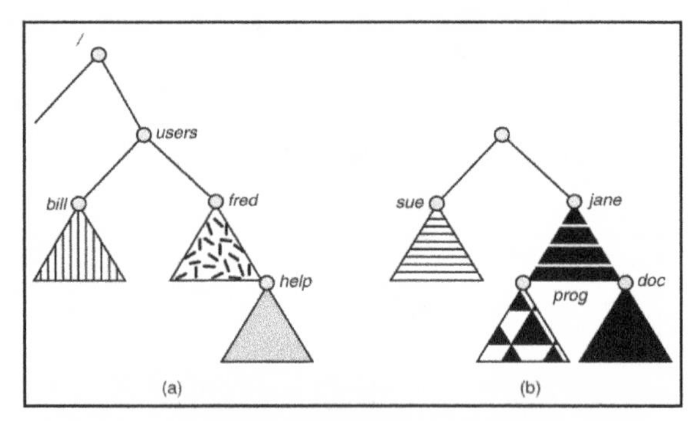

Figure - File system. (a) Existing system. (b) Unmounted volume.

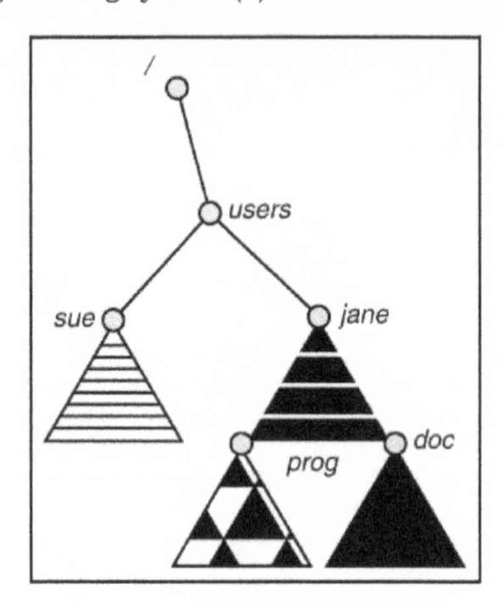

Figure - Mount point.

The traditional Windows OS runs an extended two-tier directory structure, where the first tier of the structure separates volumes by drive letters, and a tree structure is implemented below that level. Macintosh runs a similar system, where each new volume that is found is automatically mounted and added to the desktop when it is found. More recent Windows systems allow filesystems to be mounted to any directory in the filesystem, much like UNIX.

File Sharing

Multiple Users

On a multi-user system, more information needs to be stored for each file:

- The owner (user) who owns the file, and who can control its access.
- The group of other user IDs that may have some special access to the file.
- What access rights are afforded to the owner (User), the Group, and to the rest of the world (the universe, a.k.a. Others.)
- Some systems have more complicated access control, allowing or denying specific accesses to specifically named users or groups.

Remote File Systems

The advent of the Internet introduces issues for accessing files stored on remote computers

- The original method was ftp, allowing individual files to be transported across systems as needed. Ftp can be either account and password controlled, or anonymous, not requiring any user name or password.
- Various forms of distributed file systems allow remote file systems to be mounted onto a local directory structure, and accessed using normal file access commands. (The actual files are still transported across the network as needed, possibly using ftp as the underlying transport mechanism.)
- The WWW has made it easy once again to access files on remote systems without mounting their filesystems, generally using (anonymous) ftp as the underlying file transport mechanism.

The Client-Server Model

1. When one computer system remotely mounts a filesystem that is physically located on another system, the system which physically owns the files acts as a server, and the system which mounts them is the client.
2. User IDs and group IDs must be consistent across both systems for the system to work properly. (I.e. this is most applicable across multiple computers managed by the same organization, shared by a common group of users.)
3. The same computer can be both a client and a server. (E.g. cross-linked file systems.)
4. There are a number of security concerns involved in this model:
   - Servers commonly restrict mount permission to certain trusted systems only. Spoofing (a computer pretending to be a different computer) is a potential security risk.
   - Servers may restrict remote access to read-only.
   - Servers restrict which filesystems may be remotely mounted. Generally the information within those subsystems is limited, relatively public, and protected by frequent backups.
5. The NFS (Network File System) is a classic example of such a system.

Distributed Information Systems

- The Domain Name System, DNS, provides for a unique naming system across all of the Internet.
- Domain names are maintained by the Network Information System, NIS, which unfortunately has several security issues. NIS+ is a more secure version, but has not yet gained the same widespread acceptance as NIS.
- Microsoft's Common Internet File System, CIFS, establishes a network login for each user on a networked system with shared file access. Older Windows systems used domains, and newer systems (XP, 2000), use active directories. User names must match across the network for this system to be valid.
- A newer approach is the Lightweight Directory-Access Protocol, LDAP, which provides a secure single sign-on for all users to access all resources on a network.

This is a secure system which is gaining in popularity, and which has the maintenance advantage of combining authorization information in one central location.

Failure Modes

When a local disk file is unavailable, the result is generally known immediately, and is generally non-recoverable. The only reasonable response is for the response to fail.

However when a remote file is unavailable, there are many possible reasons, and whether or not it is unrecoverable is not readily apparent. Hence most remote access systems allow for blocking or delayed response, in the hopes that the remote system (or the network) will come back up eventually.

Consistency Semantics

Consistency Semantics deals with the consistency between the views of shared files on a networked system. When one user changes the file, when do other users see the changes?

UNIX Semantics

- The UNIX file system uses the following semantics:
- Writes to an open file are immediately visible to any other user who has the file open.
- One implementation uses a shared location pointer, which is adjusted for all sharing users.
- The file is associated with a single exclusive physical resource, which may delay some accesses.

Session Semantics

- The Andrew File System, AFS uses the following semantics:
- Writes to an open file are not immediately visible to other users.
- When a file is closed, any changes made become available only to users who open the file at a later time.
- According to these semantics, a file can be associated with multiple (possibly different) views. Almost no constraints are imposed on scheduling accesses. No user is delayed in reading or writing their personal copy of the file.

AFS file systems may be accessible by systems around the world. Access control is maintained through (somewhat) complicated access control lists, which may grant access to the entire world (literally) or to specifically named users accessing the files from specifically named remote environments.

Immutable-Shared-Files Semantics

Under this system, when a file is declared as **shared** by its creator, it becomes immutable and the name cannot be re-used for any other resource. Hence it becomes read-only, and shared access is simple.

Protection

Files must be kept safe for reliability (against accidental damage), and protection (against deliberate malicious access.) The former is usually managed with backup copies. This section discusses the latter. One simple protection scheme is to remove all access to a file. However this makes the file unusable, so some sort of controlled access must be arranged.

Types of Access

The following low-level operations are often controlled:

- **Read** - View the contents of the file
- **Write** - Change the contents of the file.
- **Execute** - Load the file onto the CPU and follow the instructions contained therein.
- **Append** - Add to the end of an existing file.
- **Delete** - Remove a file from the system.
- **List** -View the name and other attributes of files on the system.

Higher-level operations, such as copy, can generally be performed through combinations of the above.

Access Control

One approach is to have complicated Access Control Lists, ACL, which specify exactly what access is allowed or denied for specific users or groups.

The AFS uses this system for distributed access.

Control is very finely adjustable, but may be complicated, particularly when the specific users involved are unknown. (AFS allows some wild cards, so for example all users on a certain remote system may be trusted, or a given username may be trusted when accessing from any remote system.)

UNIX uses a set of 9 access control bits, in three groups of three. These correspond to R, W, and X permissions for each of the Owner, Group, and Others. (See "man ***chmod***" for full details.) The RWX bits control the following privileges for ordinary files and directories:

bit	Files	Directories
R	Read (view) file contents.	Read directory contents. Required to get a listing of the directory.
W	Write (change) file contents.	Change directory contents. Required to create or delete files.
X	Execute file contents as a program.	Access detailed directory information. Required to get a long listing, or to access any specific file in the directory. Note that if a user has X but not R permissions on a directory, they can still access specific files, but only if they already know the name of the file they are trying to access.

In addition there are some special bits that can also be applied:

- The set user ID (SUID) bit and/or the set group ID (SGID) bits applied to executable files temporarily change the identity of whoever runs the program to match that of the owner / group of the executable program. This allows users running specific programs to have access to files (while running that program) to which they would normally be unable to access. Setting of these two bits is usually restricted to root, and must be done with caution, as it introduces a potential security leak.
- The sticky bit on a directory modifies write permission, allowing users to only delete files for which they are the owner. This allows everyone to create files in /tmp, for example, but to only delete files which they have created, and not anyone else's.
- The SUID, SGID, and sticky bits are indicated with an S, S, and T in the positions for execute permission for the user, group, and others, respectively. If the letter is lower case, (s, s, t), then the corresponding execute permission is not also given. If it is upper case, (S, S, T), then the corresponding execute permission IS given.

- The numeric form of ***chmod*** is needed to set these advanced bits.

-rw-rw-r--	1 pbg	staff	31200	Sep 3 08:30	intro.ps
drwx------	5 pbg	staff	512	Jul 8 09.33	private/
drwxrwxr-x	2 pbg	staff	512	Jul 8 09:35	doc/
drwxrwx---	2 jwg	student	512	Aug 3 14:13	student-proj/
-rw-r--r--	1 pbg	staff	9423	Feb 24 2012	program.c
-rwxr-xr-x	1 pbg	staff	20471	Feb 24 2012	program
drwx--x--x	4 tag	faculty	512	Jul 31 10:31	lib/
drwx------	3 pbg	staff	1024	Aug 29 06:52	mail/
drwxrwxrwx	3 pbg	staff	512	Jul 8 09:35	test/

Sample permissions in a UNIX system.

Windows adjusts files access through a simple GUI:

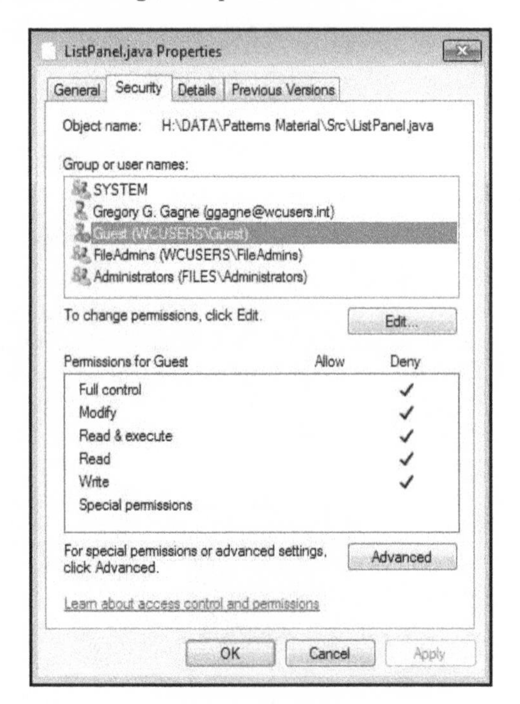

Figure - Windows 7 access-control list management.

Other Protection Approaches and Issues

Some systems can apply passwords, either to individual files, or to specific sub-directories, or to the entire system. There is a trade-off between the number of passwords that must be maintained (and remembered by the users) and the amount of information that is vulnerable to a lost or forgotten password.

Older systems which did not originally have multi-user file access permissions (DOS and older versions of Mac) must now be retrofitted if they are to share files on a network.

Access to a file requires access to all the files along its path as well. In a cyclic directory structure, users may have different access to the same file accessed through different paths.

Sometimes just the knowledge of the existence of a file of a certain name is a security (or privacy) concern. Hence the distinction between the R and X bits on UNIX directories.

File-System Implementation

File-System Structure

- Hard disks have two important properties that make them suitable for secondary storage of files in file systems: (1) Blocks of data can be rewritten in place, and (2) they are direct access, allowing any block of data to be accessed with only (relatively) minor movements of the disk heads and rotational latency. (See Chapter 12)
- Disks are usually accessed in physical blocks, rather than a byte at a time. Block sizes may range from 512 bytes to 4K or larger.
- File systems organize storage on disk drives, and can be viewed as a layered design:
    - At the lowest layer are the physical devices, consisting of the magnetic media, motors & controls, and the electronics connected to them and controlling them. Modern disk put more and more of the electronic controls directly on the disk drive itself, leaving relatively little work for the disk controller card to perform.
    - I/O Control consists of device drivers, special software programs (often written in assembly) which communicate with the devices by reading and writing special codes directly to and from memory addresses corresponding to the controller card's registers. Each controller card (device) on a system has a different set of addresses (registers, a.k.a. ports) that it listens to, and a unique set of command codes and results codes that it understands.
    - The basic file system level works directly with the device drivers in terms of retrieving and storing raw blocks of data, without any consideration for what is in each block. Depending on the system, blocks may be referred to with a single block number, (e.g. block # 234234), or with head-sector-cylinder combinations.
    - The file organization module knows about files and their logical blocks, and how they map to physical blocks on the disk. In addition to translating from logical to physical blocks, the file organization module also maintains the list of free blocks, and allocates free blocks to files as needed.

- The logical file system deals with all of the meta data associated with a file (UID, GID, mode, dates, etc), i.e. everything about the file except the data itself. This level manages the directory structure and the mapping of file names to file control blocks, FCBs, which contain all of the meta data as well as block number information for finding the data on the disk.

- The layered approach to file systems means that much of the code can be used uniformly for a wide variety of different file systems, and only certain layers need to be filesystem specific. Common file systems in use include the UNIX file system, UFS, the Berkeley Fast File System, FFS, Windows systems FAT, FAT32, NTFS, CD-ROM systems ISO 9660, and for Linux the extended file systems ext2 and ext3 (among 40 others supported.).

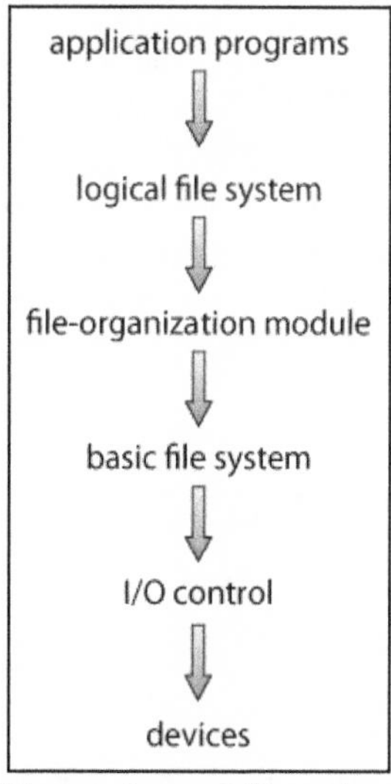

Figure - Layered file system.

File-System Implementation

Overview

File systems store several important data structures on the disk:

- **A boot-control block**, (per volume) a.k.a. the boot block in UNIX or the partition boot sector in Windows contains information about how to boot the system off of this disk. This will generally be the first sector of the volume if there is a bootable system loaded on that volume, or the block will be left vacant otherwise.
- A **volume control block**, (per volume) a.k.a. the master file table in UNIX or the superblock in Windows, which contains information such as the partition table, number of blocks on each filesystem, and pointers to free blocks and free FCB blocks.
- A directory structure (per file system), containing file names and pointers to corresponding FCBs. UNIX uses inode numbers, and NTFS uses a master file table.
- The **File Control Block**, FCB, (per file) containing details about ownership, size, permissions, dates, etc. UNIX stores this information in inodes, and NTFS in the master file table as a relational database structure.

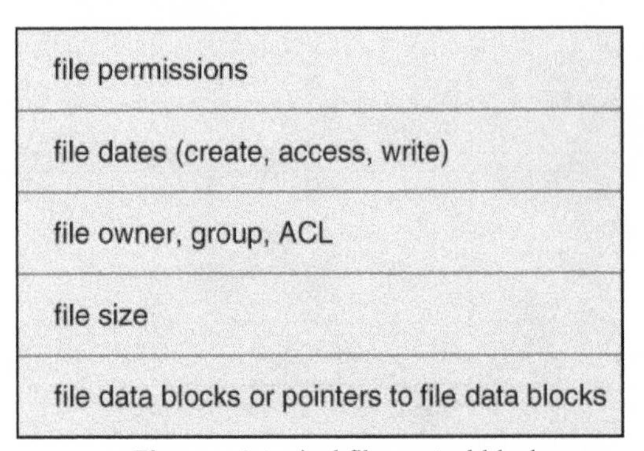

Figure - A typical file-control block.

There are also several key data structures stored in memory:

- An in-memory mount table.
- An in-memory directory cache of recently accessed directory information.

- A system-wide open file table, containing a copy of the FCB for every currently open file in the system, as well as some other related information.
- A per-process open file table, containing a pointer to the system open file table as well as some other information. (For example the current file position pointer may be either here or in the system file table, depending on the implementation and whether the file is being shared or not.)

Figure illustrates some of the interactions of file system components when files are created and/or used:

- When a new file is created, a new FCB is allocated and filled out with important information regarding the new file. The appropriate directory is modified with the new file name and FCB information.
- When a file is accessed during a program, the open( ) system call reads in the FCB information from disk, and stores it in the system-wide open file table. An entry is added to the per-process open file table referencing the system-wide table, and an index into the per-process table is returned by the open( ) system call. UNIX refers to this index as a file descriptor, and Windows refers to it as a file handle.
- If another process already has a file open when a new request comes in for the same file, and it is sharable, then a counter in the system-wide table is incremented and the per-process table is adjusted to point to the existing entry in the system-wide table.
- When a file is closed, the per-process table entry is freed, and the counter in the system-wide table is decremented. If that counter reaches zero, then the system wide table is also freed. Any data currently stored in memory cache for this file is written out to disk if necessary.

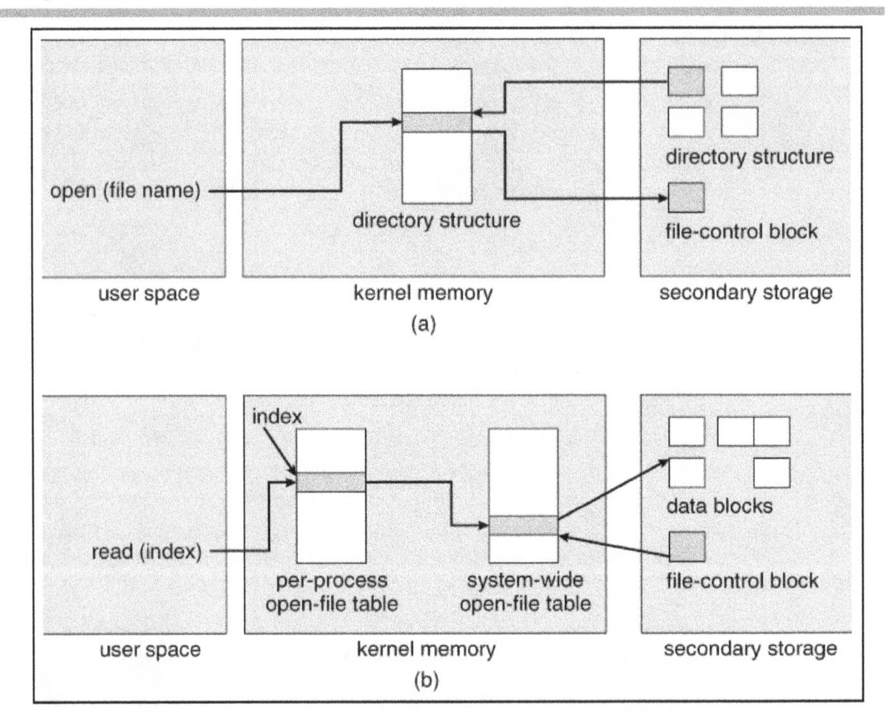

Figure - In-memory file-system structures. (a) File open. (b) File read.

Partitions and Mounting

- Physical disks are commonly divided into smaller units called partitions. They can also be combined into larger units, but that is most commonly done for RAID installations and is left for later chapters.
- Partitions can either be used as raw devices (with no structure imposed upon them), or they can be formatted to hold a filesystem (i.e. populated with FCBs and initial directory structures as appropriate.) Raw partitions are generally used for swap space, and may also be used for certain programs such as databases that choose to manage their own disk storage system.

Linux VFS provides a set of common functionalities for each filesystem, using function pointers accessed through a table. The same functionality is accessed through the same table position for all filesystem types, though the actual functions pointed to by the pointers may be filesystem-specific. See /usr/include/linux/fs.h for full details. Common operations provided include ***open( ), read( ), write( ),*** and ***mmap( ).***

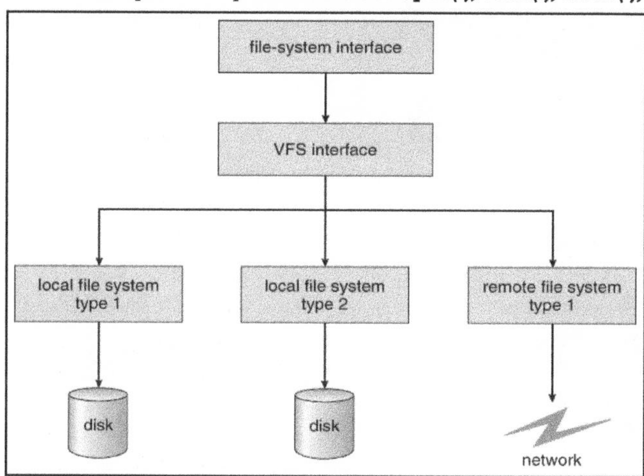

Figure - Schematic view of a virtual file system.

Directory Implementation

Directories need to be fast to search, insert, and delete, with a minimum of wasted disk space.

Linear List

A linear list is the simplest and easiest directory structure to set up, but it does have some drawbacks. Finding a file (or verifying one does not already exist upon creation) requires a linear search. Deletions can be done by moving all entries, flagging an entry as deleted, or by moving the last entry into the newly vacant position. Sorting the list makes searches faster, at the expense of more complex insertions and deletions. A linked list makes insertions and deletions into a sorted list easier, with overhead for the links.

More complex data structures, such as B-trees, could also be considered.

Hash Table

A hash table can also be used to speed up searches. Hash tables are generally implemented in addition to a linear or other structure.

Allocation Methods

There are three major methods of storing files on disks: contiguous, linked, and indexed.

Contiguous Allocation

- Contiguous Allocation requires that all blocks of a file be kept together contiguously.
- Performance is very fast, because reading successive blocks of the same file generally requires no movement of the disk heads, or at most one small step to the next adjacent cylinder.
- Storage allocation involves the same issues discussed earlier for the allocation of contiguous blocks of memory (first fit, best fit, fragmentation problems, etc.) The distinction is that the high time penalty required for moving the disk heads from spot to spot may now justify the benefits of keeping files contiguously when possible.
- (Even file systems that do not by default store files contiguously can benefit from certain utilities that compact the disk and make all files contiguous in the process.).

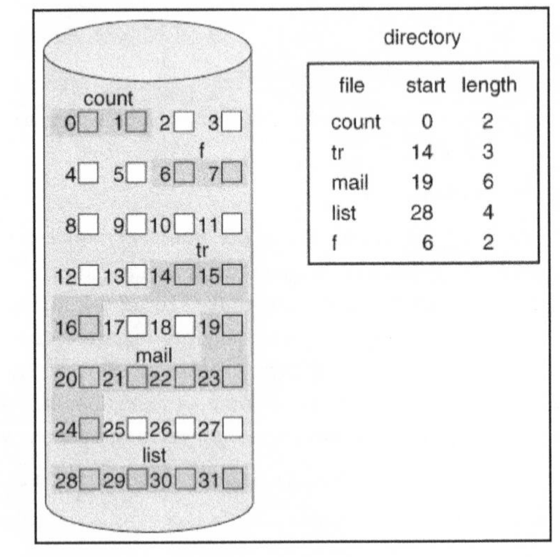

Figure - Contiguous allocation of disk space.

- Problems can arise when files grow, or if the exact size of a file is unknown at creation time:
- Over-estimation of the file's final size increases external fragmentation and wastes disk space.
- Under-estimation may require that a file be moved or a process aborted if the file grows beyond its originally allocated space.
- If a file grows slowly over a long time period and the total final space must be allocated initially, then a lot of space becomes unusable before the file fills the space.
- A variation is to allocate file space in large contiguous chunks, called extents. When a file outgrows its original extent, then an additional one is allocated. (For example an extent may be the size of a complete track or even cylinder, aligned on an appropriate track or cylinder boundary.) The high-performance files system Veritas uses extents to optimize performance.

Linked Allocation

Disk files can be stored as linked lists, with the expense of the storage space consumed by each link. (E.g. a block may be 508 bytes instead of 512.)

Linked allocation involves no external fragmentation, does not require pre-known file sizes, and allows files to grow dynamically at any time. Unfortunately linked allocation is only efficient for sequential access files, as random access requires starting at the beginning of the list for each new location access.

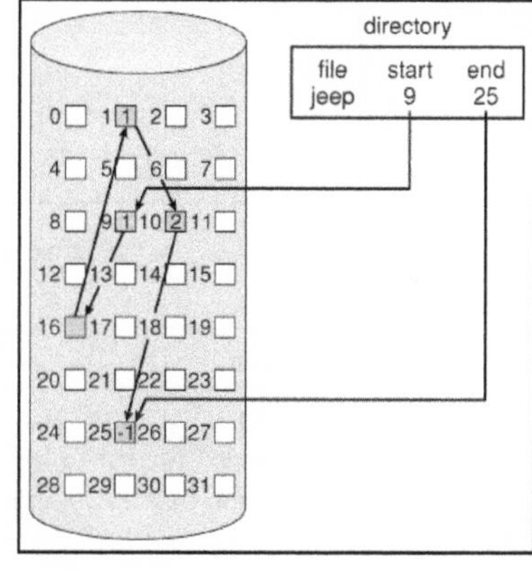

Figure - Linked allocation of disk space.

Allocating clusters of blocks reduces the space wasted by pointers, at the cost of internal fragmentation. Another big problem with linked allocation is reliability if a pointer is lost or damaged. Doubly linked lists provide some protection, at the cost of additional overhead and wasted space.

The **File Allocation Table**, FAT, used by DOS is a variation of linked allocation, where all the links are stored in a separate table at the beginning of the disk. The benefit of this approach is that the FAT table can be cached in memory, greatly improving random access speeds.

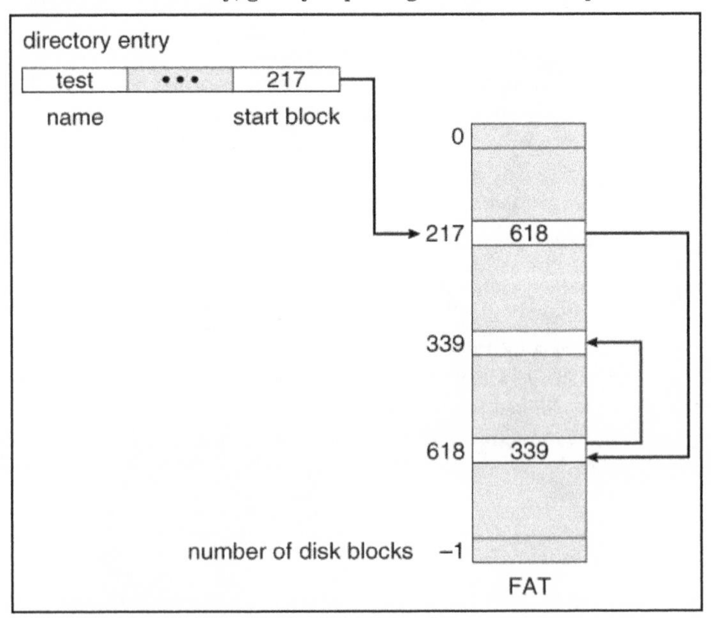

Figure : File-allocation table.

Indexed Allocation

Indexed Allocation combines all of the indexes for accessing each file into a common block (for that file), as opposed to spreading them all over the disk or storing them in a FAT table.

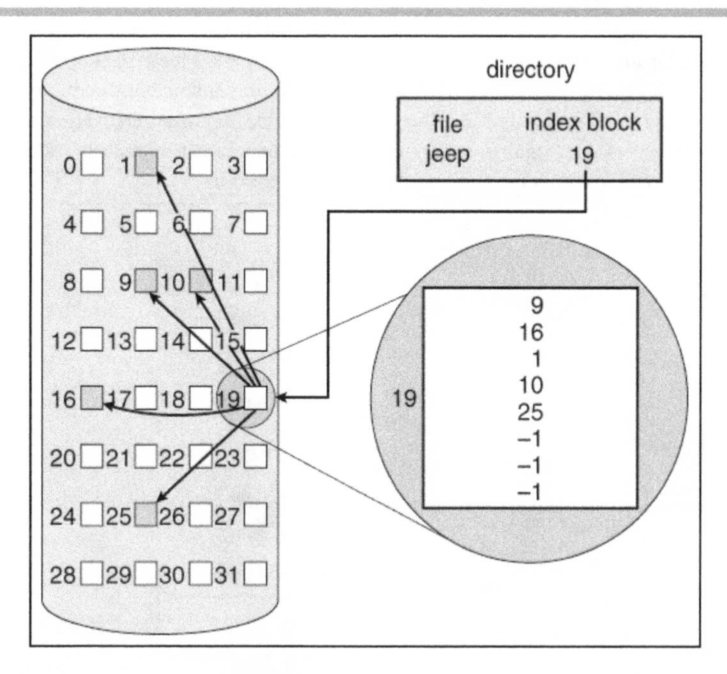

Some disk space is wasted (relative to linked lists or FAT tables) because an entire index block must be allocated for each file, regardless of how many data blocks the file contains. This leads to questions of how big the index block should be, and how it should be implemented. There are several approaches:

- **Linked Scheme** - An index block is one disk block, which can be read and written in a single disk operation. The first index block contains some header information, the first N block addresses, and if necessary a pointer to additional linked index blocks.
- **Multi-Level Index** - The first index block contains a set of pointers to secondary index blocks, which in turn contain pointers to the actual data blocks.
- **Combined Scheme** - This is the scheme used in UNIX inodes, in which the first 12 or so data block pointers are stored directly in the inode, and then singly, doubly, and triply indirect pointers provide access to more data blocks as needed.

The advantage of this scheme is that for small files (which many are), the data blocks are readily accessible (up to 48K with 4K block sizes); files up to about 4144K (using 4K blocks) are accessible with only a single indirect block (which can be cached), and huge files are still accessible using a relatively small number of disk accesses (larger in theory than can be addressed by a 32-bit address, which is why some systems have moved to 64-bit file pointers.) .

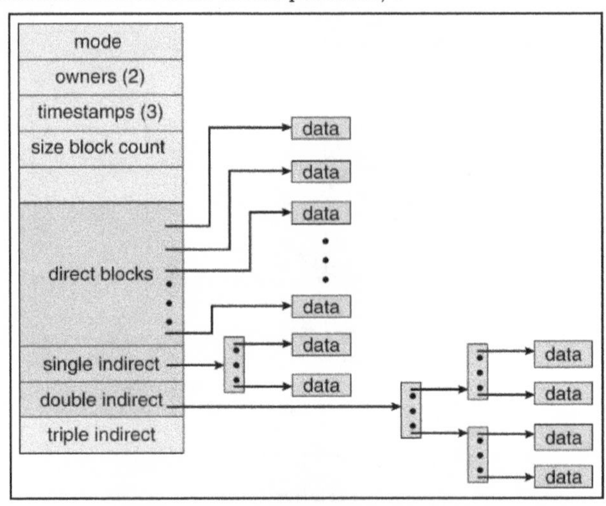

Figure - The UNIX inode.

Performance

The optimal allocation method is different for sequential access files than for random access files, and is also different for small files than for large files.

Some systems support more than one allocation method, which may require specifying how the file is to be used (sequential or random access) at the time it is allocated. Such systems also provide conversion utilities.

Some systems have been known to use contiguous access for small files, and automatically switch to an indexed scheme when file sizes surpass a certain threshold.

And of course some systems adjust their allocation schemes (e.g. block sizes) to best match the characteristics of the hardware for optimum performance.

Free-Space Management

Another important aspect of disk management is keeping track of and allocating free space.

Bit Vector

One simple approach is to use a bit vector, in which each bit represents a disk block, set to 1 if free or 0 if allocated.

Fast algorithms exist for quickly finding contiguous blocks of a given size

The down side is that a 40GB disk requires over 5MB just to store the bitmap. (For example.)

Linked List

A linked list can also be used to keep track of all free blocks.

Traversing the list and/or finding a contiguous block of a given size are not easy, but fortunately are not frequently needed operations. Generally the system just adds and removes single blocks from the beginning of the list.

The FAT table keeps track of the free list as just one more linked list on the table.

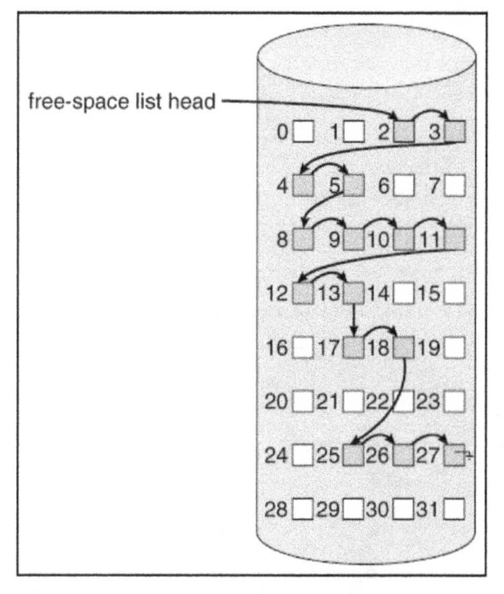

Figure - Linked free-space list on disk.

Grouping

A variation on linked list free lists is to use links of blocks of indices of free blocks. If a block holds up to N addresses, then the first block in the linked-list contains up to N-1 addresses of free blocks and a pointer to the next block of free addresses.

Counting

When there are multiple contiguous blocks of free space then the system can keep track of the starting address of the group and the number of contiguous free blocks. As long as the average length of a contiguous group of free blocks is greater than two this offers a savings in space needed for the free list. (Similar to compression techniques used for graphics images when a group of pixels all the same color is encountered.)

Space Maps

Sun's ZFS file system was designed for HUGE numbers and sizes of files, directories, and even file systems. The resulting data structures could be VERY inefficient if not implemented carefully. For example, freeing up a 1 GB file on a 1 TB file system could involve updating thousands of blocks of free list bit maps if the file was spread across the disk.

ZFS uses a combination of techniques, starting with dividing the disk up into (hundreds of) metaslabs of a manageable size, each having their own space map.

Free blocks are managed using the counting technique, but rather than write the information to a table, it is recorded in a log-structured transaction record. Adjacent free blocks are also coalesced into a larger single free block.

An in-memory space map is constructed using a balanced tree data structure, constructed from the log data.

The combination of the in-memory tree and the on-disk log provide for very fast and efficient management of these very large files and free blocks.